Goodbye, Mango Sergeant

Memoir of a Jamaica Trench Town Boy

Keith Walker

with Z. Nia Reynolds

H
HANSIB

Hansib Publications Limited, 2010
P.O. Box 226, Hertford, SG14 3WY
United Kingdom

Email: info@hansib-books.com
Website: www.hansib-books.com

A catalogue record for this book is
available from the British Library

ISBN 978-1-906190-39-2

Printed and bound in Great Britain

I am but a speck of dust occupying time and space,
and in time I will disappear without evidence or trace
that I ever existed or that I had ever occupied this time or this
place.
Hence this book is my immortalisation so that in 200 years when
all who existed today have gone, there will be this evidence for
those future men and women from different races and
backgrounds to read and understand about themselves,
even though they had not existed in my time and or indeed in this
place.

Keith Walker

I would like to extend my heartfelt thanks to Nia for guidance, support and contribution to this project. I would also like to thank my wife for allowing me to write my story and for her contribution in the editing of this project.

Keith Walker

CONTENTS

1

Trench Town

Trench Town, in the heart of Kingston, was where I was born and where I spent a good part of my formative years.

Like thousands of the other children in the area, I had been delivered at the "Lying-In Hospital", as they used to call the Kingston Public Hospital, which was situated almost in the heart of the overcrowded public housing scheme that was home to so many people.

I remember that in the tenement where we lived there were all these rooms next to one another with one long veranda at the front, and a family lived in each room. And the strangest thing was that there were all these women, single mothers with their children; the men were never around.

Occasionally you might find a family which would occupy two rooms and the man would be in the background somewhere. Chances are he would be in the army or away at sea: on a boat, and he would turn up out of the blue, maybe once every two months, stay for a couple of weeks, impregnate his woman and disappear again – that's how it was.

So, in that yard, there were lots and lots of kids and their mothers. More often than not we kids would be left on our own. We had to survive on our own and that meant we had to learn to grow up pretty fast.

As boys we were very mischievous, and we used to go underneath the houses and look up through gaps in the flooring to see what was happening inside the other rooms. As highly-inquisitive youngsters we would take it in turns to peer between the cracks to spy inside those mysterious, pokey little rooms because we would notice that some man would turn up and disappear inside with a young woman, perhaps a friend of your mother or another one of our neighbours, and the children would be told to "go and play outside". So, whenever that happened my friends and I were given the usual command to disappear, we would dutifully comply, but instead of going off to play we would sneakily slip under the house to see what they were getting up to inside that room, and we would learn things. Yea, forbidden things, and of course we used to talk and laugh about it. That was our entertainment.

I think we must have been about nine or ten then. In Trench Town you had to be grown up by the age of eight in that kind of ramshackle, overcrowded community where there wasn't much in the way of privacy or molly-coddling.

Everybody seemed to live on top of one another and it was a place where everybody's business was like public property, even though some people tried in vain to keep themselves to themselves.

Me and my gang – the other children I hung around with – were very young. We were a rag-tag band of brats, some with runny noses or bloated stomachs – what we called "bang bellies". Most of the time, the bloating was caused by malnutrition or worms.

We used to hang around together for company and, to some extend, for protection because life in the ghettos was often quite dangerous. We were just little boys and the bigger boys used to pay us little attention, as long as we kept out of their way.

We would all be in this yard and they would officially be in charge of us, although most of the time we were just left to our own devices, to play and to fend for ourselves. They were carving out their territory and establishing their power bases, and we were busy mimicking them with our own little turf wars.

When the big boys were around we would disappear but when they weren't we would go under the houses and investigate those secretive assignations taking place inside the rooms whenever a woman and her "gentleman caller" were alone together. Apart from fighting, getting beaten up and, in turn, beating up some fellow smaller than you, there wasn't much else to do besides spying on what was euphemistically known as "big people business".

Sometimes we would follow the big boys and see what they were getting up to – whenever they weren't fighting that is. It was certainly interesting. But the funny thing was that you didn't realise then that you were poor; you didn't realise that life was tough. You just took things as you found them and lived a day at a time.

We knew that there were times, during the middle of the day, when it was hot and you were thirsty; very thirsty and hungry, and you would go in the house to see if there was anything to eat or drink and sometimes there wasn't any food or drink there.

At other times there would be food but if there was nothing available we would go next door to my mother's friend, Miss Pee, a very kind lady, Indian, I think, with long black curly hair. She was always smiling and was very popular with the local fellows. We'd knock on her door to see if she had anything to offer because she was very generous to me and always seem to have things available to share with us. Miss Pee always had a little more than my mother and was generous to me and my brother.

And the good thing about Jamaica back then, was that people wouldn't let you starve even though, like you, they didn't have much. They were always happy to give you something, whether it was a Bulla cake (a simple flat cake made from sugar and flour with the faintest hint of baking soda) which you would eat with a piece of cheese or some butter (if you were lucky) and drink some sugar and water, "beverage" as we called it. So, hard as things were, we could always get something to fill the gap and quench our thirst and then we would go back and play again. We spent pretty much the whole day playing in that yard: Cowboys and Indians, cops and robbers, marbles, or fist fighting, that sort of thing.

If the boys had a toy gun, we'd play with that, otherwise we'd use sticks, while the girls amused themselves with skipping games or playing with imaginary dolly-babies and played at keeping house. We boys would break up their games and they'd get mad and go off in a huff, leaving us to become more and more unruly until we'd be fighting each other.

At first there was no school. What I remember was that I think my mum had problems with her relationships and I suppose that with her being a young girl they took advantage didn't they? And being attractive they did take advantage of her and left her with these two kids, my younger brother, Ken, three years my junior, and me to bring up on her own.

Eventually we left that tenement, moving from Trench Town to Jones Town, but it was a similar set up: poverty-ridden and overcrowded. We had the yard in between two rows of single rooms with a common veranda running across one end of the yard linking both rows of rooms. There was the cooking area and these large sinks to the front and at the back were big tubs and toilets.

We occupied a room which was big enough to accommodate three people. My mother had the bed and my brother and I would sleep somewhere else in the room, usually on the floor. My mum had to go to work so I was in charge. Well, I had to be in charge; I had to be the man of the house and protect whatever we had otherwise the big boys would come inside there and help themselves. Some of them behaved as though they were living out their Cowboys and Indians or cops and robbers game for real, beyond playtime.

I think it was around this time that I started school. Whatever age I was, it was around the time that we moved to Jones Town. My mother had a good friend there, that's why I think she uprooted the family to this Jones Town which she might have thought was a better class of ghetto.

I can't really describe my mother except to say that she could be hard on us sometimes and she always seemed to be under pressure. It probably stands to reason that my mother Willel was always stressed when you look back at the situation but at the time you didn't think; you didn't understand.

Here was this beautiful young woman, more or less a kid herself, left with these kids and no man to provide for her or her children. So, she had to fend for herself, and life was hard.

They used to call me the "Jamaican Buck", whatever that was supposed to mean. In fact, years later in England before I got married, when I was introduced to my future mother-in-law, a Trinidadian, she looked at me for a bit then said, "He looks like a Jamaican Buck". Apparently it was a particular look. Maybe it was the eyes, the physique or the mannerisms. I had no idea then and I am none the wiser now about what a "Jamaican Buck" is supposed to be like, except I was always branded as one. I suspect it has the suggestion of a kind of sexual animal.

There's something about Jamaicans and their nicknames. A short man is bound to be called Short Man or, ironically, Tall Man; whilst a one-legged man will be known as "One-y" or "One Foot". There's no point protesting or getting upset about it. In Jamaica, whatever name is attributed to you becomes yours as much as the name you were christened with at birth; and whether to your face or behind your back, you are going to be called by that name. So, you just have to get used to it.

My mum had a lot of friends that were half Indian, although they used to be called "half coolie" or "coolie royals". I don't know why, but that's what they were called. And they all lived there with us, sometimes staying in our place as if they were part of our family and they would often feed the two of us whenever our mum was away.

However, most days before my mum would go off to work in the morning she had this big, thick drinking glass that she used to fill up with oats then top it up with water and put it in the ice box (I don't think we owned a fridge back then). At lunchtime I would add condensed milk to that mixture, blend it up with more water and ice, and that was lunch. Before that, breakfast was maybe a mug of green tea and a piece of hard dough bread.

The routine was that you would wake up and go outside – everything is done outside – washing and everything. She would go off to work and then my day would start.

At the top of the long veranda running outside our room towards the road were these two rooms where a family of eight were living. They had two little girls and one of them liked me but she had six brothers who always wanted to fight me. I had no choice, I had to fight them; you were not allowed to be a wimp. So, every morning rain or shine you would wake up, do your bits and pieces and, before long, there was a fight.

For some unknown reason a boy would come up to you and say something like, "Give me money, no!" or "What you doing with my money?" before snatching your cash from you, and that would start a fight.

Normally I would be fighting with one my own age and his big brother would be there egging him on and if I'm on top of him, he'd pull me off, so it's an unfair fight. But I had to fight that Eight Family every day. I don't know why but I always had to fight them.

Afterwards, their sister, the girl who liked me, would come and more or less apologise and take care of my injuries. But then, the next afternoon, if they're attacking my brother, I'm in there fighting for him and for me, and I'm fighting the boys from the Eight Family or the one over there from the Four Family, but it's not just them fighting me, it's whoever else they can get as back-up, and this goes on every single day in the yard. We grew up with a culture of constantly having to defend ourselves. It was, without doubt, the survival of the fittest.

We might have been at school then, but I remember the times when we weren't at school. Perhaps we were on holiday but we didn't have a holiday from the fighting, and we didn't really go anywhere else apart from that yard.

Since moving we lived on Fourth Street where there were these different yards. And in each yard families were fighting each other over simple things; sometimes quite viciously, and in the evening my mother would come home and ask what had happened. My brother and I would re-enact every detail, spicing things up if we didn't know the facts or if the truth wasn't dramatic enough.

Ordinarily, we hardly saw the adults or were aware of their activities but I remember in our yard there was a woman who, every so often, would take off all her clothes and just walk about the place stark naked. Maybe the heat had got to her and given her heatstroke but they reckoned that she was mad.

Suddenly, no one is fighting any more; we would all start looking. She would be shouting and carrying on; pacing up and down and a lot of adults would be looking as well. Some of the fellows would say, "A nice piece of batty that, no?"

They would just hang around and laugh and make lewd jokes and the other women would be embarrassed and call out to her to put her clothes on, but the men would say, "Leave the woman alone no, let her have her freedom. Let freedom reign", things like that. And, like the men, we little boys would enjoy the spectacle of this crazy woman exposing herself and carrying on.

The thing about Jones Town and Trench Town was that we grew up fast because we'd see sex happening quite often. We'd see girls and boys round a corner "doing it" and the girl would be shouting and carrying on and maybe she is being raped or maybe not, we couldn't be sure; and another time a girl would see us and she'd tell us, "Go away, bwoy, go away!", and you'd think maybe it's not rape since she's shooing us away because she wants to continue doing what she's doing.

So, sex was something that we grew up with; we'd see the adults "doing it", we'd see chickens, and dogs "doing it" and we'd see the older boys and girls also copulating. And, as a growing boy, you'd feel like something was happening to you; a sensation that made you think that maybe you should be involved in that sort of thing as well, but in those days it was only the more forward guys who were sexually active.

We younger boys, if we weren't fighting or peering under the rooms, would be sitting around talking or having a snowball or snow cone, which is shaved ice shaped into a ball and then covered with syrup. That was yummy and very, very refreshing, particularly when the sun was at its hottest.

My mother worked at the Ministry of Health, which was down town. She took me there once or twice but I don't know what she did there, maybe a little clerical work or a menial type of job. She was just an ordinary young lady who was presumably attractive enough to be employed there, but no type of high flier or 'career girl'.

Years later when we had left Trench Town, I realised that the area was perhaps the worst part of Kingston to have grown up in, but for us it was normal way of living. We would see people hanging out of their window half naked; carrying on, making love, men fighting, women cussing, labrishing* or gossiping. Another time you would be walking around and someone might show you a gun and you'd look at it fascinated and then just move on, or you'd see guys squaring up for a fight with machetes (cutlass), which was normal.

It never occurred to me then that these were dangerous things that could kill you; it was just part of everyday life in that environment. But, years later when I went back to Jamaica for the first time after about 15 years of living abroad, I was appalled to see these guys with sharp, sharp cutlasses and they'd be talking to you and gesturing and waving this thing in your face, and I'd be thinking, "Watch what you're doing with that", and suddenly I realised the danger of living there in the ghetto, where people are living on top of one another and it's like a pressure cooker.

As a boy I had lived with that every day and barely thought anything about it. I wouldn't wish that kind of upbringing on any child, but I suppose it toughened me up. Can you imagine you're fighting every day over here and you go to the next tenement and you're fighting there, too? Some kid and his friend would find a reason to fight: you're looking at his girlfriend or – it doesn't really matter the reason – they'd start a fight just for the sake of it.

In the evenings all of us from Fourth Street would be going down past Fifth Street and we're one big group now; very much together as a gang, and it was territorial.

At weekends, usually in the evenings, we used to go to the cinema, the Rialto, a big cinema up in Half Way Tree, and we'd get dressed up as best we could and go in one mass movement as the Fourth Street Posse. You would never go on your own, it never occurred to us to go on our own; we'd go in a group of 50 or 60 of us walking to the cinema, going to see some big film – or 'flim' as we used to say in those days – maybe a cowboy picture, which was popular in those days. But we'd also go to meet girls from other areas and that would start a fight because you'd checked out the wrong young lady and some big guy would take exception and he'd get up, come over and say, "What you looking at me woman for?"

I would only have been about 12 then, and he'd start pulling me up by my shirt collar and the guys from your gang would break out and then a big fight would start and there would be up to a hundred of us brawling until it was broken up by the police.

Yet all we had wanted was to go to the cinema and in the end we would scatter and find ourselves back in our territory at Fourth Street to chat about it. This is how life was in the ghettos of Kingston.

* Labrishing – Chatting expressively, usually spitefully about a neighbour or friend

2

School Days

Going to school in that area was a challenge; I got "sanded" twice and nearly died, and caned more times than I can remember.

My mum couldn't afford to give us much stuff so I had one pair of shoes which would take me everywhere, and a pair of khaki uniform for school. I would only wear my shoes whenever I was going somewhere special: to school, the cinema, funerals, or to church, otherwise we were walking barefoot around the place.

I was looking forward to going to school for the first time. Trench Town School, as I later found out, was quite tough, but then it was just somewhere different from the tenement yard.

Now, to get there you had go pass Fourth Street, Fifth Street, Sixth Street, another street and another street (presumably seventh and eighth) and you'd arrive at the school.

When you were on your way to school you would notice that all the lads from the various streets were in their gangs, and in the break time – recess – you would see them all in groups talking about such and such from Fifth Street over there, and so on.

So, we're in groups and we check out our groups' girls or we check out the girls from another group and that usually lead to a lot of hassle. Somehow, there's this girl from our tenement yard who happens to be going to the same school and she liked me and I liked her, and this was an opportunity to spend time with her away from her brothers.

It was always good to have a friend from the gentle sex as they tended to keep you sensible and kept you out of trouble, but, in Kingston, it was almost impossible for a young man to escape trouble in one form or another, although we were only children. I remember once I was almost beaten up just for being on the wrong side of the tracks.

There was a famous Jamaican cricketer who had died in a car crash in England and they'd brought his body home to Jamaica for burial. It was lying-in-state somewhere near Trench Town, and everyone was supposed to go and see it and pay their respects or view the body out of curiosity, or whatever, but it was a big occasion.

Anyway, some of us from Fourth Street and Fifth Street decided to go as well. Now, because it was so hot we didn't walk up on the road, we went along the gully, which was like an area of wasteland where the sewers ran adjacent to the road. The gully is wide and made out of concrete, but there's water running down the middle making it much cooler than overhead along the roadway.

And, walking along the gully, the chances are that you're going to see other guys down there as well. Somehow, I must have got separated from the others and I ran into a gang of boys from another street. And, as was to be expected, they backed me up in a corner down there.

The cry went up: "A Fourth Street bwoy, here!"

There I was on my way to pay my respects to a dead son of our native land and here was a bunch of guys getting ready to put my lights out, so I ran like hell, jumped up out of the gully and eventually got into a place where there were lots of people. I just mingled a bit with the crowd until I felt safe enough to walk around and go and look at the stiff who was on display.

I don't know what I expected to see, really, but it wasn't all that great: just a huge coffin with the top part turned up so you could see this once distinguished cricketer's bloated, grey-coloured face and pink lips. He didn't even look like a human being. I didn't feel numb; I didn't feel anything, and after a while I decided to look around the grounds of the pavilion. Suddenly, these guys backed me up again.

"You still on your own, yea? What you a do on your own?"

"Come to see...come to see..."

Shock, fear, whatever it was, had taken my voice and I was stammering some nonsense that I couldn't quite finish.

"What you got in your pocket?"

"Nuthin'... nuthin'."

"Give me your money!"

And about six or seven of them just started: "Give me your money, Give me your money".

"Me no have no money."

"Turn out your pockets!"

So I turned out my pockets and what I had in there were my comics and a few coins. It was very important to buy these comics once a week or every fortnight. I can't remember what they were, but they were a very significant thing for any boy to have, so that when you got back home you would sit down under some shade and really enjoyed reading them, but this was a stick up and I had no choice but to hand over my prized possessions. I felt the loss of the comics more than whatever little money I'd had to surrender.

They took everything, even my penknife, and pushed me around a bit. What was I going to do? I'm on my own. You do your best to leave in one piece, although, walking back home in the hot sun you wish they'd left you with enough money to at least buy a snowball to stave off your severe thirst, because in heat like that you were bound to be parched.

It was a relief to get back to Fourth Street and to see some friendlier faces and they would be wondering where you'd gone off to but you realise how stupid it was to have been caught on your own, off guard, so you don't even bother explaining about your brush with that gang.

Those sort of things happened virtually every day, so there was no point complaining; fighting and bullying were just a way of life. You even had to be on your guard at school, where you were supposed to be learning something and you were trying, but someone would always say something in the class to try and distract your attention, so there would constantly be arguments and the teacher would have to break us apart. Most of the time the job seemed to be more about peacekeeping than actually teaching, but there were times when you wanted to get on with something constructive and have a break from all the hostility.

On one such occasion, this guy was annoying me and kept saying, "Let's meet up after school" but I didn't pay him much attention. I knew he didn't want to discuss the finer points of school life; he wanted to fight. He wasn't one of my Fourth Street group so I knew I was going to get support from my gang once we did get outside.

In the classroom there was a lot of finger pointing and carrying on but nothing happened. Still, they don't forget these things: name-calling, finger pointing and poking would always lead to big fights, especially if someone said something unpleasant about a person's mother. You don't do that; you don't talk about a person's mother, that's taboo and there's always a fight no matter where or when. The teacher would break it up and then, detention. I remember being in lots of detentions not because I'd done anything wrong but just for trying to defend myself or my mother's reputation.

I was usually picked on because I was from a small family, but I remember one time in particular when this guy was irritating me while I was doing some geometry. I had a compass in my hand and he kept on and on; it was so annoying. Suddenly, bam! I rammed the compass through his hand and he wailed, Waaah!, and there was blood everywhere. I hadn't meant to hurt him; I'd probably reacted to try and scare him off or shut him up but ended up stabbing him with the compass. The teacher came running and pulled me away and sent me to see the headmaster, Mr Denton.

I was put in detention and whipped with the cane. He bent me over the table and whipped me on my bare backside. Usually, during canings, what we used to do was put the exercise book in our pants and when we got caned we wouldn't feel it much, but this time he pulled my pants down and beat me till my arse was raw. That headmaster was very strict and, in those days, they could do what they liked and the cane was used a lot.

A note went home to my mother: "I shouldn't have attacked someone like that", that was the other part of the punishment from school but forget about that; my mum beat me on top of the caning. When I got home I gave her the note and she read it and thrashed me in a fierce temper, lashing me with her tongue as well as her belt. After the beating she called me all kinds of dreadful names and compared me to my "good-for-nothing-father", whom I had never even seen in my life.

The next day, everything continued as normal, but the boy's gang decided that they were going to get their revenge. They were out to get revenge and teach me a lesson, so what I used to do to avoid them was, if school finished at three I would make sure that at quarter to three I'd take my books and put them in the toilets, and then at five to three I'd say I was going to the toilet and then I'd slip out before school was dismissed; I've gone home and then in the morning I'd get in early. I kept this up for a while, but in the end they caught me off guard. They never forgot what I had done to that irritating kid.

They way-laid me one Friday when I had been chosen to run in some sports trials. Afterwards, a friend and I were on our way home when this deceitful guy called out to me: "Hey Keith, what happen? Come over here, man."

So I went over and he started smiling, "Hey! I hear you've got a gold tooth. Open you' mouth mek me see it."

Of course, I didn't have a gold tooth, but for some reason I just opened my mouth. Suddenly, whoosh! They sanded me – threw a handful of sand in my mouth – which blocked my throat. The boy had hidden the sand in his hand behind his back and, when I'd opened my mouth, had chucked it in to choke me. It was a trap; the whole thing had been planned and was something that I'd never expected.

There I was going home with my friend but they'd planned to get me back for attacking this guy with the compass, who was a friend or relative of theirs. I'd more or less forgotten about the incident, so they got me off guard.

I tell you, I thought I was going to die. Sand went down my throat and I couldn't breathe. Gulp! Help! I was choking with this sand and I was frantically trying to get it out and trying to breathe; the situation was desperate. I think my friend must have called out to some grown up who was nearby: "Help, he's dying", so this big woman came running over. "What's wrong with you pickney always fighting one another...", and she took me round to the cistern in a yard and poured water down my throat and slapped my back until eventually it became unblocked and I could breathe again, but I was in such a state.

The guy who was with me took me home and I went to bed and a lot of people from the tenement yard came over and were talking about how they'd almost killed me and my favourite little girl came round to look after me and in the end the Aunts came over to give me some medicinal stuff and everybody had their own remedies and decided that I should "drink this" or "sip that" and go to sleep. Then when my mum came home she was frantically asking: "What happened? What happened?", and when she got the story you could see how frightened she was, so much so that I didn't go to school for a couple of days.

That incident made me very, very suspicious of certain people displaying any sort of kindness towards me; I'd see that as a threat: somebody's tricking me, so from that day I was always very wary of anyone being too nice. If you're always too nice I'm going to be suspicious about what your true intentions are, because the boy who sanded me was pretending to be nice and friendly, but was in fact devious and deadly.

Soon after that, the school sports day came about and I was competing in the athletics. Now, at the school the teachers were there as your protection. If you were going to be beaten up and the teachers were close by they would protect you because in those days the kids are not going to beat up the teacher as they do nowadays.

So, we had sports day and on this occasion you'd have your girlfriend on your arm and you'd both be eating ice cream, you'd have some money saved up for that as well as peanuts because that's the day for you to splurge and show off. And in the games you'd run, you'd jump and you'd do all these things to try and make a name for yourself and get your peers and girlfriend to pay you even more attention.

Jumping is what I was good at, mainly the high jump. I wasn't very good at the running, though, I was always beaten so I gave up on that. And with the long distance races, I always used to run out of puff, so forget that. I think maybe because I was undernourished: I wasn't being properly fed, that's why I wasn't so good at the running. But the competing aside, the main thing was to be with your girl; someone to relax and pose with. You would be admired for that, but more to the point, you had someone who cared about you and that was worth a wall full of sporting trophies.

Now, looking back, I do understand why these young lads in Jamaica find themselves in gangs; find themselves doing things they don't want to do just for survival each day. It's because they don't have love and opportunities. It's nice if they have girlfriends, it's not the sex it's a friendship which has a calming influence on things. It's someone who'll look after you and you know she will be kind, and it's important. When you have that you can move away from the gangs as much as you can, although you can't always move away from them entirely because they're like your family; they support you against other attackers, particularly when you are outside your own territory.

3

Kidnapped

I met my father when I was about 11 or 12.

Life for us in Jones Town was no different from one day to the next. As lads, we would fight almost every day, and it was normal, but sometimes we'd get money and could buy something and share it among ourselves, or there was another diversion to break up the monotony.

One very hot afternoon something very different happened. A big black Ford car slowly rolled up and stopped in front of our yard and three guys got out. They had on their dark felt hats and dark suits and were dressed like real gangsters, and this very light-skinned guy, who seemed to be the leader of the pack, looked at me and said, "You're Keith, ain't you?"

I said, "Yes, I am Keith, how do you know me?"

The fellow said, "Me a you' father you know."

And everyone went, "Wow!"

I've got big respect now; all eyes are on us. And he asks if I want to go for a drive, "Bring three of your friends". Off we went, four of us squashed in the back with this man: me and my brother Ken and two others.

I couldn't stop looking at him. He was a red-faced, red-skinned man with straight brownish, mouse-coloured hair, strong Negroid features, and an especially flared nose. But it was the hair that struck me. In those days people used to say about me, "Him have nice hair, eeh?" And they used to play with my hair because it used to be very, very curly. I don't know, maybe that was something I got from my father. Now that I'd actually met him, it all started to make sense; my identity started to make sense.

They say he was from Cuba. Perhaps he was born there and had found himself in Jamaica like a lot of Cubans did in those days. Anyway, his friends called him Red Man. I don't think he minded. In any event the name suited him.

So, there we were, driving along in this car and I'm as proud as anything because everyone's looking; admiringly, and I couldn't feel more pleased; as though, finally, I am somebody. Then my father asked, "Where's your mother?"

"She's at work".

"Well, she's got to look after you, you know, 'cause she's not looking after you very well."

The whole thing is surreal. Up to now it's been just my mother, my brother and me. Now, suddenly, I have a father. He's on the scene, I won't say back on the scene because I've never known him, and from the way he's talking nothing's right, but he's obviously empowered to fix things.

Just looking at him, you could see that he had money; the car alone spoke volumes, and there were his cronies to jump at his every instruction. He was tall and slim and his complexion was so light that I assumed he must have been mixed race. He was a handsome man, with the kind of lady-killer looks that I suppose most women would have fallen for, although, back then, a man could have been as ugly as sin and as evil as the devil but as long as he had a car and money, women would have thrown themselves at him. I don't know the circumstances that had brought him and my mother together, but I could hazard a good guess at what had caused them to become estranged.

He took us down to a little restaurant in town.

"What do you want?"

I saw the big poster for Coca Cola.

"What can we have?"

"You can have whatever you want."

So I ordered Coca Cola – the first time I'm having Coca Cola. We would see it advertised at the cinema while we would be drinking sugar water, but now we get to order Coca Cola and two pieces of carrot cake with the icing on top. You would see that on the poster as well, but that's the closest you'd get to it because you would have to make do with Bulla cake, plain old Bulla, until now, and all four of us are sitting down and we're really eating and drinking like we're starving. Then we finish and he says, "Boy hungry you know. Your mother's not looking after you, bwoy."

Then he asked, "What else do you want?"

And, man, ice cream, we wanted to have ice cream! Buckingham ice cream. I think it was rum 'n' raisin and it was nice. I remember he put me on his lap and said, "You can steer" on the way back and I'm thinking this is a big man, a big man.

And now when my mum came home we were all excited and respected! We've got the respect of everybody in the yard – "His dad is a bad man, you know, and three of them came here with them felt hats and such looking like something out of the gangster films in the cinema".

That's the impression you get, gangsters in their felt hats, and with a car like that – Al Capone. I had big respect for a whole week, and no fights for a whole week. And people were saying, "You know he's got a gangster father". Just before Redman left he said he'd come back and see my mum, but by the time she came back from work he'd already gone. And so when my mum came home that evening I told her what happened and she was livid!

"And you went with that good-for-nothing-man? You know you're not supposed to go in a strange man's car!" And she gave me the works, a real tongue-lashing. And I'm thinking, "But he's my dad". So I said it.

"What the hell do you know about your dad?"

On and on she went, humiliating me and calling me ungrateful. I felt so small.

He did come back one evening to see her and she gave him the usual blah, blah, but then she went off with him. I don't know, he must have just flashed the cash and here is a single young woman who is struggling to bring up her children on her own and there's her old flame from way back when and he turned up and after she gave him what for they disappeared in his great big car and she choose to forget what a scoundrel she thought he was. Anyway, the appearance of my father was the first time I really got any respect from the others in the tenement yard.

Of course I wanted to go away with him. I wanted to share his lifestyle. I'm also thinking of my brother because he's got to come with me as well. He had a different father to me so I don't think Redman would have been interested in bringing up another man's child.

So now my parents are getting on again, but something else happened. There was another man who also felt that I was his son, and he came on the scene and confused me.

My parents didn't reconcile their differences. I think he had his place and a wife somewhere in the country, and he just came to see my mum, his old flame; you know, having his cake and eating it, that sort of thing. And I think she might have been upset with him and got in another man who said that I was his son. Perhaps she introduced that to make my dad jealous, but it backfired.

What happened was I think this guy's mother wanted to have a grandson, so he used to come by and take me to his place in Trench Town, Jonestown or Denham Town, I can't remember which, to meet his relatives and they were quite nice. Where they lived was a house, a proper house, it wasn't a tenement like ours, and that was quite respectable. It was so pleasant to go into a house with a separate sitting room, separate kitchen, separate bathroom, you know, for me that was something and they had their own private yard, so that was impressive, too.

The fellow, my "dad", let's call him John, took me to his house to meet his mother, supposedly my grandmother, and I thought, well, I don't know what to tell my mum. In the end I didn't tell her that I went to John's mother's place, you didn't tell her that sort of thing just in case she hit the roof. I hadn't forgotten how she'd over-reacted when I told her how I'd gone off with the other "dad", the gangster-looking one with the big car.

And then, one day, this guy John and his mother said to me, "You know, why don't you come and stay with us in the country?" and I thought about it and thought "Yea, fine".

So he came to the house and convinced my mum that I should stay the night with him and his mother, but didn't mention anything about going to the countryside. Anyway, early, very early the next morning "Daddy" John drove his mother and me to the country in his car. It was a fantastic journey! Seeing miles and miles of grass and trees and animals – I was enjoying it so much that I didn't remember about my brother or the fact that he would have loved to be there too. This was like a beautiful dream I was having. As far as I was aware, we were driving for a whole day when we left Kingston.

Tranquillity is where we went. To get there we passed a place called Annatto Bay and from there we went up into the hills to this place called Tranquillity and the old lady said, "This is where you're staying now."

I wasn't happy about that. One day, two days, became three days, four, and by now she was finding a school for me to go to. So, I was in this remote place, in this house, in this yard with people I supposed were my grandmother and her son, and this "father" wasn't around much but would occasionally turn up. Before long, I was already a regular at the church and Sunday school, and then the old lady arranged for me to go to the local school. I didn't want to but I had no choice.

Sometimes, there would be a relative or friend of theirs who would come by with some children for me to play with, and I thought that I'd get to know people around the district but it did not turn out that way. My grandmother started off being OK, but she was very strict, moody and not much fun. As time went by she became more and more strict and would sometimes lock me in the house. I felt like a prisoner. She always used to beat me if she felt that I was ungrateful for something or was not performing some task she'd set me. Physically, she was wiry and was of fair complexion but her son, on the other hand, was dark-skinned and mandingo like.

It wasn't long before I realised that I had been kidnapped. I really was trapped. Here I was, in this place; I couldn't go outdoors on my own, she would take me to school, she would collect me from the school, and I couldn't really go out and meet people because I was locked up in the house.

Well, on the other hand, I'm getting food, regular food, and it's a nice place with lots of animals to see and handle. There are mango trees and lots of other fruits you could pick and eat. So, from that perspective it was good, but the fact is I started thinking about my mother, my brother and what was happening back home; I was homesick.

After about a month in this place I realised that I was not going back home, perhaps never, all because this man's mother wanted a grandson and he reckoned that maybe I was his son, so this was supposed to justify their action in abducting me. As a child, I was confused by it all and just accepted the situation because I didn't know what else to do.

It wasn't all bad, though. She used to take me with her to the market down in Annatto Bay where she used to go to sell her mangoes and other provisions. I used to be there with her and the other market traders used to cook breadfruit and other "hard food" like yam and sweet potatoes and serve that up with fish or a savoury meat dish like curry goat. So, market day was fun and exciting for me, and in the evenings we'd all go back up to Tranquillity, packed up in the bus, everyone squashed in like sardines.

Once or twice a day there was a bus that would come up to Tranquillity, which was at the end of the bus route, and the driver and crew would take a break, before returning to Kingston.

So, as usual, I was taken to school and there were strict instructions from my "grandmother" to the teacher that I shouldn't be allowed to do this that or the other, and definitely not go out into the street. With her it was all discipline: I couldn't see people, I couldn't do this or that, I had to learn this and that, I had to obey her every instruction; I had to be seen and not heard.

Unusually, I was coming from school on my own this particular day and this bus suddenly stopped and pulled up beside me. The bus driver looked out and said, "Aren't you the boy in the paper? Isn't your name so and so? Aren't you kidnapped? They say somebody kidnapped you and everyone's wondering where you are. So this is where you are."

I said, "Yea! I wanna go back to my mum."

Apparently, I'd been reported missing and it ended up in the

Gleaner newspaper and this driver recognised me, but that was quite a few months after I'd got there.

It hadn't really occurred to me to try and run away. And go where? I was in the middle of nowhere, in this quaint-sounding little country village, a far cry from my tenement home in Kingston with people who were supposed to be my family, and all I could do was accept it. I kept hoping that my mum would come for me, but as time went on I realised that wasn't likely to happen. I convinced myself that life was not too bad, except that I was restricted from making friends and did not have my mother around.

I did miss my mother and my brother, but when I mentioned that the old lady would say, "Well, we'll take you down to see your mum soon."

She was always promising that would happen but it never did. I didn't miss what goes on in Kingston, I was quite happy to be away from all the fighting and poverty, but I desperately wanted to be with my mum and brother Ken.

Anyway, soon after the bus driver found me, a detective came up to Tranquillity with my mother and they took me away and there was a long drawn-out court case.

Once she got me back home, my mum called me all sorts of names, "Ungrateful so and so", "this and that", "so and so"; "How could you go off with that man," "Blah, blah, blah."

I went with him; so I was obviously ungrateful.

"How could you leave your brother like that?"

As I said, the case went to court. I think the "father and grandmother" may have been charged with kidnapping and there was a lot of court action that followed, but in the end I can't really say what happened exactly. As a child, I suppose they didn't think it was important to tell me the outcome, but it was certainly a high profile case at the time. It was only afterwards that I had a sense of fear about the whole thing, because we would sometimes hear about children going missing and them finding a body or body parts months or years later.

While the court case was going on, there was a lot of to-ing and fro-ing and appearances before various benches to establish my parentage; was my mum really my mum? Was my "dad" my real dad? Was his mother my grandmother? What had happened in Tranquillity?

It was decided that my mum was my mother, but that the fellow was not my real father and therefore had no claims to me. I tell you it was confusing, but, listen, when you grow up in Trench Town or Jones Town nothing surprises you, because nobody has fathers. And then there's a father who's your uncle, he comes and stays with you and he's your "Uncle So and So", and then he disappears and you ask, "Where's 'Uncle So and So?'"

And you're told, "He's not your uncle."

They tell you off. But they're the one who told you he was your uncle in the first place. And another chap might be your dad, but you hear, "Why are you calling him your dad?"

Because she'd introduced him as my dad (although of course I don't say that. I wouldn't dare). You can't win, and it all gives you the wrong impression about relationships and where you fit into things.

In the end, I was sent home with my mum. I was certainly glad to be back; seeing my mother and brother again, and even the old broken-down tenement yard didn't seem so bad after all. It was familiar; it was home, and no one was locking me up and forcing me to behave like a prisoner or a slave. But, little did I realise that I wouldn't be back home for long. My mum had other ideas – she decided to send me away to live in the country.

4

Mango Sergeant

My mother decided, as a result of the whole furore with the court case and with me being so uncontrollable in going off with strange people, that she was going to pack me off to the countryside to stay with my grandmother, that's her mother, and Aunt Adlin, mum's sister.

Mum and her friend took me to the bus stop in downtown Kingston, and I got the bus to Portland. My mother came to pay the fare and to give a food parcel and my brother was left, I suppose, with one of my 'aunts' back in the tenement.

There were no lingering goodbyes. It was quite formal, really, with lots of admonitions to "Behave yourself" and "Don't give you' granny dem any trouble".

You would think that having just got me back my mum might never have wanted to let me out of her sight again, but no. This relocation, she assured me, was for my own good. Presumably, it was the same argument the English government made when shipping off petty crooks to Australia centuries ago.

So off I went to the country to a place called Black Hill on this rickety old country bus, which was packed to the very roof with people and their cargo, including small livestock.

I remember that the bus went round and round the foot hills of the Blue Mountains; up and down narrow roads, over streams, through gullies and the bus would stop at various places to let off or take on more people, but after a few hours the bus would stop for the driver to stretch his legs and we would also get off and go to answer the call of nature before going in search of something to drink. When the driver was ready to proceed he would blow the horn and we would all bolt to get back on the bus.

The journey went on for hours, and felt like a whole day by the time we'd arrived at Black Hill, but just before you're there, the bus had to laboriously climb up a bit of mountain road called "Junction". Although it was only a short distance, it took quite a bit of time for the bus to negotiate its way up that steep bit of road, and seemed to be crawling along and then lurching backwards every time the driver changed gears. On top of that, he kept blowing the horn as if to warn other vehicles he was on the junction; and, of course, the sound of the horn woke up those of his passengers who were sleeping, alerting them that we were approaching a major bus stop at the top of the hill; whilst broadcasting our approach to anyone within a three mile radius.

I located my little "grip", the miniature suitcase my mum had loaned me for the trip, and followed the other passengers off the bus where I was met by my Aunt Adlin and a few others from her household.

After answering questions about the journey and about the family I had left behind, we set off for their house, turning off the main road and on to a dirt road, heading for a place called Rodney Hall, which apparently had something to do with slavery days and was named after some slave master or other.

So, we're off the main bus route and we're walking in the dark with only the light from the moon to provide some illumination for the journey. There were no street lights, just strange sounds that I'd never heard before coming out of the darkness: chirping crickets, flickering peeny-wallies or titibu, as the fireflies were called, and owls calling, "toot, toot!"

Then, suddenly, I saw something dart out in the darkness and my heart slammed inside your chest.

"What's that?"

Something has run out of the dark into the road and you're frightened, but then with the moonlight you see it's just a goat, and your fears are gone. So you keep walking in the dark; the stone road is damaging your shoes, and you're all going along this road which appears to be twisting round and round the mountain range, and eventually it opens up into a flat area that is Rodney Hall.

There are all these little shacks like buildings with zinc roofs from which little flickering lights are seen; just two rooms or one big room in every house and they are all separate little buildings; no bigger than boxes.

To get to our place we've got to go down a little slope off the dirt road to this little track leading to my grandma's place: two rooms: 'one a-front, one a-back'. Then they have a little thing like a shed with a zinc roof away from the main house with pots and things hanging from this slanted ceiling; you cook there, and there are two sticks on either side supporting it up to stop things from getting wet when it rains, and in the centre the iron pot is propped up on three large stones above a wood-burning fire. The toilet is further down the slope on the other side, it's a latrine and you go down there and open the door to reveal a box seat with a hole in the centre and you think, "Good gosh, I'm going to fall in!" At least those in Kingston were solid and safe; we had proper toilets there, here it's a pit latrine: just a seat and when you open it, it creaks and there are loads of flies swarming around. I am petrified that I'm going to fall in, and then there's the smell, but at night time we had our chamber pot under the bed and you would hear someone peeing: Chhhhhh! But it's the women who make the most noise, wow! The sound they make peeing in that chamber pot is so strong, and you're thinking, "Gosh, that's powerful", and then the next morning they'd come with this full chamber pot, heading towards the front door. They've got to pass you to get to the door to chuck it out, and sometimes the smell is overpowering, and you're just hoping they don't spill it over you.

Now, for water they'd use a barrel or shet pan for collecting the rainwater and a ladle for bailing it out. That was tough! Apart from the inconvenience of all of us, five or six people, sleeping in the same room, the kitchen was "down there", a short distance from the house; and the rickety latrine was "over there"; and there's a big drum with water on the other side, "over there".

Well, I am the nephew of my mum's sister, Adlin, who's living there with my grandmother. Aunt Adlin has two kids, I-man and Kenneth, who are around my age, although one was slightly older, but I am about to discover that I'm the one who will now do all the work. Every morning Adlin would wake me up, sometimes with a strap, and force me to go and do chores. I can't think of anything worse than being awoken from your slumber by someone reigning blows on you. It's always like that in Jamaica; your aunt would protect and give preference to her kids and take advantage of you, the nephew or niece they've been entrusted to care for.

What used to happen was, my mum would send things like shoes and clothes up there for me, but my Aunt would pick out the best bits and give those to her sons and I would get whatever was left. Also, I used to have to go and "drogue" the water from Medicine Hole, the water source for the village. This water was supposed to have medicinal properties, hence the name, but we needed it to wash and cook with. To get there, I would be walking barefoot on a gravel road, and then I'd go down a steep hill; all the way down to the bottom and when I am passing the large trees along the way, I would see these huge lizards turning different colours and pass slimy bullfrogs which I might even step on. "Aaahh!" It's scary, and I had to carry the shet pan, a huge zinc basin, full of water back up that hill. That pan has a number of uses: sometimes they would cook in it, and at other times it's by the side of the house collecting water when it rains. But mostly, I've got to take that down to the stream and fill it up with water and bring it back in time for them to use to make breakfast or to wash with.

I'd make a cotta, which is a padding made from cloth, which would act as a cushion when I'm carrying that pan full of water on my head back up the hill. And I tell you, it was really hard work and there were times when I'd get half way up the hill and I'd fall down, so I had to go back down the hill and it's slippery and I am sliding back down this steep hill, usually on my backside.

This was my duty, early morning, every morning. I'd have to do it before I went to school and I'd have to do it after I come back from school. They would just use up all the water and I would have to replenish it. I would ask them "why can't so and so come with me" and they'd make excuses: he's doing something else. She was really very unfair, my Aunt Adlin. She used to treat me like a skivvy and give me a hell of a life. When they had a bath I had to use their dirty bath water to wash my feet. I would be the one to go and drogue the water, but I use to get dirty water for my personal use or I would have to go and drogue more water specially for my own use. So, most times, I would just bathe in the stream at Medicine Hole on one of those water-fetching trips down there.

I was treated really badly by my own family. My grandmother was just there, she was OK, but I feel she did not want to interfere with Adlin's arrangements. Grandma was sort of kind, but I could see that she didn't want to upset Aunt Adlin or her lazy boys. Then again, maybe she did not see anything wrong with my treatment and the fact that I was always getting the worse end of everything.

I don't know how she managed it but my mum was always sending stuff; food parcels, clothing, and my aunt would choose for herself from what was there and I would get nothing or at Christmas time I know that some of whatever in the parcel was mine but I wouldn't get any or very little, the scraps, in comparison with the cousins. I was like the "Cinderella Boy", the odd one out; there was no love or appreciation.

Sometimes, however, my uncle Malton, he was really my grand uncle, would take me to his little piece of land and that was good because we'd be together cutting down things and digging things up or picking mangoes, there was a small stream at the bottom of this piece of land where we'd catch Janga – shrimps. They moved very fast but, eventually with patience, you'd catch some and cook them as a run-down stew with coconut milk and cucumber, a delicate vegetable. We'd use a tin can to do the cooking right there by the riverbank. Those were some of my best days.

As children we used to make gigs. We would get a piece of wood and cut it and carve it with a penknife to make the shape of a small pear and you get a nail and nail it into the bottom of the pointed end and somehow you break off the head of the nail and then get a piece of string and wrap the string around the nail and let it go – let it fly! And it would go round and round sometimes we would have gig fights: my gig against your gig. One used to smash the gig against the other and the one that broke last, and the player with the gig still spinning was the winner. We made it out of certain types of wood and make it as stable as possible. This would take a long time to shape the wood and get it right.

In Rodney Hall I was respected because I was a Kingstonian. I came from Kingston, so I was the man; a real novelty.

"Bwoy, Kingstonian over deh so."

"Kingstonian this and Kingstonian that" because they've never been to Kingston and they've heard great stories about it. Some of the country folks maybe have a radio which you'd hear only as crackle, crackle because of the bad reception. This was usually the source of their stories. And to hear stories was great, the only other way you're going to hear good stories is if you walk out to where you got the bus from Kingston, that's where people from the small villages met to exchange news and trade gossip.

Sometimes we would go to other villages for a change. Now, there were some nice girls living in a village some ways from Rodney Hall, half Indian girls, but they lived far down by the seaside and it was a long walk to get there and you'd pass a big water tank on the way which was used in slavery days, and in the past people from Rodney Hall used to go to this tank to get water before they started going to Medicine Hole.

Anyway, this village was closer to the sea and quite different from Rodney Hall. We would go there to swim in the sea or to check out the girls but although it was a long way it was worth it as there were different things to do and anyway the girls were beautiful and friendly.

At other times, we would just hang around in our district and play marbles or we would go fishing in the river for our lunch or hunting for wild fowl and we'd catch some and make a good meal, so there was always something to do in the country and you couldn't starve. Although you might not have been able to buy luxuries such as saltfish, flour, oil or whatever, we improvised, we would make our own cooking oil from coconuts. Looking back, it was the good life, although we didn't think so at the time.

But there were experiences that were not so pleasant. My problem was that I was always curious about people fighting and there's a mark just above my eye to remind me of this weakness.

One evening I noticed this crowd of kids coming from school as they were all in uniforms and there was raised voices, lots of shouting. I didn't go to school that day so I was not with them, but I saw the excitement and the animation of the crowd and I just started to get curious about what was going on. They were coming closer to the centre of the village and there was this commotion as two of them were fighting and were being egged on by this huge crowd that had formed a ring around them. As I moved closer to get a better look, the crowd suddenly parted and "Pow!" A stone flew out of the crowd and hit me just above my eye and I yelled blue murder. There was blood everywhere. Some of the kids helped me off the ground where I fell, but by now blood was gushing from my face. They took me home to Aunt Adlin's and she washed off the blood and, of course, there were no stitches, she just got something to cover the cut and bandaged my head and sent me to bed. Eventually, it got better but I'd almost lost my eye; a little lower and that stone would surely have blinded me.

The irony was that this one time that I was not actually in the fight; I was just a spectator for a change and was floored by this sudden action. After that I decided I must resist that type of curiosity, as it could be harmful for my health. Don't they say, "Curiosity killed the cat"?

Then, there was this guy in the village called Jackman, who was the boss around the place; he beat up everyone in the village and at school, a real bully. This guy would pick a fight every single day and earned his reputation by wasting all his opponents. He was a couple of years older than me and was bigger built, and he decided he wanted to fight with me.

Now fighting is what I grew up on in Kingston, it is the culture of the ghetto, so I was not afraid to take him on. And, as always, there was a nice girl in the village and one day I was talking to her when Jackman came over and said, "Get away from her", but that's what you always heard in Kingston anyway, and there it always led to a fight. So, now he started to get really belligerent and pushed me over, so I got up and whacked him back, and everyone cried: "Fight, fight!" and rushed over to watch and, boy, we had a fight that day; rolling in the mud and all that. I think we fought for about an hour, but I was used to fighting, it's not a big thing to me; it is the way we survived in the ghetto. So we fought and fought and I think he was getting tired and he's trying to get away and I kicked the hell out of him and then he got up and jumped on me and eventually I got him down onto the ground and pinned him into a neck hold and he's crying, "Whaaa!" And now everyone starts shouting, "Let him go, he's learnt his lesson".

Well, he was my best friend after that and I never had another fight in Rodney Hall. Anyone who wanted to fight me would have to go through him first. It was so strange, this was the bully in the district and he used to beat up everyone he challenged but because I stood up to him I got his respect and his friendship. We were as close as two crossed fingers after that. He became like my bodyguard so, of course, I didn't have to fight any more.

We used to go shooting birds with a catapult, which we called a slingshot. We'd make from two pieces of wood shaped like a 'Y' and cut off at the bottom then cleaned up with a penknife. We'd then get two pieces of rubber and fix those to each end and in the middle we add a piece of leather, put a hole in each side and tie it on to each piece of the rubber, and the stronger the rubber the more powerful the catapult is.

So, after I'd gone to collect water the two of us would disappear into the woods for a day of fun, shooting birds. We hid in the bushes and aimed, then Pam! We've shot a bird, a big juicy bird, and that's just the beginning; we'd collect a whole brace of them. It was fantastic. Once we'd collected quite a few, we would pluck them, gut them, clean them, cut the heads off and roast them right there in the woods. Whenever we went into the woods we would carry matches, a penknife, the slingshot, a cutlass for clearing a path, and a bit of salt if we remembered to pinch some from the kitchen. We'd roast the birds and eat them right there. Afterwards, we'd pick a few mangoes and eat those too.

Sometimes we would go hunting and pick lots of mangoes to eat and we would often get the runs. As boys – there were usually three of us – we'd get up in a tree, sit there and pee as far as we could. It was a competition. And sometimes we might sit in a tree to defecate and accidentally use cow itch leaf to clean ourselves, but that leaf would itch horribly and we would end up scratching like mad, so we had to be careful what leaves to pick to clean ourselves with.

At other times we would go to the river at Medicine Hole and play around in the water or torment the lizards on the way down to see how they would change their colour. We would be discussing things like wouldn't it be interesting if we humans could do that too?

But the thing is I would eat mangoes for breakfast, for lunch and for dinner. I was always eating mangoes and I could eat more mangoes than anyone else, so everyone in the village called me Mango Sergeant. In time people forgot my real name; I was just known by that nickname which stuck to me like flies to sugar.

I ate a lot of mangoes because I found it strange that you had so much around and for free. You paid for the mangoes in Kingston and if you'd ever tried to get a mango from someone's garden, the chances are they'd shoot you. But here, in the country, mangoes were as common as green lizards, and I couldn't get enough of them.

I was Mango Sergeant and everyone in the village knew me by that name, I was no longer "Kingston bwoy" or whatever else they'd called me. And, of course, the girl that Jackman and I had fought over was now my girlfriend too. Life was getting better.

I used to go to the local school, Black Hill School, and I would regularly get caned because I was always getting into trouble with the girls there. I was always late or I wouldn't turn up because these girls decided to take us to the bush to "do something".

My first sexual experience was with a half Indian girl from school called Rosita. I don't know why she liked me, but she made her intentions very plain. I used to spend all my time with the fellows but she used to pull me away and take me into the bushes and started doing things to me. She obviously knew what she was doing and little by little I cottoned on and, with her guidance, started doing things to her. It was out of this world. Wow, what was that? The sensation of excitement that came from peeking underneath the houses in the tenement yard came rushing back, except this time I was no longer a voyeur but a blissful participant.

So, I was late for school a lot, and I got caned, but after spending those mind-blowing times with Rosita, I decided it was worth it. At times if we knew that we were going to get caned we would get a particular weed and fix it into some sort of knot and throw it behind us without looking back, a superstitious rite to try and cancel the expected caning. Sometimes, if I didn't get caned, I would relate it to that action, or what we used to do as well, for a laugh, is if we saw a dog pooing we would wrap our little fingers around each other, pull it back and call out "Pone, pone" and apparently that would get the dog constipated and they couldn't continue to defecate. That was big fun and for some reason it seemed to work.

But what I found the most interesting were the girls. After that first sexual experience, I saw girls at school in a different light. When the guys were jumping around and doing things, I would be looking at the girls and thinking, "I wonder what that one is like?" I'd be fantasising. And it seems that I used to get some girls into trouble because their rivals would get jealous and beat up the girl that I was moving with at any particular time or they'd fight the girl that I was going after.

But, all that female rivalries aside, I used to get on well with all the girls. I don't know why. Naturally, I supposed it was because of my good looks, charming personality and because I treated them all – even the ugly ones – like goddesses. But the truth is it was more likely to have been about my main asset – my soft curly hair which they used to like playing with. I needed the friendship, which I got in abundance from these girls, who all wanted to pet me, and from my bird-hunting friends, who gave me a sense of belonging. Outside of that, I was treated like a servant.

Aunt Adlin hated me and she used to take me to her Seventh Day Adventist Church every Saturday. We couldn't "kindle" – light a fire – or do anything that involved cooking during daylight hours on Saturdays. Before the sun rose you could have a cup of green tea and maybe a piece of bread, but after that, nothing until after the sun set; and we'd be in church for the whole day.

I used to hate Saturdays. I hated it because I did not want to spend the whole day with this man up there in his pulpit slapping the Bible: slam!

"And the Lord said blah, blah, blah!"

And I'm just sitting there having to sit up and pay attention; you couldn't even fidget or try to distract yourself because someone was bound to notice and cuff you in the back of your head. Can you imagine that all day? A couple of hours maybe, but it's all day Saturday; all day in church and you can't escape. It's like being in prison for the whole day and this happened every Saturday without fail. It was all about church. Not that I hate church, but the fact that I had to go the whole day was like a punishment. After a while I hated it and that really put me off going to church, which is a reaction that has lasted up to today.

Sometimes I used to run away. Well, I didn't exactly run away, but I used to go and hide until they'd all gone off to church so they'd have to go without me.

I have this thing about trees and I remember this one occasion when I climbed up into this exceedingly tall tree and it was beautiful and cool up there, with the wind gently rocking in the branches where I'd settled myself. It was wonderful to be able to get away like that and escape from all the chaos and confusion in that household; just being coolly rocked in this tree, alone with my thoughts, gently relaxing. Suddenly, I fell asleep and landed with a huge bump in the little water hole just below. You couldn't really call it a stream, it was literally just a small pool of water that reached up to my waist, but it broke my fall and probably saved my life.

I woke with a start out of my slumber to find myself waist deep in water. I was totally shocked and slightly bruised. Slowly gathering my thoughts, I tried to work out how I'd got there, because the last thing I remembered was being up in the tree overhead enjoying the cool breeze. It was obvious that I could have broken my neck if that pond hadn't been there. That was quite an experience and part of me couldn't help wondering if that was some kind of divine retribution: my punishment for trying to get out of going to church.

Anyway, as a result of getting up so early and having to drogue this water every day and getting my head constantly wet, I got catarrh, and I think my mum eventually realised that I was being ill-treated. People would write and tell her or they would tell her when they saw her, mainly because they expected something from her in return, so they would try to be nice to her: "Boy, they treat the bwoy bad, you know! I mean every morning him have to go drogue the water and the lazy Ken and I-Man don't do nothing and your pickney is always the one working."

So, after all the various tribulations down there in West Portland, my mum surfaced one day to find out what I was getting up to and my aunt told her that I was too bad and they couldn't control me. I was never bad, boisterous maybe, but never bad.

The real problem, of course, was the unfair treatment; they worked me so hard that my health began to suffer: the catarrh was getting worse, caused by constantly having to carry water on my head in the early mornings and late evenings, plus being barefoot all the time, even to the point of going to school without shoes to save on the leather. On top of that, I was getting caned at school for being late whenever I had to go and get water in the mornings which made me late for school, so that wasn't helping either.

My mum hauled me back with her to Kingston and, for some reason, it was reassuring being back home in the tenement with the old familiar routines that I'd left behind, but, she decided she was going to send me away again. According to her, I needed the discipline and guidance of a father and, all too soon, I was on the move once more, this time to East Portland.

* Drogue – Colloquial word for carry

5

Red Man

One evening a truck pulled up outside our tenement yard and everyone rushed out of their rooms to find out what was going on. It was my dad, Red Man, with six or so of his cronies: the so-called "side men", hanging off the sides of the truck.

One of them came over and took up my little case. It couldn't possibly have been big as I didn't have many clothes: just what was on my back and my Sunday best that came out only on very special occasions.

I was looking forward to this trip, although I wasn't even sure where we were going. As far as I was concerned I was off on another adventure and the anticipation gave me butterflies in my stomach. I had heard so many good things about this man, my father: he's rich, he's got power, with people at his beck and call, and he's married with his own property.

His arrival that evening sparked major excitement in our yard, with people coming from all directions, even the other yards to poke their noses in. So, while this serious-looking, red-faced man goes into the room to chat with my mum, and no doubt to be read the riot act about how he was to control me, I was outside holding court. The curiosity was too much for the other kids.

"Who's that?"

"My dad!"

"Oh, he's got a dad."

"Yea."

And I'm beaming from ear to ear because this is all about me; I'm respected, admired and even envied. It's just like before when he had come and taken me out for a drive that day. I had a father and, what's more, I was going away with him, so things were looking up.

Finally, after about 20 minutes, he marched out, still wearing his long, serious expression, with not a word to anybody, jumped into the truck and we were off, with the kids from the yard creating a commotion and running alongside the vehicle. Meanwhile, I was trying my best to act cool, as though this sort of thing happened to me every day.

The first stop we made was for something to eat: patties and Coca Cola from a little bread shop down town before stopping by Coronation Market to collect the market traders, the so-called higglers, that he had brought up to Kingston on the truck earlier that morning. By now, they would have finished doing their selling and would be buying sugar, flour, salt-fish and other foodstuffs to take back home to Portland.

We pulled up at Coronation Street and he and a few of the side-men disappeared into the market to go and buy what they wanted, or to go and see their girlfriends. What really scared me though, man, were those people with their sharp machetes, these were sharp, sharp, sharp, the traders would be walking through the market talking loudly and threateningly to some person and swinging their tool as though it were primarily a weapon:

"You better pay for what you did tek..."

"You ordering something or you just looking?"

"Just looking."

"Cho! Go and look somewhere else if you not buying. This is not a side show!"

With all the arguments, conflicts and joviality going on, the market did indeed feel like a kind of a theatre show. Somehow I found it fascinating, but the sight of those gleaming, razor-sharp machetes flashing in the air put the fear of God into me.

You could see that business was brisk, but it felt like an intimidating place to be, especially if you were a child and didn't know what you were doing or where you were going. Besides, raised voices and sharp machetes felt to me like a potential recipe for disaster.

All the while we were there in the market I was getting to know the side-men, the fellows working for my father who were more like older boys, really. They were bigger than me, but were

44

still like children in some ways. They were following this man's every move like he was the Pied Piper or something; everywhere he goes, they go, and anything he wants done, they're quick to oblige, and none of them want to displease him or get a public tongue lashing from their boss.

"Hey bwoy, what happen?"

"A Red Man son this, you know."

"Yea? A Red Man son, for true?"

And they're starting to look out for me, which I liked. It was reassuring; I felt as though I belonged to the club, but then, lest I should get too familiar, they would say things like: "Better not leave him on his own because he might decide to run 'way".

"I suppose him going to be bad like him father! As bad as Red Man – a gal in every district, ha ha ha."

And they'd have a good laugh about that, so it feels more like they're babysitting me rather than seeing me as a peer.

Well, by now, night had fallen and the higglers all started climbing on to the truck and sitting down on some planks the side men had laid out. I was going to be in the front but I asked if I could ride in the back so my father's main man swapped places with me so I could sit in the back with the other boys and these higgler women who are all talking and making plans.

Before long, they're asking me about Kingston; what Kingston gals are like and other things boys like to chat about, and what I noticed about driving in this truck was that suddenly I am outside of Kingston and it's dark; pitch black, as all the street lights and signs have mysteriously disappeared and all you can hear is the noise of the truck, "Whooowww!" And we're going fast, very fast and, then, I noticed the mountains in the dim moon light and the hills bordering Kingston, and it was spectacular, so different to any view of the city that I'd seen before, although it was not that far out from where I had lived for so long.

The talk then ranged from the sublime to the ridiculous and back again but I'm the main topic of conversation, the butt of the humourless, and at times, vulgar jokes. Throughout it all the governor, Red Man, hardly spoke. He was doing the driving with the windows down and concentrating on the road while getting through what seemed like a chain of cigarettes.

Then we were driving by the sea with the cool breeze assaulting our faces, and it was just beautiful powering along in the pitch darkness apart from the beam of light from the truck, and above we could see hundreds of stars like silver coins in the night sky.

I was excited but I didn't know what to expect. Occasionally, we would stop and Red Man would get out of the truck and disappear, either to meet with one of his many girlfriends who ran one of his businesses, like a bar or a dance hall, or to collect money or deliver orders. While he's round the back taking care of business, some of us would get out and go inside the bar area for something to eat and drink while others would make their way over to where they were selling jerk pork or some other delicacy, until we heard the honk, honk of the truck's horn when Red Man was ready to move off.

Eventually, the boys told me that we were approaching Hector's River, on the border between St Thomas and Portland, which was our destination. They pointed out that you could always tell when we were making this approach because the rough St Thomas road we had been riding on suddenly became nice and smooth. The Ken Jones Highway, they called it. Ken Jones was the white *backra**who had lived in the area and owned a sugar plantation in years gone by, perhaps as far back as slavery time.

This is the highway that would take us straight into Hector's River and we drove up to a little district after travelling on the coastal road for a bit. This spot along the coast was beautiful; right by the sea where the waves were crashing on to the rocks sending salty spray splashing on to us, even though we were quite high up above the coastline. We drove up to this shop in the centre of the village above which Red Man and his wife lived and below that to the back of the shop was where his uncle, wife and their children lived.

So my dad and his wife lived upstairs and opposite there was a building with lots of sawdust where he kept ice which he

Red Man

and Shortie would sell to the district and they seemed to be the only ice business for miles. I discovered that the sawdust is used to stop the ice melting and the next morning Shortie, who ran the shop, and Uncle James, Redman's brother, or one of his other people, would drive the truck to distribute the ice to the surrounding villages.

My father introduced me to my stepmother and told me to do whatever she said because she ran the house. The stern look on her face told me that I had no choice. Apparently, they had been together in England for years until he won big on the Irish Sweepstakes, scooping a whopping £30,000, which was a huge fortune in the UK in the 1950s, and even more so in Jamaica.

In those days, you could buy a house for £500 and apparently where he was living in Camberwell, south London, his friend had told him that he could buy a whole street but instead he and his wife decided to return to Jamaica to live in the area where he had grown up and to build his house and settle down with his wife and family, although Miss Inez was barren. Of course, he had children outside the relationship, me, for example, and later I would discover that I was not the only one. So, now, here we are in Hector's River at his uncle's place while his own house was being built at a place called Compound, which was about a mile or so from the shop.

The next morning, after the pleasantries and a lovely breakfast of fried plantains and eggs, Miss Inez dictated the house rules which were ok, I had no problem with any of that, and then I was introduced to my cousins: Laurel, who would turn out to be my best cousin, she was lovely and very bright, and Kenneth and Horace and of course Shortie, Timothy and others. The Halls were all hard-working, studious types and their father, Cyrus, wanted them to be doctors, lawyers or other professionals.

Then I had to go and register at Hector's River School, which was the lower school, and just above it, on a hill, you could see the high school, Happy Grove High.

When I started at the school I met the headmaster and his wife but I was introduced by my dad, who said, "This is my son

Keith Clarke". His name was Clarke and my mother's maiden name was Walker, so it seems that when she went to register me, she'd registered me as Walker. Although I thought it strange that for all these years I was known by one name and suddenly, as if in the blink of an eye, I have become someone else, however it didn't impact on me too much as I was assimilated into the society, and, in many ways this was a whole new experience; a whole new life, so the name change didn't really matter.

Around the school was an area of land where we would do our farming as part of our lessons in agriculture. It was a proper little farm where we grew fruits like paw paw, sugar cane, kitchen vegetables, all types of foods and we actually learned about things like grafting and creating hybrid fruits, like grafting sweet orange on to lime to produce a sour orange.

The school was on one level with various classes determined by imaginary boundaries and you went from one class to the next, according to your achievements. I wasn't very book smart but these relatives of mine were very clever. As it turns out, Hector's River has produced some of the most brilliant people in Jamaican society, like Olympian athletes, doctors, pilots who have distinguished themselves in the American and Canadian air force, and one or two scientists.

Strangely enough, some of our relatives were Chinese. Mr Chin down the road ran a shop, and somehow he was related to us. Then the Halls, whom I have just mentioned, were Indians, and they owned the shop below our apartment and there were about ten of them in the Hall family. So, suddenly, I've got ten cousins and it's great because most of them are boys so I can be in whatever group I want and have a great time with my cousins.

It didn't take long to work out that my step-mother hated me and my dad knew this, so he would send me over to his uncle's shop where I had a slate so that any time I wanted anything to eat I could just go and get what I wanted and he would pay my bill at the end of the month. I wasn't spoilt, but he made sure that I never wanted food because Miss Inez was the sort of person who would hold a grudge for one reason or another and punish me by denying me food.

My dad was a quick-tempered man, who, ironically claimed he loved women and hated to see them ill-treated but thought nothing of beating his own wife with a strap every drunken weekend. He used to drink quite a bit, particularly at weekends, I suppose he might even have been an alcoholic; you could smell him coming into the house, and he was supposed to eat but he didn't eat just drank quite liberally so that took its toll on him and his health as well as his marriage.

Redman always had a few girlfriends locally and Miss Inez found out about one of them and confronted the woman who was supposed to be pregnant and when my dad came home that evening he beat her very badly and cursed her, calling her barren mule and other shocking names. I remember the day when he beat me in my back so badly that I've still got the scars to show. What happened was that a girl down the road really liked me and kept trying to get close to me but this particular day I was with the guys and didn't want her following behind me. After dark, yes, but not openly in the middle of the day when I was with my friends; it was embarrassing and the guys kept teasing me, so to get rid of her I picked up a stone and pretended to sling it. This was so insane and it slipped out my hand and must have just grazed her but she made a big drama out of it, claiming that I had knocked her down with a big rock stone. She told her father, who complained to my father and that was it. When Red Man came home he didn't say a word, he just walked in one afternoon while I was waiting for Cookie, our cook, to finish my lunch he grabbed a belt with buckle and let fly as he beat me with it: bam, bam, bam, bam! He was like a robot; there were no words, no explanation, just violence as he peppered me with licks. I jumped up and tried to escape through the window but he came after me with the strap, hitting me so hard that he tore off a piece of the skin in my back.

I was a mess of shock, pain and humiliation. I had been subjected to acts of spitefulness from my peers and even from my aunt Adlin, whose punishment included sending me to collect water from a pond a quarter mile away in the middle of the night, but I had never experienced such raw brutality, and for what? On the basis of hearsay, someone had said I did something and that was enough for my father to condemn me with no benefit of the doubt.

My only refuge was to escape and lick my wounds. I did so by climbing a big ackee tree in the yard with a whole heap of foliage to camouflage me. I climbed right to the top and stayed there for the whole day. They couldn't see me but I could see everything that was going on down below; people moving around, coming and leaving, frantically looking for me.

At one point Red Man showered and disappeared in his car, which meant that he was going out. Whenever he took the truck that was work because he drove the truck to go and distribute ice or to transport higglers from one place to another. The car, now, was used for his own social manoeuvres. The minute he left, I came down from the tree and went into the house where Cookie took pity on me.

"Ah, let me see your back, poor chile," she said, and put iodine on my cuts and bandaged up my back. Boy, it burnt like hell and I cried like a thousand Tarzans. Then Cookie started interrogating me about why did I have to knock down that gal and I asked what gal? She said the gal down the road, Mr so-and-so's daughter. I kept protesting that I did not, but she insisted, "Yes you did" and said that was why my father was mad. Cookie added it was a good thing I had run so that he could have time to cool down.

I didn't see Red Man for a whole week after that. Whenever he came to the house I would disappear and climb back up into my tree to hide and keep a lookout. The best part was that I didn't need to confront that miserable old man and risk his wrath again and, secondly, nobody knew where I was.

Then one day the girl must have relented and told somebody that the incident didn't happen like that and how the stone must have just brushed her but, as far as I was concerned, the damage was already done. I think the main thing was that I had wounded her pride. She fancied me and I didn't mind, but I just didn't want her cramping my style when I was hanging out with my friends. Stone or no stone, by slighting her I had sealed my fate

Relaxing on the porch of my father's house in Hector's River

and she was determined that I should suffer. Well, Red Man took care of that and to this day I still have the scar to prove it.

Eventually, I settled into a routine: having a hard time with Miss Inez, some good times with my mates, and my dad, whenever he was about, would call out, "All right, boss!" Those few words were symbolic: they indicated that he was warming to me – that's when he was not drunk. Most times, he was somewhere in the district propping up some bar, drinking and laughing with his pals. He was notorious for the booze and the ladies. Boy, he could drink. He'd drink like a fish! He'd start on a Friday night and keep going through to Sunday morning. If he was going out of the district he'd drive his car but on those occasions when he took the car he'd end up in an argument with his wife because he was obviously going out to enjoy himself and she wasn't going with him. I think he preferred the company of his pals on those occasions and his wife being with him would cramp his style, so most times he'd drive the truck whenever he was going out with the guys to show that he was working, but you could tell whenever he came back that he was drunk because you could hear the truck labouring along in first gear, he was obviously too drunk and incapable to change up, so the vehicle was just churning along.

Mostly, he'd go to Flat Grass drinking with his mates or in the opposite direction, which led down to Morant Bay or somewhere where he had his clubs or bars. Otherwise, he'd go to see his friends elsewhere in the district where a whole lot of guys would congregate around him and they would be drinking, talking and laughing as though they hadn't a care in the world.

I worked out that if I ever wanted anything the best time to ask was then, so I would wait until he was with his mates drinking and I would go over and say, "Dad, can I have..."

"Oh, yea, yea..." and he'd pull out his money, but if he was on his own, you'd hear, "What you want it for?"

But he never asked any questions whenever he was drinking with his friends. So that's the time when I'd go and ask for money and I'm sure he'd later regret it but he would show off to his mates by giving his son money, "The boy needs to have some fun, here son." So, I'd take advantage of those moments.

The churning grind of his engine on his way home would always warn us when he was drunk, so we could prepare ourselves for his drunken mood swings. To butter him up, Miss Inez would cook his favourite food for him but he wouldn't eat because he was too drunk or sometimes he'd come and start eating and maybe she'd say something to him like, "Awy, you've been? To see some woman?!" And he would snap back at her and leave the food, taking himself off to bed in a huff.

He was constantly in arguments with her, almost always about some other woman. The thing is we knew that he had got some young girl down the road pregnant and I knew he had another one like that in the next town. Miss Inez decided to beat this pregnant girl from down the road and she would talk about it endlessly; hassle him about his infidelity, and he would say to her, "Well, woman, you barren, ain't you, you can't have no kids," really goading her, and that would lead to a fight. But she would always rile him up. So on those occasions, he would go out with his friends, if only to get away from her nagging and have some fun.

* Backra – Derogatory Jamaican term for a white boss, used during slavery

6

Love is Deceiving

My first real love was a beautiful half-caste girl at lower school. She was from a family of six, with a white father and black mother, Mr and Mrs Oricas, and their four lovely daughters. I can't forget them; they were stunning. He was a busha* man and they lived in Flat Grass, which was the next district from where we lived in Hector's River.

My best mate then was a boy called Ken. It was interesting that he had the same name as my brother, because in the time that I lived in Hector's River he became as close to me as a brother. His family was very poor, so he came and stayed with us, sharing my room and practically living at our house.

Ken had five sisters and he was the only boy. His father was away in the army and every time he'd come home he'd impregnate his wife and disappear again. But they were really, really poor and couldn't afford to eat, so with Ken coming to live with us there was one less mouth to feed. The two of us were always together. If people saw me, they'd see him, otherwise they'd be asking, "Keith, where's Ken?" or "Ken, where's Keith?" Everyone expected us to be together all the time.

When he came to live at our place he had his chores to do and he'd get his pocket money the same as I would, and, although he only lived about couple of houses down the road, he rarely went there, except occasionally to see his mum.

We didn't have too many chores to do because there was a cook and a maid, but my job was to clean the 20 steps up to the veranda. They didn't design the house properly, so when it rained all the water settled there so we had to clean them, water her plants, weed up the garden, and polish the verandah floor until it shined. Miss Inez was always sending us out to "pick up the yard", which meant cleaning up all the rubbish around the enclosure.

But chores aside, Ken and I liked the Oricases and decided that they were going to be our girlfriends. My girl, the youngest, was also the cutest; a real beauty with long, sleek hair all the way down to her lower back. The other girls at school hated these beguilingly beautiful sisters; naturally they were jealous but, like most of the boys, I was smitten. It was the first time that I had ever loved a girl and I wanted nothing more than to always be with her to pet and protect her.

Her name was Jean and I became her friend and her protector but I never had any intimate thing with her. Ken did and I went mad. I thought he liked one of the other sisters but it turned out that he liked the little cute one too, and we had a massive fight over it. He turned around and told me "smell this", unzipping his pants and holding out his manhood.

He said: "I've just been with her. Smell this if you don't believe me."

I said, "Which one?"

"Jean".

"What!"

I was dumbfounded. Not my little cutie. This was my Jean; my own jewel that I had just put on a pedestal. I walloped him. We fought and the two of us fell out for days. I couldn't come to terms with it. I just thought she was the most perfect girl, but after that I decided she wasn't so perfect after all. Maybe she went with him because she thought going with him was the same as going with me, I don't know; maybe he made the whole thing up, I could never be sure. He was supposed to be my friend, why would he say that? If he was supposed to be my friend how could he possibly have had sex with her knowing how much I loved her? Some friend, but then friends are like that; they let you down. It didn't make sense, but like a real brother might have done my loyalty was more with him than her, so our falling out did not last too long. I forgave him but could never look at her in a loving way ever again. In fact, I hated her and stopped talking to her. The poor girl couldn't understand why I'd gone off her; she seemed genuinely perplexed and confused. That made me wonder if Ken had really told the truth, but I gave him the benefit of the doubt, reasoning that perhaps she was a bit more forward than I had imagined. Anyway, I gave her up and took up with one of her other sisters instead. These girls were the cream of the crop and, for me, since my friend had "done it" with her, that was the worse thing; she's spoiled so she's his now. But that was the first time I was in love and it ended in heartache and bitterness. The second time was with this Chinese girl but it did not last long or amounted to much.

Where we were in Kingston my mum's friends were Indians so I got involved with Indian girls, and when I went to the country the first time there were lots of Indian girls there too. But Indians or Negroes I didn't mind so long as they were attractive, that's all I really cared about. Anyway, a Chinese family came to Hector's River and this girl was a stunner but I learned from the experience with Jean that if you liked something enough then you had to sample it because if you don't then somebody else would end up sampling it instead and once that happens, it is now spoilt. After all, they say the first cut is the deepest.

Some people would call this double standards. Why should girls keep themselves pure while guys get to move around with lots of different girls? But it wasn't like that. Most of the time, it was the girls who took the initiative. A girl would fancy this guy and she would do things with him and then, later on, she would decide she didn't fancy him any more and move to somebody else and do the same thing. Like most guys, I wanted to be with a girl who was a bit more tame and reserved.

Other girls were for fun but a "love girl" was supposed to be yours exclusively. So, that experience of first love was a big disappointment. I began to think that a pretty face was one thing but a good character was another thing altogether, and I decided to be more careful about how I selected my "love girls" in the future.

When it came to sex, it was the maid who broke me in. She was called Tenabutt. I don't know why they called her that, but she was in her twenties and I was maybe fifteen. She lived on the premises in a small house, which was more like a one-room shack, behind the main house.

In the evenings, the cook would disappear home to her family but Tenabutt was free and single; she would go out and have a good time and then she'd come back late in the night to her little shed. If she had any fellows in there we wouldn't have known because she'd do it late at night when we'd all gone to sleep and they'd have to leave before daylight. She knew my dad wouldn't have allowed it and would have sacked her. They called him an "Ignorant Man" because he was quite strict and wouldn't have accepted that sort of thing but Tenabutt was careful with her romantic liaisons, at least to keep them hidden.

Anyway, that's where she lived and sometimes we'd go inside there when outside was hot like hell and we'd sit down and chat with her about this and that, have something to eat, and it was cool; a nice little den to escape to.

Behind this shack there was a little farm where we had all sorts of fruit trees: paw-paw, banana, coconut, one or two pineapples, naseberries, mangoes, and so on, and these other big, tall trees which I loved climbing so that I could enjoy the view for miles around and watch the sea. Sometimes, from all the way up where we lived we would get the spray from the sea when it was really rough.

Tenabutt use to work with Cookie, doing most of the menial jobs like making coconut oil, which she did about once a week, and I helped out by collecting the coconuts from the trees on our land.

One day we were alone in the house. The others had the day off and my father had gone to market. I think my stepmother had gone with him to do her clothes shopping in Kingstown. So, Tenabutt and I were there alone, and she came in from outside, took all my clothes off and inspected me; then took her clothes off and, of course, things happened: she seduced me.

Put it this way, she was sort of training me to know what to do; it was supposed to be every schoolboy's fantasy. But she had a terrible reputation with the guys in the village because she was a "loose gal" who went with anybody she took a fancy to, and I was shocked when I found that out. I mean there was this older girl doing things to me I never knew was possible and I just accepted whatever she was doing although I was petrified but too scared to protest.

It was nothing like the gentle, fun times I'd enjoyed with my girlfriends when I was staying at my grandmother's and Adlin's place in Rodney Hall. This was exciting but somehow it felt dirty and illicit and I had no respect whatsoever for the young woman who had decided to provide me with my education in carnal knowledge.

* Busha – Jamaican word to describe a white plantation supervisor

7

Chicken Thief

On our way home from school most days we would buy sugar cane, if we had money, or we waited until the trucks from the cane fields were passing on their way to the factories in St Thomas and we'd run and grab a long shaft off the moving vehicle.

At other times, we used to hop the trucks and ride from one place to another, but that was dangerous and I remember on one occasion I almost got killed. I'd hopped the truck for a joyride and fell off. Bang! I landed on the hard asphalt.

The wheel of the truck just brushed along my hairline: Whoosh! Half an inch closer and my head would have been crushed like a grape. It was luck. Or perhaps there was somebody up there looking after me.

We used to hop on to those trucks either to get somewhere when we didn't want to walk in that hot sun, in the middle of the day, wearing that hot khaki uniform, or when we wanted to "sky-lark", but the day I fell off and had that shock I decided that in future I'd walk to where I was going. We still pinched cane from the truck but my near-death experience made me more circumspect about joyriding on the cane trucks.

Ken and I used to go to these young people's social evenings that were put on by the Quakers who ran Happy Grove School and the local missionary church. They organised these young people's groups every Thursday night but some of the guys would use them as a cover to meet their girlfriends and disappear with them behind the gravestones and do their business.

These evenings were supposed to be social fellowship at the minister's house for the better behaved boys and girls from the local schools who would go up there, have refreshments and learn about various things, so we looked forward to that.

The fellowship was designed to teach us about Quaker values and their way of life, and the good thing about it was that we were right on top of a hill overlooking the ocean and we'd sit there and watch the big ships, the luxury liners, going by far out into the darkness illuminated by the light emanating from inside those liners. We could only imagine what lavish activities were taking place on board, and then we would see the container ships going by as well. I don't think they could see us waving to them because we were so far away, but it was good just to sit there and relax, admiring the view and dream about faraway places; it was beautiful. This contrast quite well to where I was coming from, that sprawling, suffocating hothouse called Trench Town; this was luxury, man.

The only problem I had in Hector's River was with my stepmother. She gave me a lot of bother. I remember one time we were supposed to be going away on a school excursion and I was having a new khaki suit made specially, so I went to the tailor and he took my measurements but she went there afterwards and got him to make the suit twice the length and size. Why? So I could grow into it maybe? The suit was huge, I couldn't and wouldn't wear it; it was embarrassing.

She said to me, "Either you go in that or you don't go at all."

Of course I couldn't go. She was so spiteful.

We lived in a half-acre of land where my father had built the biggest house in the area with all his cars and trucks on display at the front. Everyone of importance would come over, which added to his standing in the community. Miss Inez was in the church so on Sundays we had to be washed and dressed in our "Sunday best". We boys were not allowed to shower inside the bathroom, only adults and the girls had that privilege, we had to bathe under the outside pipe which afforded fun and laughter for the local girls and embarrassment for us. Our shoes had to be cleaned and shined till you could see your reflections in them, and we walked along with our bible in our hand going to the Quaker church and along the way we'd meet other families we had not seen all week. These Quakers (like the guy on the oats packet) were from Canada and America. They ran the church but had also established the school, which, naturally, they ran with Quaker's values.

The pastor would visit our house some Sundays and have a nice meal while we watched. He'd turn up after church and Miss Inez would make us fix our clothes so we looked smart and sit watching while he ate and drank almost everything. Then, after he left, we could eat the leftovers.

Apart from my stepmother I had no problems living at my dad's house. I was like a child in a candy shop most of the time; there was food for the asking (apart from when my stepmother rationed me), girls for the taking and good friends to hang out with.

Aside from Ken, I was lucky to have two other mates who lived opposite: Big Man and Little Man. Ironically, Big Man was the little one and Little Man was the big one, but they were both big guys and much older than me. They were my partners in crime whenever Miss Inez would 'vex me', I would exact my revenge by thieving one or two of her chickens and running off into the bushes behind the house for a cook up.

You see, she kept chickens in the yard, coups and coups of these fast-growers, as they called them. She would get these small chickens and fatten them up within weeks and sell them. It was a good money-earner for her but every morning it was me who had to wake up early to look after her chickens – clean up the shit, wash out the coup and feed them. She did nothing except collect the eggs, which was the nice part. So, whenever I wanted to get my own back for some punishment she had doled out to me, I'd take one or two of her chickens and run to the bushes round the back with Big Man and Little Man. They were the ones who had told me, "You've got to hold dem by the neck otherwise dem will mek noise".

So after I raided the coup, grabbing the chickens by the neck, we'd vanish into the woods and they would kill, pluck the feathers and skin the birds, set up the pots on the fire with three big stones underneath to balance them and then make these big, broad dumplings to go with the curried chicken. Those guys were master cooks and that food was the best yard food you could get: dumplings and curried chicken. Revenge was sweet indeed.

The first time we did that was because I figured that I was doing all the work and this woman was getting all the profit; I wasn't getting anything out of it, not even lunch sometimes, because she wanted to punish me, so I would take my "pay" by cooking her chickens and having a good time with my friends.

After eating, we would climb up in a tree and sit in the branches just chatting, with the wind blowing through and keeping us cool, Big Man, Little Man and me. Those days were good fun, and were among the highpoint of my time living with my father. I could never sit down with him and just "shoot the breeze"; he wasn't that sort of man. I don't think I ever had a proper conversation with him, boy to man or man to man, for that matter. To some extent Big Man and Little Man filled that void.

When we were still living above the shop, I remember one morning waking up and feeling movement; the building was shaking as there was an earthquake and everybody rushed out into the street and the women were wailing and crying with their hands on their heads, "We're all dead now!" As the quake went on for what seemed like a long while people were rushing around and everyone was panicking.

What happened was that a strong earthquake had hit the eastern part of Portland and it created a massive crack in the road. At the time, my fear was that the crack would run right into the sea and carry us with it. I think after that incident my dad must have speeded things up because it was dangerous living up on top of that building, so soon after the earthquake we moved to the brand new house that he was having built. It had tiles on the floor, an inside toilet, shower, bath and all those nice facilities, and a cistern outside for washing clothe and showering for us guys. And with the girls there we boys had to go and have a shower underneath that cistern right there in the open every time exposing our selves to be ridicule of those young girls.

Hector's River was, for me, a great place for growing up. It was there that I first learned to ride a bike and to swim. Well, it was learning after a fashion, because how they would teach me to ride was by taking me to a point where the road was highest and put me on the bike. They would then push me hard and I would take off like a kite amid a load of commotion and encouragement and eventually I crashed at the other end with the twisted bike underneath. That was the first time they tried to teach me to ride and I ended up with cuts everywhere. Once was enough. I decided to leave bike riding to the older boys after that disastrous introduction.

Sometimes we would go to the River to look at the salmons swimming up stream. We weren't really fishing, just sightseeing, but most of the bigger boys would be jumping in between the salmons and swimming with them. I'd just be sitting at the side admiring their antics because I'd never learned to swim. They would shout to me: "Come on in, come on, come in".

But I'd call back, "oh, no, I can't swim. Ah!, come on in, it's fun; you'll have a laugh, man", they'd say.

I didn't know how to swim, so I decided I would just sit and watch, but they decided they were going to teach me and I was happy about that but did wonder if it would be like teaching me to ride the bicycle. I had just taken off all my clothes except my underpants when all of a sudden, Whoosh! Someone just pushed me in. I let out a mighty scream, "Whaaa!" and I was in the middle of the river panicking with my arms flapping and screaming for help, "Help, help!" But they were laughing and shouting, "Swim man, swim, swim". That was their idea of teaching me to swim.

Somehow I managed to make it to the bank and grabbed a clump of land and held on to it for dear life, panting and puffing with my heart racing thinking that I had nearly died. All the way to the riverbank I thought I was about to drown because the water was going into my mouth and I could feel myself weakening. No doubt they were thinking it was because I wasn't swimming but I knew it was because I didn't know how to swim. Despairingly, I started flapping my arms in a mad frenzy and by the time I got to the edge I was exhausted. I had made it and now was determined to hold on tight and never let go, all the while puffing and panting to catch my breath. After a while one guy came up to me promising to help and said, "I'm going to be on the other side, you swim over to me and I'll help you." But I thought I'm not going to trust these guys again, I'm hanging on to the bank, but then I started thinking about how I was going to get out of there since the bank was too steep to climb and the only way out seemed to be over on the other side of the water. I rested a little while longer and then I took off, with my arms flapping in a furious "swimming" action, which was more splashing than anything, while paddling with my legs like a frightened bullfrog with my head held high out of the water, it must have been a sight to behold.

The rest of the guys were shouting, "Come on, come on", but I was getting so frantic and tired. I managed to splash my way to the guy who said he would help but every time I got close to him, he kept moving back and saying, "you've got to do it harder and faster". Anyway, somehow I made it to where I could stand up and get out. And, as I stood there panting and sighing like I'd just escaped my death, I thought I'm never going to do that again so I stayed in the shallows while the other guys swam about in the deep.

The next day we went down to the seaside to fish and then they decided to go for a swim in the river, so we jumped into the water and I paddled about in the shallow end while the other guys were showing off their swimming skills and calling out to me, "Come on, come on, you can do it."

And some were shouting back, "Oh, no, no, him not going do it him too scared."

There was some of my stuff over the other side that I was supposed to get so I thought I'd get out, walk up the bank and go over there the easy way. When I got there the guys said, "Hey, you must learn to dive as well" and one of them pushed me back into the water, once again I flung and flung my arms; flapped and flapped and wore myself out again trying to swim. Yet again I made it from one end to the other and while I was there recovering, I thought I'd try again, so I flapped my arms quickly and kicked my legs furiously and managed to get from the deep part into the shallows. Then I thought that wasn't so bad?

So that was the sum total of my "swimming lessons": the guys chucked me in the water a few times where I struggled and splashed for dear life until I reached the safety of the bank. I was never a confident swimmer; I preferred to start at the deep end and swim into the shallows.

It was a very difficult formative experience but that's how I learned to swim – sort of – at Hector's River.

While I was living in Hector's River, I used to go to a place called Nuts River, where my other grandmother, Grandma Tee, lived with her husband Mr De Pause and his son, Leon, from another relationship.

I enjoyed visiting my grandmother on their huge farm where they had a big house and kept horses and so on. There was a big neiseberry tree and I would just go in the morning and have loads of these fruits before breakfast, it was lovely going to their farm and seeing rows and rows of banana trees and pineapples. Everywhere you looked you could see bananas just hanging off the trees and rotting on the ground because there were just so many of them.

They had two racing horses and Leon just put me on one of them, Fleet Wing, and said, "Let's go" but the horse took off like a rocket and I'm over here and I'm over there; it's galloping and throwing me in all different directions and I didn't know what to do to get it to stop. I'd never ridden before but he had assumed I knew how to ride. Eventually we both ended up in the bush covered in bruises and scratches. It reminded me of my experience when I was learning to ride a bicycle; that was just as disastrous.

It was such that I never tried horse riding again; I decided I'd had enough, once thrown was once too often as far as I was concerned. In the end I was rescued by Mr De Pause and I went on his horse with him using a rope to pull the horse that I should have been riding as we rode back home. After a day went by Leon, who had given me my first horse riding experience, said, "Look, try the donkey", and I did, and it was much better. For a start it was lower and they had attached two baskets on either side to support me so I could just sit in the middle and direct my little donkey where I wanted him to go. I ended up riding the donkey most days, but never bareback like they did; I always had to have a saddle.

My grandmother used to take her provisions to sell in Kingston and I went with her a few times whenever I was going to see my mum, who got on really well with my Grandma Tee. Mr de Pause and the others would take us down to the main road where we would get the bus to Coronation Street market in Kingston. We'd go early in the morning when it's cold, you wouldn't believe how Jamaica can be cold; very cold sometimes in the early mornings, and we're there waiting wrapped up in sheets until a bus turns up and of course the driver would turn up hours late. Nevertheless, we were grateful to see the bus, we'd get in the bus and it's nice and warm in there with all these people huddled up close together.

Grandma Tee had a little stall in the market which she'd open up and put her things on display and then, after we'd been there for most of the morning, my mum would come down there and they would talk about whatever. It was nice to see my mum and to catch up on news about my brother Ken and the others in the Kingston tenement. It was only then that I realised how much I'd really missed them, although not enough to want to go back with her. I was getting close to my grandmother and was enjoying my childhood in the country. I wasn't waking up every day wondering who I was going to have to fight or whether I was going to have enough to eat; all that was taken care of.

They were all generous in the market, "Oh, so you're Mrs de Paus's grandson, you want this or you want piece of that? Sit down here so no?" It was nice being spoiled for a change and it was definitely something I could have gotten used to.

So, we would go to Kingston occasionally to do this marketing and I would go back and stay with Grandma at her farm up there on top of this mountain, which we would reach at the end of a long, winding dirt road from Morant Bay, dotted with a few houses and the occasional shop and a vast expanse of hills and valleys.

I enjoyed going to Nuts River as I felt freer than I ever had; there was none of the pressure that Miss Inez put on me. I enjoyed it while it lasted but then I found out that I had to go back to Hector's River. Anyway my grandmother and I had a very good bond and I cared a lot about her.

It was good when I went to Nuts River, although Mr de Pause's son got more privileges but there was no animosity between us; we were just two lads enjoying life and having all kinds of adventures.

Here it is quite different to my father's place in Hector's River where, once or twice I said I was going to run away and I packed my things because I was having such a difficult experience with Miss Inez.

I said, "I'm off, I can't take this anymore I'm going back to my mum", and I'd take my stuff and hide up in a tree. I wanted to run away but I kept thinking where the hell am I going to go? I didn't know how to get to Black Hill from where I was in East Portland and of course life wouldn't be better with Aunt Adlin. I couldn't go back to my mum because I didn't know how she would have reacted. So, in frustration, I gave the impression that I was actually running away by packing my stuff and hiding it in some bushes near the property, and then I'd disappear up a tree until late in the night. When I was ready for something to eat I'd creep down and sneak out the back yard to the shop down the road to get food from Shorty, then go back to hide up in the tree again. I would stay there until way up in the night when everyone had gone to bed then I would creep down and if Tenabutt wasn't in her little house I'd go inside there and stay until the morning and be up before anyone woke up and I'd quickly go and gather the mangoes and neiseberries that had dropped off the trees overnight and eat them for breakfast before disappearing up the tree again to my hideout. As far as they were concerned I was away for a couple of days. By now Miss Inez would have been getting worried because if my dad came back and asked for me she couldn't say, "He's run away." My old man would have been furious.

By now, when it was becoming too tedious and lonely being stuck up in that tree, I would come out of hiding looking haggard and tiptoe to collect my stuff from its hiding place. I would turn up, put on quite an act like the Prodigal Son returning home after spending time in a far off place. Everyone started screaming how worried they had been about me and how relieved they were that I was back. I put on a dejected expression and said I couldn't find how to get to such and such a place and so I had returned. As far as they were concerned I had gone for days, they weren't to know that I had been up in a tree all along, hiding and watching what they were doing. I'd see people come and go and I'd hear everything they were saying; it was the perfect deception.

Now I was "back" they couldn't do enough for me; Cookie rushed around preparing my favourite meals, and even Miss Inez made an effort to be pleasant, which was completely out of character for her. I just lapped up all the attention and commended myself for my superb acting skills.

* Sky-lark – Innocent fun, mocking about

8

Psychic Powers

Miss Inez, my stepmother, could not have kids and I think she took it out on me for the girls in the village who were going off with her husband, my old man. She started to hate me for that, although it's obviously was not my fault I must have represented what could or will happen as a result of those liaisons. Well, she had to take it out on someone, I suppose.

Perhaps I reminded her of the child she could never have but, whatever her rationale, she didn't hide the fact that she couldn't stand the sight of me. And there was something else about me that met with her displeasure; she was convinced that I had special powers, like I was some kind of psychic or obeah* man.

The thing was that at certain times I would "see" or experience something that was somehow a bit extraordinary. I remember one time, for example, when I went into the woods with these guys. It was a beautiful day and we were hunting for wild fowls with our slingshots and generally getting up to our usual antics when, suddenly it started raining in a sudden downpour that arrived without even the slightest hint of a warning. Straight away I shouted out, "Come on you guys, there's a shed around the corner, let's go and shelter there."

My mates all stopped and looked at me curiously.

"What shed?"

They knew those woods as well as I did, perhaps better because they'd been in the area longer, but convinced that I knew what I was saying I sped off ahead. We ran and ran and there it was, a shed around the next bend in this virgin woodland, and we rushed inside to shelter from the torrential downpour which was getting worse with crashing thunder and flashes of lightning.

We sat in the shed reminiscing and plotting new adventures while the heavens gushed like a waterfall. Afterwards, when the rain had cleared and we pulled ourselves up to set off again, the others asked me "How did you know there was a shed around here? We've never been here before. Have you?

It was true, I had never been to that part of the woods before; none of us had.

"You don't know anything about this area," one of them said.

I nodded. "I know."

"Then how did you know about the shed?"

I told them truthfully, "I don't know."

That was it, I don't know how I knew; it just came to me. It was as though something said to me, "There's a shed there," and I just accepted it.

Call it intuition, called it premonition, I don't know what it was or where it came from, and at the time I didn't even have a name for it, all I knew was that I just knew something at a particular moment when I needed that knowledge, and I never doubted the information or questioned where it had come from. Interestingly, the insight was never wrong.

Soon, the others started telling people in the village about these strange experiences and my stepmother would think I was weird and, on top of her other grievances, this phenomenon made her even more hostile as well as suspicious of me. As far as she was concerned, I was "odd". It wasn't true, I was just a normal boy, but maybe something had happened to trigger those occurrences, something quite natural that we don't have any way of explaining. But the reaction was one of fear and finger-pointing over something that, after all, didn't do any harm. I was labelled mad, bad and dangerous by my stepmother. I think she enjoyed finding ever more reasons to mistreat and ostracise me.

On top of everything, I used to have dreams, strange, bizarre, fantastical dreams about finding a treasure trove. I especially used to dream about "Panya Jar"*, these supposedly mythical jars packed full of gold that were buried centuries ago by Spanish buccaneers in the olden days when Jamaica was overrun by pirates.

One night, I dreamt an old Spaniard wearing a funny hat sitting under a tree close to the old church in Hector's River. The old man gestured to me and said, "Come." In my dream I went to him and he said, "You dig there, you will find a Panya Jar with money."

When I woke up I was excited but, funnily enough, I was full of trepidation as well. The dream had seemed so real that I felt as though I had really lived the experience. I had to tell someone and in my state of exhilaration I blurted out the story to my stepmother, of all people. I could barely finish speaking when she railed at me and whoever else was within earshot, "You see what I say 'bout this bwoy? Me tell you there's something strange about him! Maybe it's to do with his madda, maybe she was an obeah woman!"

I stood there shocked with my mouth wide open for what felt like minutes. How could she react like that when I was only relating a dream? Besides, why did she have to drag my mother into it? It was hurtful but the lesson was to learn to keep my big mouth shut; henceforth I would keep my dreams to myself. I felt a little like Joseph the dreamer from the Bible, who put his foot in his mouth when he told his family about his fantastic dreams about being better than they were. Look what happened to him – his brothers ended up selling him into slavery. I thought better of telling my friends about the dream, which I was convinced was more like a vision, because the fear was that they would have said, "Come, let's go dig it up." I was too scared to do that, not because I was worried we wouldn't find anything – on the contrary, I was afraid in case it was there! Then Miss Inez's prognosis about me being some kind of voodoo child wouldn't have been too far wrong would it?

I had heard people talking about the Panya Jars. They used to say that when the Spaniards died their people used to bury them with their riches. To me, those stories were more than fairy tales because I used to have these dreams that frightened me because they were too realistic; they were nothing to do with imagination or wishful thinking and I had no control whatsoever over those strange revelations.

In the end I never went to dig for that treasure that the old Spaniard told me was buried close to the old church so I'll never know if I could have found Spanish bullion, but lots of things like that used to happen. I've got a scar on my right hand and even that came about as a result of these strange little incidents that seemed to have no logical explanation. Every time I see the scar on my hand, I remember that it was all supposed to have been a dream.

What happened was that my best friend Ken and I went everywhere together. Both of us had our cutlasses, sharp little machetes for chopping down vegetation and cutting up things like sugar cane and coconuts around the yard and in the woods. We were like two overseers on the property, going around fixing things and whenever someone asked us to do something we'd take our cutlasses and do that, so our tools were useful and conveyed on us a certain sense of power.

One time I dreamed that it was a beautifully hot day and we were out as usual making ourselves useful with our sharpened machetes, when suddenly it became absolutely dark. It was as though within the blink of an eye it had gone from daylight to midnight, and Miss Inez said, "There's a storm coming".

We all ran indoors and, low and behold, there was lightning, thunder and heavy, driving rain which went on for a while and then, just as suddenly, it stopped raining and the sun came back out again. The heavy sudden downpour had caused the banana trees in front of the house to collapse and Miss Inez instructed us, "Unno go and clear up the banana tree, cut it down and remove it from there." So, Ken and I dutifully grabbed our cutlasses and we start chopping, chopping, chopping and suddenly, wham! His cutlass cut me on the back of my hand.

"Whaaah!" I screamed so loudly everyone must have thought I was being murdered and I was bleeding and bawling so much that there was quite a commotion with everyone in earshot running to see what was happening. Just then, I woke up. What a relief, it was only a dream.

Anyway, some time later, it was a nice day and we were all sitting around relaxing on the verandah and I was telling Ken and Miss Inez about that particular dream. Miss Inez was her usual cynical self: "Ah bwoy, mek you always come out wid them fool-fool things? What you doing talking about things like that? Go away, go pick up the yard."

Ok, nobody wanted to listen to my story so I skulked off to tidy up the yard, as usual. Ken eventually joined me and the two of us went around doing what we normally did. Suddenly, the place went dark and someone said, "Ha, there's gonna be a storm".

Then, bam! Immediately there was thunder, lightning, rain and we rushed inside and sat down. This time now, it was not a dream; this was real. And it went on and on with the thunder clapping and lightning flashing and eventually, just like it had happened in my dream, the storm stopped and the sun suddenly came out.

Miss Inez said, "Unno go and clear up the yard, move them banana trees from there."

So we went and got our cutlasses.

No, no, I had not realised that this was deja vu, this is the funny thing.

Ken and I started chopping up the banana trees and suddenly, Pow! Ahaaaaa! He chopped me on my hand and just as suddenly it all came rushing back to me.

"Oh, my God!" The realisation dawned on me that I had just lived out every single detail of the dream that only a short time ago I was relating to the others. It was uncanny. Miss Inez thought I was absolutely strange and Ken was rushing around in a state of shock trying his best to stop the bleeding. Eventually, Miss Inez glared at me with a peculiar expression before she decided to come and administer some first aid, bandaging the wound and putting the hand in a sling, but all the while she was doing that she was mumbling to herself about how strange I was and what manner of evil I was bringing into her house with my outlandish experiences.

There were also a lot of other things that happened, like experiences which gave me the impression that I had been to places that I'd never been before. I used to keep those things to myself; shut them inside of me. I wouldn't tell anyone because I was "strange" enough; I didn't want to give them any more ammunition to further condemn me.

It was mainly my stepmother who made me feel strange about myself; I really got on her nerves. She thought I was a peculiar lad doing strange things and this particular experience was the icing on the cake for her because she remembered that I was telling her about the dream and she had dismissed it and said, "oh, this fool-fool bwoy", and suddenly the very thing we were talking about unfolded right before her eyes.

I even used to have a lot of that same thing going on in school. Sometimes I would wish something would happen and it would come true, like if a boy was troubling me I would just think, "I wish he would fall down and break his damn leg!" And he did. When that happened, I was upset; that was a bit scary and I'm thinking to myself, did I do that?

I used to wish for bad things to happen and they did so I had to be very careful about opening my mouth; careful of what I was wishing for. It came to the point where I was very afraid of my wishes coming true. It didn't make me feel powerful, it made me feel very much afraid because it was like it wasn't me, it was somebody or something controlling me and so because of that I was not very happy with the power or ability, whatever it was, so I tried to suppress it.

Still, there were occasions where Miss Inez would give me a hard time and I would say, "I wish, I wish my dad would just do something", because I wouldn't have anything to eat or she would punish me in some spiteful way and I would wish for some sort of intervention. That happened one day when my dad came to me and said, "You know what I'm gonna do? I'm gonna go to Shorty and open a book for you because they tell me that sometimes you don't get any food and for whatever reason I think you should still get your meals even if you're bad." So he set up an account for me with Shorty, who manages his father's, Mr Cyrus's, shop down the road, so that at any time I could take my friends there and order all sorts of food. That was a thing I'd hoped would happen, it was just like an intuition, and it happened but mostly it was like something attracted me, like a number would attract my eyes; it's like it's dancing in front of me telling me "pick me, pick me" and I would follow the thought and it would pay off. If I ever tried to do it logically it never worked but when I followed my intuition, it always paid off. Anyway, I suppressed those things and, thankfully, they don't happen any more. However, in my youth I felt that I could actually influence things and I was scared of that power, or that ability, but now I just think maybe it was all just coincidence after all and that I didn't have any of the influence I imagined I had, although years later during my time in England I had some supernatural experiences which reminded me of the time I spent as that "strange boy" who seemed to have the power to make his own dreams and wishes come true.

* Obeah – witchcraft, magic
* Panya Jar (sometimes called Spanish Jar) – This was believed to be treasure that the Spaniards (colonists, pirates and buccaneers who had colonised Jamaica) use to bury underneath some landmark, such as a certain tree. It was thought that the spirits of these people could "dream" to a chosen person among the living about the whereabouts of this buried treasure, which was usually stored in a container called the Panya Jar.
* Madda – Jamaican colloquial word for mother

9

Boarding School

As school children in Hector's River it was always our ambition to progress to college and beyond. At the lower school it was drilled into us that we should strive to go on to higher education, which meant graduating to the high school up the hill and after that we were expected to finish up at a university in Kingston, the USA or Canada.

Indeed a number of children from our school ended up at some of the leading educational establishments in the country, places such as Titchfield in Port Antonio, Calabar and Excelsior in Kingston, and other top institutions, and afterwards they were destined for UWI – the University of the West Indies – in Jamaica, or other universities abroad.

One or two from my year were given scholarships to study in the USA, including my cousin Laurel, who won a scholarship to study science at an American university. She eventually graduated as a microbiologist and stayed on in the United States to further her career.

I found it very difficult to match up to the brilliance of my cousins but, for some unknown reason, the teachers expected me to be up to their level. From my point of view it wasn't hard to see how much of an advantage they all had which gave them a big head start on me. I mean, they were a focused group of individuals from a stable family background, whose futures were probably charted out from birth. They attended school in a structured way and had their parents and all their brothers and sisters to help them along. They weren't fighting just to survive each day but where I had come from I was fighting just to go to school; fighting just to get home from school and then, suddenly, I'm in this different environment, a quiet family-oriented setting where children going to school is normal and they expect me to slot in at the top of the class and everything to be just so. I became a rebel because I wasn't as good as they were or as brilliant as the teachers expected me to be.

The truth is I was pretty awful at maths and dreaded the lessons and more so because I was put in the class with Laurel and others like her who were top of the class. She tried to support me sometimes when the teacher asked me a question she'd whisper the answer to me. But if I answered the teacher would say, "She told you, didn't she?" And I'd be embarrassed again. I'm always embarrassed by my shortcomings, so when Laurel was moved up and I was kept back I had a sense of relief; I didn't feel as much pressure after that. She was promoted to where she deserved to be but I was put down into a class where they thought I should be and, of course, I was like the biggest boy in that group and felt like a dunce.

The teachers expected too much of me without taking my background into account. With a little more interest and patience, I might well have caught up on the academic side, but, still, I could play cricket and I excelled at that, so I wasn't so useless after all. I decided to focus on the practical things, like sports, cooking and farming and did very well, so I tried to excel in those areas. I just couldn't do the academic stuff, or maybe my confidence had been undermined.

Soon after I returned to Hector's River from spending time with my grandmother in Nuts River I noticed that most of my school chums had started to go off to college, including some of my own relatives. The problem was that I wasn't smart enough; I wasn't in their league, so I wasn't sure if I would get a chance to go to college like the others. However, a college called Xavier, a private high school in Kingston, was offering scholarships so I applied and was awarded a half scholarship. I later found out that there's no such thing – as so-called half scholarship is just another way of getting you to pay, but I was excited. "Yeaah, I'm going to Kingston, to Xavier High. I'm getting away from the country bumpkins back to my old stomping ground!"

When the time came I went with my father on the truck and all the side-men came along for the ride. So I went to this school and my dad talked to the headmaster and later I was introduced to various people there. I was going to be living on the development as a boarder so they took me round to what was like a big house, with the girls on one side and the boys on the other. And at the back is a massive kitchen and dining area and the House Man, who looks after the boys, is living there, as is the House Woman, who takes care of the girls.

So, there I was, I'm established now, I'm going to High school and I'm going to learn Latin – "amo, amas, amat", as we would repeat by rote – and I'm enjoying the snobbery. And enjoying the boarding as well, which is fantastic. I like being back in Kingston because I get to go out to the sports grounds and sometimes there are different competitions going on, which is exciting to watch or take part in.

And then there were the girls. We guys valued every opportunity to get together with them because they separated us and the only time we got close to the girls was in the classroom, but the teacher was always very eagle-eyed so we didn't really get to mix with them. In the evenings when we had our meals, we had a session where we used to sit together underneath the trees and we would briefly talk to them but aside from that we were just kept apart, so much so that the headmaster would patrol the corridors in the evenings so we couldn't meet.

Anyway, this headmaster had his own agenda regarding those girls. I didn't know that he had fancied one of the girls at the college. I was naïve because I liked that particular girl too, and we used to send little notes to each other, although we couldn't get to see each other except at dinner time when we would play footsie underneath the table and look longingly into each other's eyes.

That was exciting but frustrating because we couldn't meet up to talk or hold hands; we had to use other ways of communicating by gestures and little notes saying things like, "I like your eyes" or "I like your dress", or whatever. There was nothing to say who had sent it, but she knew. It so happened that the House Woman must have told the headmaster to watch me because she thinks I'm having an affair with one of the girls.

So, I was being watched and one night I was in my bed sleeping, while outside in the corridor people were walking up and down and this particular girl must have come out to go to the toilet and someone must have seen her and said she was coming out of my room. The headmaster and other staff came knocking and so I ended up being grilled or being accused about what they thought they saw and she was in another room also being interrogated. The headmaster sent for my father. I had broken the rules: I "had a girl in my room".

My gosh, I was shocked and confused! I mean I liked her and I may have touched her hand maybe once, if that, but that was it.

The whole thing was that this headmaster himself took a fancy to this girl and wanted to have something going with her and I was in the way and he wanted me off the premises so he cooked up the story that this young lady and I were together in my room, that way he could create an incident which get me out of the picture. I had been framed!

My dad came to town with all those boys on his truck and after speaking with the headmaster came to the conclusion that I was indeed getting up to no good in college. He put on a front with the headmaster about it being a serious matter and how disappointed he was, but really, he thought it was funny, in a nudge-nudge, wink-wink, kind of way; how bad It was going off with the "headmaster's daughter" right under the headmaster's nose so those were the lies the headmaster gave my dad. I think Redman was secretly proud of that and went round telling all his friends what a little rogue I was. I became the butt of their jokes; how the apple doesn't fall far from the tree; I was obviously my father's son.

In the end it was decided I wasn't going to be expelled from the school but I was expelled from the boarding. I would be a day student so my dad arranged for me to stay with a lady who lived three streets away from the college.

The place seemed nice enough when I went there but this guardian was a Bible-bashing Pentecostal Christian woman and every night, around seven o'clock, I would have to go with her and her friends to this little church. She had a car and we'd drive to collect her church sisters and they would cram in while we ventured downtown to attend this late-night church service which was a heap of wailing and commotion and didn't finish until around three o'clock in the morning. I just fell asleep there as I needed my rest to be alert at college the next day, but we did that at least four or five times a week and she wouldn't leave me on my own because, you see, I was the "tearaway"; I needed religion to save my errant soul because of what I was supposed to be doing with all those young girls. Therefore, I must be in church to stop me corrupting anyone else, so now I am spending my evenings in church with this lady all the time, seeing all these people being baptised in the pool that was underneath the floorboards near the pulpit but despite their persuasion I didn't want to be baptised and objected whenever they mentioned it.

Just picture the scene: this Bible-thumping pastor shouting and railing from the pulpit with the people all clapping their hands and wailing, and I'm thinking "I've my lessons to do, what am I doing here?"

Eventually, I told her that I was tired and fed up with my lack of progress at school and it was because of the late nights at her religious services, so she suggested that when I came from school I would go straight to do my homework before going off to the church. It wasn't exactly the solution I was after, because we were still out late into the night, most nights. And I knew that it was late because when we were coming home the dust carts were on the road. Not surprisingly, I was falling asleep in class because I couldn't get much sleep at night. Finally, I told Red Man that I couldn't take it any more, so he relented and found me some other lodgings downtown.

After my experience at Xavier High boarding, I decided to keep away from girls because my association with them was getting me into too much trouble.

I was taken to live with a new family where the guy reared pigeons, lots of pigeons. I don't know what he did with them but I used to enjoy going to the coop to watching those birds performing their antics and listen to them cooing: "Cooo-cooo". I don't think he used to race them; he might have been supplying them to the local Chinese restaurants; who knows!

The woman, who became my new guardian, had these four strikingly beautiful daughters – just the way we guys in Jamaica like them: fair skinned, straight nosed and with long wavy hair. They were also very nice people, but I was petrified that I might be framed again so I don't think I managed to get close to any of them. It was ironic that I should have been kicked out of boarding school for allegedly fraternising with a girl against the rules, and here I was put up in a house with four beautiful young women to tempt me.

They were practically white, half-caste people who were trying to live above their means. However, I remember the mother was very pleasant and even encouraged me to take out her daughters to the cinema or to the beach, but I was hesitant, embarrassed, and always mindful that others were monitoring my behaviour. It took all the courage I had to decline her kind offer.

Anyway, my guardian must have fallen out with her fellow and so we had to leave that property which was owned by the ex-boyfriend. We moved to Vineyard Town, which was regarded as a better address in Kingston, and that's where she rented a very large house, five bedrooms and a roof garden. It was a new house, detached with garage and off-street parking, and there was even a maid's quarter. I don't know if she managed to pay the maid, or "helper", as we called her, but poor as a person is there is always someone poorer that you can help, so she managed to get someone to help her out around the house, and perhaps paid her in food and board.

So we all uprooted and moved there, but she had to pay high rents and I assume she felt quite comfortable with the commitment because she was getting a regular boarding allowance for me from my father, and she also did some work downtown now and again.

One of the daughters, the older one, Pauline, was also working, I'm not sure what job she was doing but she was of that age and I suspect with her good looks and light-coloured complexion she was probably in a bank or fashion store serving customers. The youngest of the daughters, Jennifer, was my age and particularly attractive. They were all beautiful girls and I enjoyed their company, it was good just to be around them and at times I was jealous when they were in the company of other young men.

Anyway, I settled in with the family but this woman was always in debt, particularly because she liked expensive furniture. I don't know why she couldn't do the housework herself, but she didn't do much around the house either; there was the helper to do that, so she could play at being poor-show-great. It later transpired that my guardian's new boyfriend worked on one of those merchant ships which visit the Jamaican ports and he would stop by whenever he was in Kingston. She would have a great time going out with him and buying lots of things and after spending a few days he would disappear again until the next time, which would be months at a time.

I presumed that he must have been her favourite man, although not her only paramour, and whenever he came by it was fun and she would be glowing with excitement but the sad thing was that she would hide from all the people coming to the house to collect the money she owed them, and she would tell me to tell them that she wasn't home when all the while she'd be hiding in the back somewhere.

This lady was always dodging the furniture people and all the other creditors that she owed money to, including the rent man. And I remember once these bailiffs came by and took away all our furniture; it was so embarrassing. But, somehow, she landed on her feet and managed to get some more furniture and we were back to normal again for a while. Well, it was interesting living there, and sometimes I would wish I had the money to give her as I enjoyed seeing her happy. Somehow we managed to eat and she would always find some guy who would want to look after her, presumably because she was attractive and charming, as she laughed a lot despite her difficulties.

Now, one thing I liked doing was fishing, and there was one of her guys who also liked fishing and together we would go towards the airport some nights, to fish among the mangroves from the bank of the airport road and make a huge catch of snappers. Afterwards we'd go back home for a fish feed; it was good fun for all the family.

On numerous occasions I would lend my guardian my allowance knowing that I would never got it back.

Rarely did I go out anywhere after school to spend it as I usually went straight back home, but occasionally I would go to the cinema to meet up with my school chums and take in a movie. If we didn't have money, one person would inveigle his way into the cinema then open the back door for the rest of us to sneak in; sometimes it worked, but mostly we got collared.

I remember one night I wanted to go to the cinema, this particular film was coming which was to do with some young woman, I think it was called Lolita or Emmanuelle, something like that. It was one of those French films and all the guys were talking about it because it was supposed to be very sexy, and I'm going to go and meet them at the cinema but I don't know how I'm going to get in because I'm broke having given my allowance to my guardian.

While I was on my way, I saw a lady coming towards me from the shadows and just for a split second I thought to myself, What if I grab her handbag and run? I could find some money in there to pay for my cinema ticket, but it was like someone kept saying to me, "No, no, don't do that, that's not you."

This thought was going through my head as I walked towards her, but as I got up to her I just passed with a broad smile and said, "Good evening", she nodded and I continued on my journey, but it was amazing the thought processes that must go through one's head before you make a decision that could have a major effect on someone else's life as well as your own.

In this case I saw someone that I thought was vulnerable and who had what I thought I needed to satisfy my requirement, but then my conscience, my better judgment, told me that it was not right, the woman needed her money as well and she may have got hurt if I had robbed her, and I wouldn't be able to live with myself. So as soon as I got up to her I greeted her with a broad smile, "Good evening". She responded and went on her way and I was much relieved and proud of the action I had taken.

I got to the cinema and there were other students there from college and we all tried to get in but the ushers told us that we were too young as it was an adult film. And of course I hadn't thought of that!

After all that, we got there and we found out we weren't old enough to get in. So we thought maybe the older-looking boys could pay to get in and then they'd open the side door for me and the others to slip in and sit down with our group and enjoy the film, but, on this occasion there were too many of us and the ushers had all the doors covered so I didn't get to see that racy French film that all the older guys were raving about.

My guardian's oldest daughter used to go out with a soldier from Up Park Camp, the military training centre, which was not too far from where we lived. She was attracted to this soldier boy and he used to turn up in the evening and sit around and wait for us to disappear before he slipped into her room for some intimacy. However, I remember one night – it was so funny – while I was in my room reflecting and he was coming late that night for some intimacy. I could hear him rustling through the bushes towards her room which was two doors away from mine. I heard him gently knocking, tip-tip-tip tip-tip-tip, so I listened and I heard him whisper, "Come round the back." And I thought, jokingly, when he was passing my window I would just throw some water over him to cool his ardour. There he was like a snake in the grass and I wondered if he was as lousy in combat as he was at being an undercover lover.

So, she went round the back and I could hear her tip-toeing to go to him. Her door opened and she went out and immediately there's a whole lot of shushing: "Sssshhh!" they made so much noise trying to keep quiet it was comical! So these two were carrying on inside there and, being the mischievous person that I was, I thought I should do something to attract everyone's attention, like pretending that I heard a prowler, so that the others would come rushing out of their rooms and then knock at her door and see him hiding in there. Then I thought no, give the young man a break, but they were there for most of the night and early next morning I heard, ssssshhhhh! followed by more loud rustling in the bushes as he was shuffling off back to camp.

I was either jealous or I felt that really and truly that shouldn't have happened because she was such a nice girl whom I regarded as being like a sister, and, because of her wholesome-looking appearance it didn't occur to me that she got up to that sort of thing but I suppose we all have needs.

I knew what those soldier boys were like, it's this one tonight and somebody else tomorrow night and so on; it's never serious and I felt I should protect her. Anyway, the next morning at breakfast I asked her, "Did you have a good sleep, Pauline?"

And she said, "Yeah."

So I said, "Really? Well, I did hear some noises."

"Did you, what sort of noises did you hear?"

"Some noise like someone was crying or something."

And she just said, "No-one was crying" with such a serious face, not Pauline.

Anyway, she obviously got the message that I knew what went on and she looked a bit embarrassed and was extra nice to me so I wouldn't talk about it further and reveal her secret assignations.

Interestingly enough, her mother was a bit like her, actually. They were all very promiscuous but you could understand: they were looking for love. A bit like me, I suppose, never having had a family as such, with mother and father together, I suppose in their case if their parents were together things might have been different. As it was, the mother was struggling and it was tough for them financially and emotionally. The little bits of money she kept borrowing from me were always to "pay the milkman" or clear this or that debt. The thing is, I never got any of it back but then again neither did any of her many creditors, so I was in good company.

10

Tetanus or Obeah?

One of the good things about being away at school was getting back home to Portland in the holidays. Being back at Compound at the family home with Red Man and Miss Inez, meant re-establishing links with friends and cousins and, of course, we had a lot to talk about – a lot of catching up to do.

They too had come back from their different colleges, some from Titchfield or Calabar, and others from Wolmers or elsewhere. So, we would all sit around on the playing fields at Compound and talk about our colleges and what we did and so on. We would do that for a little while and then get back into our usual groups and continued to do what boys and girls do. We boys: myself, Ken, Big Man and Little Man started roaming again, occasionally checking out girls from Bell Castle and Flat Grass, or getting up early to go swimming or to search for things washed up on the beach from the previous night or even some early morning fishing.

A popular place where we used to fish was along an area of sharp, jagged stones atop of a slender pieces of land jutting far out into the sea near the Hector's River border where we would land large snappers and smaller jack fish.

If we managed to walk right out to the end we'd find these wonderful fruits called sea grapes growing on those rocks, and we'd pick lots of them to nibble on. Out there the sea is deep on either side of those razor-sharp strips of land, but if you think about it, it was crazy for us to be out there, because not only was it dangerous to walk on those sharp stones without shoes, but looking back from the furthest point seemed like miles all the way out into the sea. But we used to go all the way out to the end and fish, here the sea would be splashing up over our faces and soaking our bodies. We'd enjoy that particularly when the sun was hottest; we never thought of any danger.

Those stones we walked on were very sharp indeed caused by the constant wearing away by the sea and I don't know how we managed to walk barefoot on that piece of rock without doing serious damage to the soles of our feet.

I went back to Hector's River years afterwards and remembering the good times I'd had on those rocks, but this time wearing strong leather boots, I ventured on to those rocky surfaces as I had done all those years ago as a boy, and my nice leather boots were shredded on those very sharp stones. And I was thinking, "I'm sure we were barefoot in those days."

Cho! We never wore shoes anyway when we were going larking about, so how did my feet survive that? Somehow, we got used to that. Of course, we were more concerned about the hot sun so the leaves of the sea grape shrubs came in handy for sheltering from the direct sun and heat out there on those rocks.

It was just us boys fishing and having fun, going with hooks, a stone and a piece of plastic line. The stone was used to throw out the line away from the rocks and a piece of wood attached to make the lines float just below the surface. We'd tie the stone on to the plastic line and attach two hooks, bait them and throw out the line and wait for something to bite. It wouldn't take long before we were pulling in our fish and taking them off the hooks.

I suppose the freedom and the joy of being away from adults and the peace and relative quiet, coupled with the possibility of landing a good catch, were the reasons we spent so much time on those hazardous rocks.

What did bother us was when we had to go back onto the mainland. It is said you should never turn your back to the sea. Why? It is believed that when you do, the sea always rages up furiously and surprises you from behind and a large wave can knock you senseless into the water. Actually, I never thought of why, we just accepted that maxim and tried not to tempt fate by turning our backs to the sea. I can tell you, walking backwards or sideways along that sharp, slippery footpath was not an easy thing to do.

We would go back and cook those fresh fish and eat that with roasted breadfruit, and that was a typical day. And, of course, in the evenings we'd go and check out the ladies but we had to be careful because if we became interested in a popular young lady we could end up having a fight because the chances were that she was already someone's girlfriend, (no different from the ghettos). So we would show respect to him by ignoring the young lady whenever the boyfriend was around. But, of course, that didn't prevent the girl with the boyfriend from seeing you whenever her fella was out of the area – out of sight as they say.

I remember one Saturday back home at Hector's River when Miss Inez had gone off to Kingston. Now, on those occasions when she'd go away for a couple of days at a time, it was Cookie who was left in charge, and she always had Tenabutt, the helper, under orders to make sure she did the washing and other heavy chores. She would keep an eagle eye on her and prevail on us to behave in a grand show to assert her authority as the one in charge of the household.

Miss Inez and Dad would leave on Thursday evening, taking the higglers with them to Kingston for their marketing and shopping expeditions, and come back on Saturday night.

This particular Thursday, they went off and left us kids in the charge of Cookie – me and Ken, as well as Miss Inez's nieces, Shirley and Paulette. Normally, as befitting my nickname of Mango Sergeant, I'm the first one up looking for those mangoes, which had fallen off the trees overnight, to enjoy before breakfast but this Friday morning I couldn't get up; I was in excruciation pain. The others were already at the table and were calling me to come and eat breakfast and so on, but I couldn't get out of the bed. I was in terrible agony, and very hot with fever.

What happened was a few days previously when I with some friends were playing around at the lower school at Hector's River barefoot, having taken my shoes off to play hide and seek underneath the school building where as it turned out a lot of old wood, rusty nails, old cans and other debris had been discarded. I had trodden on one of those rusty nails and was told then to pound the affected area with a stone to get rid of the poisoned blood and I would be all right, but the rusty nail had gone way into the flesh and this created problems.

Anyway, by Friday morning, I was sweating and feeling weak. Cookie came in the room, checked my condition and panicked: "Lord, oh Lord, the bwoy's burning up," she cried.

By now, all the other kids and Tenabutt had gone about their business and she didn't know what to do so she boiled up some herbs for me to drink and tried to cool down my temperature with cold towels pressed on my forehead, but I was still sweating and burning up in that bed. I was very thirsty as well and she gave me all this stuff to drink which didn't seem to make any difference.

Finally, she went down the road to tell Mr Cyrus and the other people down at the main square that I was badly sick. When she came back, Cookie asked, "Let me see your foot."

When I held it out to her she shouted, "Oh my God, it swell up like a jackfruit!"

Then she wailed, "Oh, my God, dem obeah the bwoy, dem obeah the bwoy! Now what we going to do?"

So, everybody was there speculating that I had been the victim of obeah and Cookie being Cookie went and got a piece of salt pork fat and fried it up in hot oil and slapped it on my foot.

"Aaaarggghh!" I screamed as I felt the pain shooting up my leg. I thought it was going to knock me out, leaving me unconscious, so I twisted and turned as she struggled to hold me down and keep the pork on my foot. Eventually, she tied it on and left it there to, somehow, draw out the poison. I don't know if that was a good thing to do or not but, eventually, I slept or must have passed out and when I came round I twisted and groaned restlessly for the whole night.

The next day, all the friends and family came by to have a look and suggested what they thought should be done, and some were talking about obeah and how to counteract it and most people seemed to be into those hocus-pocus things.

You see, what had happened was that a few months before, my father was coming back with his "boys", the side-men, from where they had gone to deliver ice. He might have been drinking no one was certain however his truck knocked a man off his bicycle. The truck had come round a corner and accidentally knocked the guy off his push-bike and, unfortunately, he died. As it turned out, the chap was an obeah man from St Thomas. Now, after the accident they found a lot of stuff on this man which proved to them that he was an obeah man and they thought that maybe his people were after my father or people close to him to get their revenge.

Anyway, I remember the day when they were going to court and, of course, my dad had witnesses that it was an accident but all the same these people came up to the house and they had this fire going with some strange smelling stuff in there and they told us that for the whole day when my dad was at court we had to put this foul-smelling object into the fire and not to let the fire go down until after the court session, so we did as we were instructed.

I can't remember who organised that "science" activity, as it was called, but I think some relative did as they felt that since the victim was an obeah man we had to take precautions to counteract what the opposition was doing because his people would no doubt be working obeah against us to ensure that my dad was found guilty.

Anyhow, word came back from court that he was found not guilty. So some people decided that because my dad was cleared, the dead man's people were clearly trying to obeah me to get back at my dad for the incident.

The next morning when I got out of bed my foot looked like a jackfruit, a huge fruit that is as delicious as it is bulging and ugly to look at, and when this lump of flesh resembling a blood clot fell out of my heel where the nail had been, everyone was amazed. There was initial relief that what Cookie had tried to achieve with the pork fat may have worked, but this made relatives became even more convinced that my sickness was caused by obeah. Those relatives who were into this obeah business turned up and started doing this mumbo-jumbo incantation in the house. Now, I don't remember any details about it, I just know that it was happening. Meanwhile, I was in a bad way and getting worse.

By late Saturday afternoon I was really in a terrible state; burning hot and with ague, as they called fever in those days. Anyway, my dad came back earlier than he normally would have done and as soon as he got there the word got around that his boy was dying because "them obeah him". By now things were blown out of all proportions but luckily he had the good sense to grab me up and take me to hospital. Out on the truck it seemed as if everybody in the district piled in and off we went to St Thomas, which had the nearest hospital to Hector's River.

As we got there the huge group of people with us pushed their way into the hospital and the doctors and nurses managed to clear a path, grabbed me and put me into a bed where they pumped some white stuff into my veins to try and bring down my temperature which was much too high. If nothing else, that was going to kill me. They gave me all sorts of injections and I had to lie there in bed and after about an hour or so the doctor said to my father and the others that they were to take me to see a certain German doctor near a place called Boston.

To reach there, we had to go back through Hector's River, past Long Grass, towards Port Antonio. By now I was feeling a little better, but on the way a strange incident happened. Something flew into the cabin of the truck, which someone caught, and the people said something like, "You see, this is a sign that this boy has been obeahed".

Anyway, we drove back through Hector's River and there was such commotion as we passed through the district again with plenty people crammed into the truck with the horn sounding as we drove pass towards Port Antonio and down a track to this little place to see this German doctor who was perhaps a Nazi hiding out in Jamaica after the war, for all we knew.

Anyway, we sat down and my father explained to the doctor what had happened and he got the guys to hold me down while the doctor pumped some medication into me. It was painful and I was crying out, but I couldn't move because they had pinned me down. I don't know if the doctor took something out and put something in, but the process was very painful. After about ten minutes when he'd finished, I gradually felt a really cool breeze over my face, and then someone called out, "You alright?"

"Yea", I smiled, "I'm all right".

It was a feeling of great relief and my dad took me back home and I felt so good after that I even requested food.

Not too long after that incident my mother decided that I should come up to stay with her in England where she had by now been living for some time. While I was living with my dad, she had apparently sent my brother Ken away to stay at his grandmother's house in Black Hill, while she made all the preparations to travel to "foreign". Once all the arrangements were in place and my brother and I had settled in with our respective foster families, Mum had left to go to England to find a better life, not just for her but for us as well. There were opportunities abroad and the idea was to work, save the fare and send for us to join her and take advantage of those opportunities.

Consequently, my dad had to get my passport sorted out and what-not, and I remember going to all these various ministries and various officials; from one place with people in suits to another place with people in suits, and I had photographs taken and injections as prevention against whatever was needed at that time before going to this place where, eventually, I got a passport in my christened name of Walker. So, that was that, I was on the move yet again – this time, to England.

11

Going to England

For me, going to England was an adventure; everything for me in life is an adventure. I'm going overseas. It's exciting! Wonderful things happened overseas. My dad, who went overseas made money and came back to waste it in Jamaica, but, it had all happened overseas, so, for me it's something exciting; something that I wanted to experience.

Well, my documents were all sorted out and the day I was supposed to leave Jamaica was very, very hot. Kingston was especially hot; hot enough to melt the tarmac. I had my little grip* and was dressed up for foreign travel. I must have been about 17, and the year was 1964 – it was around the same time that Jamaica won the Miss World beauty contest in England. Wow! And I was going to this wonderful place the motherland called England.

So, there I was kitted out in my Sunday best and ready to go, saying goodbye to everyone: grinning from ear to ear and telling them, "I'm going a-foreign, now".

There was no send-off party. People just said, "Bwoy, enjoy yourself, you know, and keep in touch. Watch out for them foreign gals, you want to be careful with them." Stuff like that.

So, we got to the airport – Palaisadoes airport as it was then- and went through the formalities, got on the plane and sat down and, oh my Lord, there were all these Jamaicans; some women with their hands on their heads, nervously praying and carrying on because they were fearful of flying, some looking anxious as though they were about to throw up, but I was just casual. Am I supposed to be frightened about this? No! It is exciting; I'm actually going to go in one of those huge silver things I had seen flying up there.

You see all these people, some of the men suited up, some women wearing "tie-heads"** and some looking petrified, while others praying and some talking loudly, possibly out of dread: So now I am thinking "I hope this flight is alright you know as there is enough going on to make you shit scared"; some of the praying is for the pilot, I just took it all in and then dismissed it, made myself comfortable and took in all the to-ing and fro-ing going on around me.

Suddenly, the plane lurched forward and took off, as the plane gradually took up speed going down the runway all these people like a panic beehive, their voices are now raised, and so I'm thinking, "Wow!" it's going so fast and suddenly, we're in the air and I looked out the window and Jamaica is getting smaller and smaller, the buildings are becoming minute and, then, eventually, the country is just a little dot of a place I can see below. I start thinking, "Wow, is that where I'm from? It looks so small." And then I'm thinking, "I hope they know where they're going." Until at last I decided, look, I'm here already, there's nothing I can do about it, so I just sat back and enjoyed the ride.

After a while, the air stewards came round with drinks and things to eat, so I'm used to it now, I forget that I'm flying. For me, it was good fun but for the older people I think it was nightmarish and frightening.

I thought we were going straight to England but we weren't. After we had drinks and something to nibble and I began to get used to those people around me, we landed in New York and were all told to get off the plane. So we disembarked and walked to a certain place where we had our documents checked and collected our suitcases. We were all escorted to a different plane for the flight to Heathrow, London airport, and as I got on and looked to my left and to my right, for the first time in my life all I could see were white faces, more like pink lobsters; lots and lots of blank white faces and not one smiling face in sight. And they're all looking straight back at me; I suddenly started to feel nervous and uneasy as I went to sit down.

This plane was a bit different: bigger and a bit more organised and they were all white people, crew and passengers and the few of us blacks from Jamaica all sat at the back of the plane. I remember wanting to go to the toilet but that meant going towards the front and as I moved forward all these white people were once again staring at me with eyes like darts – it was a complete culture shock. Up to this point, I have been accustomed to seeing lots of black people and, occasionally, you'd see a white face but, on this plane, there were hundreds and like an undulating sea of white faces all looking at you and none of them looked pleasant; nobody smiled, I couldn't imagine how the other blacks were feeling but the coldness made me uncomfortable. Their expressions were as if to say, "What is he doing here? How dare he travel on the same plane." It was intimidating, so much so I quickly went to the toilet and swiftly went back to my seat.

The plane took off and there we were on our way to England. I slept, woke up, ate something given to me by the stewardess but some black people had brought their own food, which they shared out among themselves, this was a little amusing as it seems food was available to all travellers.

Anyway, the next morning, we landed at Heathrow, and that was another culture shock. We had to go through the system again and just as on the plane, there were all these white faces and not one friendly face among them. I cleared customs and then went outside and am anxiously looking and looking but can't see anyone I recognised, then suddenly I saw my mother among the waiting throng, I rushed over to her and she was there with a man, someone who was apparently kind enough to drive her to come and pick me up.

And they're asking me: "How was the trip?" And the man is telling me how careful I have to be in England because "them prejudiced", and so on. But, the thing that struck me was when we went out of the building to the car, I thought, "My gosh, the clouds are down too low," as though the sky had fallen. But it was fog. There was fog everywhere and we're driving but we can't see, at least I can't, and it was cold, and I'm thinking, how can the driver see where he's going? I'm convinced there's going to be an accident, but, of course, they're used to it all.

Eventually, we got to Camberwell, in south London, where my mother was living. When I got out of the car I looked up and down Coldharbour Lane and saw all these identical houses. Every one of them looked the same! About a mile of houses, all looking the same, and I'm thinking, how are they going to know which house is which, since they all look alike? Then as we got inside our house there are all these Jamaicans in most of the rooms in this house, and they're calling out to me, "hey boy you come to the cold country?" And I'm thinking to myself, "I certainly have. Why did I leave Jamaica?" where are these opportunities and will it ever get warm?

My mum lived in the basement of this house. She had her bedroom and a little room, and the little one was suppose to be mine I assumed until my brother, Ken, came up. Then, presumably we would share the big room and mum would move into the little room.

So, everything happened in those two rooms: they're dining room, play room, bedroom and lounge and there's one communal kitchen upstairs with the toilet outside in the garden and wash basins on the landings. Well my mum had a little black and white television so there was something that I could be interested in and get a little bit of enjoyment and education from as this was like a view from a window into the society and yes we did see some nasty things.

Anyway, I'm getting settled in and mum takes me to meet some of the other people. Every room has a different family. In this room, there are three adults living there; that room has three people living there, a father, possibly a wife and a daughter, and so on throughout the house, and then there was this one kitchen on the ground floor, we all had to share this and there's a curtain behind which is a bath and that's all we had to bathe in for every family in that house. So, on a Sunday morning, you're frying up your chicken and behind the curtain, someone's taking a bath.

As it happened, I was sharing a room with a fellow who worked nights because the small room was too small for a bed. He would sleep during the day when I was out and at night I would have the bed when he would go to work. So we're sharing the room in that way and weekends are a little strange because he's home then, so we have to manage by sharing the bed. But the biggest shock came when I discovered that the toilet was way down the bottom of the garden and I'm telling you going outside to the toilet was bad enough but inside that toilet was cold in the middle of winter. I would just run in, do what I had to do and run back out quickly; wash my hands in a basin on the landing, everything else was in our rooms. So that was my first introduction to this place.

Well, having got here and since I had some money I decided to go to the shop, which was about three blocks from where we were living. I left the house and it never occurred to me that I should make a mental note of the door number, so I stroll out to the shops and bought some comfort food but getting back I realise I could not find the house. I am on the street looking for some clue but all the houses look the same and I'm thinking, "What do I do?" here I am I'm outside in my tropical clothes shivering and freezing in this god forsaken place, eventually, I knocked on a door for help and a white woman opened up glared at me and just slammed the door in my face.

Obviously, it was the wrong house so I just kept walking up and down the road until I saw somebody I recognised coming out of a house, and that was the way I got back home. The lesson there was that when I go out I must remember the house number because they all looked the same and people are not as helpful or as friendly as back home in Jamaica.

Then, there was the church. Right opposite us there was this big church and there was a lady friend of my mother living in our house who had a daughter called Brenda, a very nice girl. Brenda was a church girl and every Sunday she would go to this church opposite so knowing I was new to the place she asked me if I wanted to go to church with her. When I looked at her and figured out that I could be on to a good thing, I smiled to myself and said, "Yea, definitely, I want to go to church". Now, I didn't like going to church because of my experience back home, but she was worth going to church for – I mean – with.

So, I dutifully went and sat down at the back (my place is always at the back, I don't like the front). So this white pastor was on the pulpit preaching and there was a black deacon and a white deacon who greeted us at the door and as the service got in full swing someone suddenly called out, "Hallelujah, Ooo!" and someone else called out " I am ready to receive you" and now the black folks are working up to a crescendo as they're getting the "holy ghost" and talking in tongues and becoming animated; similar to what I have seen happening in churches back in Jamaica. However, the white folks were a bit shocked by all this carrying on and the pastor was up there motioning to the deacon to tell them to quieten down and the deacons were going and trying to calm things and these people are getting worked up even more and they started calling out as they get the "holy Spirit". The pastor went quite red as he struggle to get people to shut up, telling everyone to be quiet and that they can't make noise in the church, but, by now the noise is loud, filling the whole church with this feverish rejoicing, and it was embarrassing.

The pastor didn't know what else to do so he quickly finished the service and we went, but once outside the church I couldn't stop laughing because of the way this pastor reacted to something that, to me, was quite normal. I told Brenda that these things happened all the time back home; didn't they understand? And she said, no, they're very conservative in this country around their fellowship, but it was quite an eye-opener for me and it was quite an eye-opener for the white churchgoers to see how the black people worship in church. But, as time went on the leaders and the congregation changed; the pastor and the white congregation accepted that there was supposed to be a certain amount of spirituality in church and they accepted that.

Years after I left the area, I went back to that same church and it was so strange to see the changes. It was now more Pentecostal.

Now, Brenda's mother worked on the buses as a conductor. She was quite a get-up-and-go type of person and wanted to own a house although many black people didn't own their own houses in those days, particularly a female but she was determined to break the mould.

By this time, Brenda and I were getting close (her mum and my mum were good friends so they liked the idea that we were getting on), and Brenda was around the same age as me so it was just right, because, of course, I needed someone to show me around and the winters required additional warmth.

Anyway, eventually, her mum went to the West End to arrange to purchase a house through a Jewish firm in Regent Street. But looking back to those times, she was really treated unfairly but that was how things were then. She paid over the odds for everything to get the mortgage to buy that house but that in itself was a great achievement as in the end she did get her house. It was a very expensive undertaking but she was determined to have a place of her own and eventually she got her house at Milkwood Road, Herne Hill. I could see that because she was black and female things were stacked against her and that the finance people were taking advantage by overcharging her. I remember the day Brenda and I got the keys and went to the house and decided to "christen" the place. Well, it was the first house they owned and it was the first one owned by any family that I knew in England. When they moved in we still saw a lot of each other, at least initially.

Although I missed "home" every day, Jamaica was becoming a pleasant but near-distant memory although I and the people around me were determined to hold on to our culture – our expressions, our food, and our joy of life in what was a bitterly hostile environment. Yet, for all that, slowly but surely I was beginning to get used to this place called England.

* Grip – Small suitcase
** Tie head – Headscarves

12

Brixton Blues

Time passed and summer came and I decided I was going to go out and check out the "brothers" – by which I mean the other black guys in the area. So I decided to go to Brixton because you would hear people talking about this place, Brixton, which as it happens was the other end of Coldharbour Lane, where we were living.

I got myself ready. Now, in Jamaica your shoes must be well shined. My shoes were gleaming and looking very nice and my "threads" were "crisp" – slang for saying that I was beautifully presented, even if I said so myself.

So, I'm going up to Brixton to check out the scene, I got on the 36 bus and before I could settle in a seat this white woman just looked at me mumbled something and spat at me. I was so shocked. People don't do that where I came from, what could anyone of my complexion have done to her to cause such an outrage? In Jamaica some people may not like you as a foreigner but they would never do such a thing to anyone. Despite that I collected my thoughts and asked her, "What did you do that for?" and she mumbled something under her breath about "black so and so..." I couldn't believe such ignorance, would you believe that these are the same people who are now being cared for in nursing homes by our black brothers and sisters all over the kingdom!

There I was dressed up, going out and she spits at me. I got off the bus and brushed it off and thought, "Strange people these", and just walked up to Brixton. When I got there, all these black people were hanging out. They saw me approaching and possibly looking a bit too dressed up they called out, "What happen, brother, where do you come from?"

"You just come up?" Stuff like that.

So, I'm going, "Yea, man, come from Kingston".

This is met with some excitement: "Oh, a Kingstonian!"

And so it's going on, meeting all these people and them congregating around because I'm the new boy from Kingston; the new kid on the block, and eventually it turns out that some of them are going to see a film at the cinema, The Ritzy, just at the top of Coldharbour Lane, so I tagged along.

In the cinema, we sat down to watch this film, suddenly I heard, "Pssssssshhhhhh!" It was someone pissing in the auditorium and it's running over my shoes, so I sprang up and called out, "What happen, how you can piss in a place like this?" and everybody shouted at me to shut up and sit down, so I just got up and walked out in disgust.

I got back home and told some people at the house what had happened and they told me about the difficulty of going out; certain places you don't go, like certain pubs; you've got to be careful. It was all right to go to the Irish pubs because they're classed like us; if you go to rent a room you would see signs "no dogs, no Irish, no blacks", so we're all classed in the same way. So, they told me in no uncertain terms that you've got to be careful wherever you go because these people are colour prejudiced and later on I found out that English people hated us and were blatantly racist indeed. I've been attacked a few times just for being "coloured". I knew that colour bar was institutionalised and I would feel vulnerable every time I was in a public place and even more so in the presence of a police officer as every black man was fair game as the police could do to us whatever they liked without recrimination. They knew no one in authority would ever question their actions as the authority did support them fully in whatever wrong deeds they perpetuated.

However, my first experience of real hatred was one late winter's morning in Brixton when I opened the door of what I thought was a normal café. I was hoping to get a hot drink but was confronted by a large group of black-leather-clad teddy boys whose collected stares were like sharp, hot daggers coming towards me. They glared at me with such intense hatred that I knew I needed to make a quick exit. After that encounter I kept away from those guys and from areas such as Southend or Margate in the summer months where these leather cladded bikers would go in large groups looking for trouble.

Now, when I got settled in and started going out, I eventually got pally with some guys in the house and some others in Brixton and eventually we became good friends. They used to have parties themselves or we would go to some other house parties in the area, which were really the only form of entertainment because we blacks wouldn't be welcome in the nightclubs, so at weekends we would always seek out these house parties. We would pay a few shillings to get in and we could buy drinks in there and wait for the curry goat to come round, of course the host would leave that until the latest hour possible – when the crowd had thinned out- the food was usually free. The determined ones, like me, would stay as late as possible to get my share of curry goat.

Yes, we would go to these parties, man, and you'd knock on the door.

Some guy would slightly open the door and ask, "Who are you?"

So you would say so and so person, a name they recognised invited us, and then he'd open the door. You pay your money and pushed your way in because it's crowded and it's hot in there and the music is deafening.

The heat hits you in your face, and you push and you push and eventually you come before a nice girl and you may decide to stay right where you are; the ska and rock steady music would be blasting away and the movement of the young lady close up to you would send you off into space; you are rubbing and rolling to the beat when suddenly the DJ would change the tempo to calypso with Mr Sparrow's Trinidadian tunes blasting away, so we are now jumping up and down as there is no other way to go, and shouting out the words of the tune.

The seventies were real fun times at these parties, roots reggae was becoming popular and of course during this period we had the most popular Lovers Rock music, which offered us guys the opportunity to get really close and personal with the ladies. Those parties were always crowded and because you couldn't move around in there you would find a girl pretty quickly (or even a pretty girl quickly!) and basically spend the whole time with her; it was too crowded to do anything else. And the music is blasting, man, and everyone is dancing like so, and if you're lucky enough to get a girl in front of you, oh boy! You just danced with her all night because you couldn't go any place else and the problems outside for the moment were forgotten. Eventually your hand moves from there, on her shoulder, slowly going down gradually to the booty zone and she doesn't say anything, you're testing the water and if she doesn't object you go a bit further until she reacts and you behave yourself or she loves it and you go crazy.

But those nights were good nights because you're among your own people, enjoying familiar music and you're having fun and it's cheaper than going to those clubs but the thing is that there is always evil lurking not far away, every so often we were raided by the police. Suddenly, there's a hundred police out there smashing down the door to this place and then pushing their way in with brute force, they were like rabid animals and there may be some guys round the back possibly smoking weed and they would start to panic and now everybody is trying to run away which creates a stampede and a crush as people tried to escape. The place is already packed but the police are pushing their way in anyway, sometimes they use their batons, blindly lashing out, and there's nowhere to go. They showed complete contempt and disregard for the safety of the people there. Those who have space are running and some managed to escape through a window or door at the back. Sometimes the police were just as bad as the National Front because we believed they were the National Front in uniform with a licence to do whatever they wanted, which they did and a lot of guys suffered at their behest. There is a saying in Jamaica "what goes around comes around" so I wouldn't be surprised that those same people are suffering as a result of their sinful deeds in their youth.

So, there were these house parties, or shebeens, which were mainly reggae raves, but occasionally, someone would invite me to a proper party, somewhere more organised and with less crush but always well attended and maybe, in a nice council flat with room to move about.

You'd go there and you could go out on to the balcony and find a nice young lady enjoying the cool morning air. She's not in the crowd, she's a bit more circumspect and you go and talk to her and she might invite you to a better party and you might find yourself in a place more up-market, like Streatham or Wimbledon, at a wonderful party, where the music don't assault your ear drums, there is space to move around inside the house and in the garden where the possibility exist to meet and talk with people, a party with lots of beautiful and sophisticated people and you don't have to pay to go in and where there is enough curry goat for every one to share. This was now late 1970s and the music was now more soul, although Desmond Dekker and the Israelites, Byron Lee, Delroy Wilson and of course Bob Marley with No Woman, No Cry, were very popular among black folks.

I fell in love with soul music and found myself collecting James Brown's hard dance soul records to practice my moves at home before going out to show off my dancing skills at parties. For those romantic evenings at home it would be the sweet soul music of Marvin Gaye, Al Green, Bobby Womack and, of course, Gladys Knights and the Pips with Midnight Train To Georgia and others such as Otis Redding, and later Stevie Wonder.

Eventually, my mother decided to move from where we were living at Coldharbour Lane. It was all right in that house for the friendships and so, but it was not convenient especially when my brother came up, which was a few years after me. So, we moved into a flat in Gautrey Road, Peckham, and not in a basement, a flat, which was a big step up from where we were. A flat meant we had our own kitchen, separate toilet and bathroom, separate sitting room and separate bedrooms, so, for us, that was a great luxury, but there were some bad people living in the area. A guy next door was growing marijuana and people used to say whatever you wanted just let him know and he'd get it for you. Crooks, all crooks down there I thought.

There was prostitution, drugs, everything used to go on around there in those days.

There was a house opposite our flat and sometimes they wouldn't even pull the curtain; you would see guys going up, getting their clothes off and we would look and see everything, that's when mum wasn't there but if she was home Ken and I would just pull the curtain and pretend we didn't know what was going on over there.

My friends Bunny and Bobsey would turn up on occasions when those people opposite were "performing" so we would just sit back and enjoy the show but neither I, my brother nor any of my friends got caught up in what was going on around us as we were all seeking a way of becoming successful black guys.

I was studying at Kennington College and around that time I started to make contact with some relatives that I heard I had in Streatham, people on my dad's side, so I went to see them and it turned out to be Timothy whom I grew up with in Hector's River. He actually owned the house he lived in so I used to visit often and we'd have chats about old times and about life back home in Portland. My mum then decided that she wanted to move again as the flat was expensive so she managed to get a council flat off Nunhead in Peckham, not too far from where we were living. The good thing about the rent was that it was affordable and if we couldn't pay one month because my mum was between jobs the Council would tell her not to worry about it till she could pay but my mum was always keen to pay her rent even if it meant us eating less that month.

After doing my GCE exams, I went to work for the International Tin Council. I remember going to Haymarket to apply for a job there. As always I was well presented dressed in my bits and pieces and went into this magnificent place above the Design council in Haymarket House for the interview.

An older blonde, voluptuous-looking woman, the chairman's secretary, conducted the interview. It was clear from body language that she was having something going with the chairman at the time, and apparently whatever she said stood, so she must have liked me and said, "Yes, you've got the job". It was my first job and I was elated and very grateful. So I started at the ITC working for about £10 or £15 a week as a general office boy. In the mornings when I got there I would do the post, make the tea for the officers, and go through the newspapers, whatever was required I did.

The important thing was that I had got myself on the job ladder and I had a chance to learn and build a career in a very reputable institution. I'm free now: I'm getting my own money that's the most important building block and a stepping stone to greater things. So, yes, life was getting good for this young man.

13

Saved by the Bus

Brenda (who had lived at our communal house in Coldharbour Lane, and who introduced me to the English church opposite) became my first girlfriend in England, but after her mother bought her house in Herne Hill we saw each other less frequently. However, we still had some good times and I visited her at her house as often as I could and, for a while, we had a good relationship going but then on a surprise visit to her house I caught her entertaining another guy in her bedroom. This shocking discovery caught me off guard and opened my eyes to the deviousness of some women and the consequence of being too trustful with your emotions. But, shouldn't I have learnt this from my experience in the past? Maybe I should but I didn't.

In the end and possibly caused by my recent disappointment I eventually moved out of the area to live with my cousin Timothy at his house in Streatham; which helped me to get over my recent disappointment and began having a good time with all the boys who lived there together. However, before I went off to Streatham, I remember I used to have dinner at my mum's flat in Peckham, although I was renting a small room from a Jamaican family at Valmer Road in Camberwell Green.

After dinner at moms flat and a bit of relaxation I would run the three mile or so distance every night to my room in Camberwell Green, so I was maybe the first person in London to take up jogging seriously. This was in the seventies and I remember people would look at me jogging in a curious way, as if I was a mad black fool. I really enjoyed the late night run so I would jog instead of just wait for the bus, usually at a cold and windy bus stop.

The daily routine was: I would have dinner at Mum's, then sit back relaxing in front of the TV watching some serial, maybe

Coronation Street, Love Thy Neighbour or some Peter Cushing horror, and doze off. Then I would be woken up by the high pitch noise from the TV denoting the close of transmission for that day, and rush out the flat heading for Camberwell to my bed-sit. By 11.30, either just before or sometime after the pubs would close and I would be running home at jogging pace to prepare myself for the next day and get, some sleep so that I would be up bright and fresh for work the next morning.

On my way I might see a bus and jump on it to ease the journey, and the good thing about the buses in those days is that they were open access platforms: you got on at the back and so I used to just jump on like I would do with the trucks in Jamaica but much easier. Well, on one occasion that Routemaster bus did save my life.

There was a good feeling about my nightly run. I enjoyed it and felt it was doing me good, keeping me fit, and every night I would run home in the relatively clean air, but didn't think about any dangers, like being attacked or anything like that. After all, this is a civilised country, isn't it? And there is no possibility of encountering wild, carnivorous animals,

However, I remember that on this particular night I was running slowly because I was a bit tired and sleepy. I was approaching a bus stop (not too far from Peckham police station, as it happens) when I saw from the corner of my eye a large group of white lads who I think must have been National Front skinheads. They started shouting and as they advanced towards me I could hear a crescendo of racist expletives and threats of what they were going to do to me.

Now, the pubs used to close as I said about 11.30 and that's the worse time to be out there on your own. So, I would avoid those times if I could but since I sometimes left my mum's quite late, it wasn't always possible to by-pass the nightly ritual at pub closing times.

I noticed that there were some people waiting at the bus-stop as I approached it and at the same time I became aware that those white guys were targeting me with their verbal abuses and heard their threatening words as I was running towards the bus-stop hoping to get support and possibly divert confrontation. My heart started racing, the adrenalin kicked in and I began picking up speed to avoid the rabble that was moving towards me. Meanwhile, the bus was some way back in the distance, slowly approaching.

Suddenly, the people at the bus stop disappeared, maybe fearing for their own lives. There was a black guy with a white girl; they too disappeared. And, suddenly, these skinheads surrounded me. Oh, shit! There were about a dozen of them if not more and they were different ages but each one looked mean and vicious. They were calling me all sorts of terrible names and I was shocked by all this. But the first thing that occurred to me was the survival instinct, and I was determined not to show any sign of weakness.

In those days they used to have crates of milk bottles out overnight for the milkman to collect in the morning, so I shot over to a crate that I'd glimpsed and grabbed a bottle in each hand and began mouthing expletives as I banged the bottles to break them. Those broken bottles became two sharp, potentially lethal weapons in each hand. As I smashed them I started calling out: "Ok, who's first, which one of you fuckers wants to die first?"

And suddenly the pack of animals stopped and started to stare at me. They slowly approached and some started creeping around to the side of me, others doing the same around the other side to surround me, but my back was against the wall so I could see them. They had me near enough surrounded, some to the sides, others dead ahead. Where could I run? I had to face this. It was like the Gunfight at the OK Coral or High Noon, only this was no movie; this was real and my life was on the line.

I grabbed a few bottles out the crate, and pelted some at them, smashing them at their feet: pelt, pelt, pelt, sending broken glass flying around my adversaries.

I had assumed that one or two black people would be around to give me support but they all disappeared; everyone disappeared. I don't know where they all went, but they just went; vanished.

But now these guys, probably fuelled by drink and high on racial hatred, are coming and they're closing in, so I shouted, "Right, I'm prepared to die but there's a few of you cunts who're going to be coming with me," as I launched my milk bottle missiles. And they were out to get me with their racist rants and, imagine, all this was being played out a few yards away from a police station. I'm thinking, "fuck the police", because nobody seemed to care. Finally, I thought, well, it's them and me.

I could see the Route master bus coming and I thought I've got to be on the right side of the road (I was on the opposite side), so I banged a few more bottles at them and then ran through the crowd of them like a mad man with two jagged weapons, causing the crowd to divide as I ran into them.

I saw the bus stopping then, but perhaps because the bus-stop was empty, it suddenly started speeding up – so I said to myself, "I have to catch that bus otherwise I'm dead". Somehow I had to gain more speed, so I ran and I ran the race of my life – for my life – and I managed to grab the pole at the rear of the bus and, in a surge of energy, managed to swing myself on. All the while the mob was chasing me but I got on and collapsed with exhaustion on one of the side seats. The bus conductor hovered over me and said something like, "You had a lucky escape there mate." Not that he had tried to slow the bus to assist my flight to freedom. And I thought, yes, I was lucky.

As I closed my eyes and panted to regain my breath, I suddenly had a flashback of the day I was sanded at school and had almost died when I was choking and couldn't breathe; and of the time I was chased by a rival street gang from the Kingston ghetto on the day that I had gone on my own to view the body of this famous cricketer who was lying in state.

My heart was pounding now as it was back then when I was a boy and the dangers I had faced convinced me that my life was on the verge of ending. Somehow then, as now, the will to live was somehow stronger, more formidable; I couldn't die without a fight.

After that, I went and got the biggest, sharpest dagger I could find. "Next time", I told myself, "next time I go out, I'm going to have some protection on me as it seems when danger strikes I am always on my own."

So, I used to walk around with my dagger sharpened on both side and shielded. I decided that I would not lie down and die alone; I would take at least a couple of my attackers with me, and damn the consequences if I survived.

It was a big dagger: huge and fearsome-looking, like the ones they used in the army. I would just push it in my belt and go out, simple as that.

I told my friends about the experience with the skinheads and they said, "Let's go and find them", but I said "No". I didn't want to go down that road because it would end up creating even more trouble.

But, after that, I made sure I got the bus. I didn't stop jogging, I would jog to the bus-stop but I made sure I left my mum's house before the pubs turned out. So, at ten o'clock, when News at Ten was about to come on, I would leave to go home when at least there would be a lot more people on the road and the pubs were still in full flow and the baddies were perhaps still fuelling their racism at the bar.

During the incident when I was attacked by the pack of degenerates, none had managed to hurt me, they didn't manage to get close enough maybe because I looked so vicious and I meant it; anger and the survival instinct took over, not fear.

I suppose if you read newspapers like the Mirror, which I did from time to time, you would probably see something in there about racist – or racial attacks, but in those days you were more likely to see stories in the right wing news about black people committing crimes rather than about them as victims. There were more about the blacks taking their jobs, their homes and their women but only cursory mention about them as victims or of being treated unfairly at work or by the institutions that run our society. However, we learnt to survive despite the difficulties. Camberwell Green, between Brixton and Peckham, was supposed to be an area with lots of blacks and other minority groups so we should have felt more secure, protected and safer than if you were living in a predominantly white area but that didn't prevent the racists from prowling the streets at night where individuals would be attacked at will just for being black or coloured and of course the police could not be relied on for assistance or protection.

Coming from the Kingston ghettoes in Jamaica where, as a young boy, I had to fight most days, I was well prepared and sensitive to dangers and so was always on my guard against a repeat of the incident which those skinheads put me through that night.

I resolved that I wasn't going to live in fear of racists – I wasn't going to look for trouble, but if it came, I wouldn't just run; I would defend myself. And from that incident with the skinheads, my dagger never left my waistband.

14

Young, Free and Single

So now I am living in Nunhead, south London, at my mum's home and had bought myself a car, but not just any car. It was a flaming red TR6 sports car with a convertible black hood that rolled back. That car was sex on wheels. I couldn't afford it but I decided that I needed a car and at least I had a safe place to park it at night.

I remember when I was driving my new car down to Lewisham and all these guys would cry out, "Yeah, man, cool!" Stuff like that, because it had a powerful roar and the hood was down – and, of course, the TR6 was a girl magnet as well.

In those days I had no fear. As you get older you start thinking about things you used to do and how people viewed you. But, back then, I couldn't care a damn, man. I could just about afford this car and it didn't matter that I lived on a council Estate, my car was there parked under my window, my confidence knew no bounds and I was getting popular with the council estate girls in the area. But, somehow, I wanted to know girls outside of the council environment because if they're living too close then there are going to be all sorts of problems, you know! You might get in bed with one and accidentally get her pregnant and she's right there to cramp your style and make your life hell, so I tried to keep away from those girls as I used to tell myself, "Never mess in your own backyard".

So, my girlfriends used to be from other parts of London or even as far away as Birmingham, but never from Peckham. Maybe, deep down, I was a bit of a snob, as I would only go to the local nightclub in Brixton with my "posse" to pose and smile at the adorable (and adoring) ladies from around the area but I wouldn't get involved. They could look and admire, but I was out of bounds to them.

Keeping warm in my batchelor pad in Streatham

Eventually, I moved out of my mum's place and went to rent a room with Timothy in Streatham. The cost of independence was that I had to sell my lovely car, as I simply couldn't afford it now. Living at mum's I didn't pay anything much, but now with rent, food and so on, the car had to go.

After I'd been at Tim's house a while he met a lady to whom he decided that he was getting married nevertheless Tim reckoned that the house was big enough for all of us as he and his wife would live upstairs and the two rooms downstairs where me and his friend Bernard lived would continue to rent as before. It was a good arrangement as we were company for Mrs Hall when Tim was working nights.

I occupied the front room to the main road and Bernard lived in the other one next to the kitchen at the back of the house, which was quiet and led out through French doors to the garden.

Life was fantastic because all I had to worry about was my own room and living the carefree life of a bachelor. In the room I had my heater, a paraffin valour heater which was very effective but smelt horrible when just lit. You would light the wick and although it smelt vile at the beginning, eventually that smell vanished or you got used to it and the heater would keep you as warm as toast, providing you kept the doors and windows sealed with draft excluders.

I also had my little black and white TV, a small record player and a nice comfortable double bed. What else would a young man want at his stage of life? Every morning I took the bus to Tooting Broadway to get the underground train to work at the Tin Council in Haymarket.

My line manager was very nice and very accommodating, so life was not too stressful and work was not bad either although there were one or two racists, including the accountant whose jokes were wide of the mark, I learnt to ignore them. It's amazing how different people are. I suppose it's due to their upbringing and their level of education (or lack of it).

However, I just ignored the main perpetrate because there was nothing illegal then about racist behaviour, the accountant kept talking about his time in Africa and the Caribbean and what horrible things he used to do to the natives but I just ignored the sick bastard. He used a lot of derogatory language about people of colour, but I didn't pay much attention to him and his hang-ups. I compared him with my boss, who was pleasant and respectful who was also white, and I looked at this guy: he's old and he's from the colonial era and he's got this attitude: "Ah, you're a nice white man", and that was supposed to be a compliment but something black would be uncomplimentary. I worked with him but I didn't spend much time with him apart from when I had to. No wonder I don't ever remember his name. And, of course, if he was not there he certainly would not be missed, but to me he was just an itch that I tolerated.

There was this woman from Trinidad working there as the tea lady, she was calm and approachable, being married to a Jamaican we had some common interests, she and I would talk about England and she understood my frustration. She also used to supplement my eating because I couldn't always afford lunch and the cost of travel so she saw to it that I had extra biscuits and tea and that's how I would survive through those days when funds were scarce.

I was the only other black person working at the ITC at that time strangely enough, and I suppose being a fellow, I was a bit of a novelty and some of the ladies would ask me into their offices for a chat and I found that I would get on very well with the Irish and the Malaysian girls but for whatever reason the English girls were hard to be friends with.

Our offices were on the second and fourth floors of Haymarket House and on the ground floor there was the Design Council, with the Sugar Organisation on the third floor. There were all sorts of quasi-governmental organisations in our building and some high-ranking people from various countries would visit there. Sometimes, I would look outside the window and see Prince Charles and his people going into the Design Council and some of the other staff would comment on his bald patch, which looked odd in view of his young age. Whenever he came to the Centre everyone would be pressed up to the windows to see this young bald guy in the middle of the group and they would excitedly exclaim, " Look that's him there's Prince Charles in the middle".

When I arrived at work each day I would usually take the lift, but occasionally I would run up the stairs just for fun or for the exercise. If I was in the lift and I saw another black face I would feel proud knowing that there were others there and I would start some conversation. Now, if there was a young black lady I would be even more excited.

Anyway, for the first years I worked there, I was the only black guy in the offices except for another young fellow who I understood worked as a porter in the basement. We were the only two coloured guys in the whole building where dozens of people were employed. He was pushing stuff on wheelbarrows between the storage areas in the basement from the back of the ground floor where things were delivered for the Design Council exhibition area located on the ground floor in Haymarket itself.

I got to know Paul and we became friends but he liked the women too much; they were always white and they were always blonde. He was himself a good looking guy, I suppose they regarded him as being handsome, and he liked them and they adored him, so I suppose that's all that mattered. After work, he was always with these beautiful women, many of them from the Design Council.

I used to go and see him at his house and every time I went there it was at the wrong time as he was always entertaining some good-looking blonde he had either just met or brought over from work. Paul was always with a different lady and he was always out of cash, so he was always destitute and I couldn't understand why he didn't choose women with money. So he was worse than I could ever be as far as the ladies were concerned, but to satisfy his lifestyle he was borrowing left, right and centre, even from me and I was already in difficulty. Maybe his job didn't pay him enough or maybe he spent too much on women, but he had appearances to keep up if he was going to continue pulling all those gorgeous girls.

That was work. At home, Bernard, who lived in the room next to mine, used to have his young ladies locked up in his room whenever they turned up. He was a bit shy, and I rarely got into his room to meet any of his girlfriends. And about two or three years after getting married, Tim got divorced. By then, he and his wife had two kids, and I don't know what happened but one day she said to me, "I am going. I am leaving this man!" And she cleaned the place and made everything spotless collected her kids and went back home to her parents in Brixton and never came back. There was obviously tension between them which we didn't know about but Tim took it in his stride and brought another relative, Mac, to live there with us, turning the place into a bachelor pad as before.

Now, Mac was much older than us three and felt he had to school us in the ways of the world – courting, and so on. Talk about girls – he was absolutely out of it and had few scruples where the ladies were concerned. Being married did not put him off.

Tim was also a bit of a ladies man. He would drive around at night looking for girls just after the pubs emptied out and he would pick them up and take them back to our house for a party. If it was one girl he would creep in without us knowing, but if there were three or four he would call us into the sitting

My brother Ken and I at Mum's home

room upstairs to meet them. As I like to choose my companion I would find this awkward especially if they were not attractive. I used to tell him that I appreciated my presents more if the packaging was attractive, so I would try to be sociable until it was time for them to leave, usually when the booze ran out.

I asked Tim once: "Tim how do you get these gorgeous young ladies to go with you?"

"Oh", he said, "I just drive around and try to be helpful".

His strategy was like a prospecting sales person, if you get this one fine, if not he would move on to the next opportunity until eventually he got some who were happy to go home with him. There were one or two black girls, but a lot of the time they were white women out for a good time with some black guys.

Mac was different, he would fancy a woman and it didn't matter if she was married, he'd have her up to his room. Then he used to talk to us about how to satisfy these ladies: "It's the Chinese Brush", he used to say, and told us how he used this to make these women really happy.

This Chinese Brush was apparently some sort of aphrodisiac, a liquid in a bottle he painted on his penis and left for about an

118

hour or so while he had a few drinks with the girl, got her to ditch all inhibitions and then he'd be ready for love. While he's telling me about his technique I'm thinking to myself, well he's an old guy so he needs all the help he can get, so I wasn't tempted. I'm scared because I'm wondering, "Do I want to do that? What are the side effects?" So I decided I don't need that anyway. Tim used it and Mac obviously used it but I don't know if Bernard got involved with that.

I was the youngest one of the group anyway and was expected to learn from Mac, who termed himself "the master". He used to get this thing from some Chinese shop up in Edgware. Apparently, it gave you a strong erection and made you stay hard for longer when you were having sex. I suppose it's the same as Viagra nowadays. I used to enjoy listening to their stories, but being the youngest I wouldn't always do what they did.

Tim seemed to know where there were lonely young ladies hoping for excitement, one night he said he was taking me out somewhere for what he termed a good time. Well, I was free and single, I mean I'd had this one girlfriend but we weren't really hitting it off so we broke up. In the beginning it was fun when we met but she wanted to get engaged and I thought, no I wasn't really ready for that sort of commitment. I decided that I'm young and I'm single so I'm just going to enjoy youthful activities for a while.

Tim always knew the hospitals where there were lonely girls needing to be liberated from the nurses' residence for a well-deserved break.

"Nurses, they work, work, work, and then they had nothing else to look forward to at weekends", Tim believed this, so we would go out in his car to visit those lonely young nurses and they would always be fighting to come back with us so we would choose the most attractive ones to spend the weekend with us, and at home we'd have a little party; we would organise some drinks and food and the girls would stay the night and sometimes the weekend.

The next night, if it was a Saturday, we'd all go out to a party or a club and they enjoyed that and we'd take them back to their nurses' residence late Sunday. In those days it seemed we had to go far out into the country but now we know it was only Surrey, Essex or Kent bordering London.

However, closer home would be Balham hospital in south London. That's where you had the West Indian girls so we went there to the nurses' residence and although we may have known only one girl to start with by the end of the evening we would have six or so excited young nurses wanting to come with us to whatever club or party we were going to. It would usually be to the "Q" club off Edgware Road, after which they would ask to spend the weekend at our house, and of course we would accommodate them because these girls were far from home and lonely and for most part unloved, and so we brought a bit of love and excitement into their lives and that was fantastic for us and for them, and they really looked forward to our visits.

15

Strange Coincidences

Apart from the nefarious activities around this time there were things that were happening to me here in Britain that reminded me of those incidences that used to occur to me in Jamaica. Those "funny things" that made Miss Inez accuse me of being strange or an "odd bod".

I could look at the horse racing form and say, "This one", I don't know why, "that one...that one...that one", and I would go through the card and surprisingly they would come up. In fact, I remember on one occasion after Tim had sold his house and I had moved into this other Streatham house owned by this Jamaican Leroy who himself was a regular gambler and professed to knew everything about the "gee gees", every Saturday he was in the bookie shop gambling and he would encourage me to go with him for the experience. One Saturday morning I decided to have a go at this horse racing lark so I went and got the Mirror and chose my eight selections. I was going to place my bet when my landlord stopped me for a chat, he asked, "Where yu a go?"

I said, "I'm going to do some doubles and trebles and accumulator."

At that point he interjected, "Mek me see them selection!" He studied them for a brief while then laugh out "ha, ha them a donkey man, heh-heh, what you want to waste your money for? Dem da a donkeys!"

His cynical laughter put me off, so I didn't place my bet. What happened was, at about two-thirty, my curiosity forced me to go and see the results at the bookmaker and the first out of the eight that I had selected, won, at twenty to one. The next won, at thirty-three to one. Another came in at forty to one. I couldn't believe what I was seeing.

There was still time to put on the remaining four but I just thought, no, I won't bother now, but they all came in; all eight of them came in. I was gutted. When Leroy came home I went to show him the form and the results, he said to me, "Ah, I think that's just a coincidence" What! I said all eight coincidence?

But it was odd. If I had actually placed the bets with my usual ten pence, I would have made fifty thousand pounds and I worked out then that I could have bought a house for around ten thousand, so I could have bought five houses.

I couldn't explain how that had happened. It was very odd but these things used to happen. However, I remember one occasion I was pretty desperate for cash so I went into a betting shop, looked at the names of the horses and placed a bet. I said to myself, "I'm just going to win what I need and walked out". Well, I didn't look at the form because if I looked at the forms I never win. However, I did win on that occasion, and that's what happened at times whenever I was short of cash. I used to just pop in to the betting shop, choose a horse on instinct, make some money and just walk out.

I had an aunt called Umera. We called her Aunt Umi. At one time she lived in the same building at Gautrey Road as my mum, and she could interpret dreams. One afternoon I went to Umi and told her about this dream I had about fire and other details, and as I continued relating this dream she kept saying, "That's number 21...number 32...that's number 44..." And she actually linked the numbers to various incidents from this dream I had, so I am thinking OK, I'll use the numbers in the pools for that week. I don't know why I didn't follow through, either it was too late or it had slipped my mind, but just out of curiosity on the following Saturday night or Sunday morning I checked the football pool results and "Aunt Umi, look at the result and exclaimed – the numbers have all come up!"

And she said, "Bwoy, you fool fool. Why didn't you do the pools as you said you would?" All the numbers came up as she had interpreted them, just from that dream.

I don't know how she did it but she interpreted them using some Maccabees code or some type of Almanac. Everything in that system had a meaning, like fire is 21 or whatever it is, but that was my period of strange happenings and I tried to suppress it because it was too strange and overbearing at times.

I don't think it still happens now. If I wish for something strongly enough, it may happen but then again I don't think it's probably anything more than positive thinking. It's not some strange psychic whatever, it's just positive thinking. Although, it wasn't so positive back in Jamaica when I had wished that a boy would break his leg and he did.

That was a bit scary and I remember thinking to myself, did I do that? I'm sure I didn't, it must have just been a coincidence.

It doesn't happen any more but I feel more comfortable that it doesn't because in my youth I felt that I could influence things and I was scared of that awful insight.

16

Girl Crazy

It was around this time that I met this American girl, Michelle, and guess what? She was absolutely fantastic to look at with an amazing personality; a gorgeous lady with such a great accent. For years all my girlfriends were nurses. This girl, of all those nurses, was the first of the bunch who said she wanted to get engaged to me after only a short period of us going out together. She wanted us to get married, move to the USA and live in a big house with white picket fence, blah-blah, blah-blah, blah-blah, and her mum would "love it" if I came over with her to the US and so on, but although I was keen on her I was not sure about the move to USA so after a while I decided that I would have problems with the life change.

She wanted us to go over to California where her mother was established but I was thinking about the Ku Klux Klan and lynching, and I thought I've got enough problems here. I mean, I used to read a lot about the KKK and the black people in America who used to vent their frustration by rioting every summer all over America. So I'm thinking, yea, I like you, but do I want to get involved in that crap in a land I only read about?

Anyway, her mind was made up; she decided she wanted to get engaged. She saw a ring which was given back to me by a previous girlfriend, Brenda, my first girlfriend in England. I didn't actually propose to her but her mum and my mum were good friends and as we were seeing each other she told her mum that we were going to get engaged and so I went along with the idea and got engaged. We had a little party upstairs over a pub with her family and my family, and although I wasn't really ready for marriage I felt I had to do it. After a while it became clear that it wasn't going to work and in a moment of heated temper she chucked the ring at me so I just kept it on my dressing table.

So, this Michelle saw this ring and put it on and told her friends in Balham that we were engaged. This went on for a while and she was pushing it and she'd go back to LA and kept pushing me to follow her there but I wanted my freedom to come and go as I chose. Eventually she got mad with me and my indecision and on one of her visits to my bedsit she took off the ring and in a fit of temper pounded it with the heel of her shoes into a mangled shape then chucked it at me before leaving in a huff.

Now, the thing is, I have a philosophy in life: I would never disrespect or suggest to any of my girlfriends that we break up it was always their shout as I know it would shatter their confidence if I initiate the break-up, but if I wanted to end it, I'd cause them to be irritated enough to end it themselves. They would feel bad later on and wouldn't mind being friends afterwards. So we were very good friends even after the split. A lot of my ex-girlfriends were great friends with me after our bust-up and would even go to parties with me and my current girlfriend with whom they would become friends with also.

My American girl wanted to get engaged and so we did but then after about a year I could not take the pressure anymore and must have said something like "I'm not really ready for this" or "I'm too young for marriage" and she got mad and went back to LA for good. I just put the mangled ring back inside this ashtray where it stayed and then I got myself back in circulation as an unshackled bachelor.

I've always had a bevy of young ladies that I would go to parties with but getting "engaged" was something that I felt needed to be done to satisfy or appease the young lady I was going with at the time. However after that American horror story I started going out again with Tim and the other guys until I met another young lady who was also very keen on getting engaged. What's the matter with these girls? She too was a nurse but she had a different approach which was to come and meet my mum and introduce herself as my future wife. I was hoping that we would be just two young people having fun, but no! She wanted more.

Millie was from Birmingham, where I had some relatives and whenever I visited relatives in Birmingham she would turn up to socialise with my relatives up there, and of course they loved her; but once again I wasn't ready for a serious type of commitment. Anyway, she eventually came to visit me at my rented room in Streatham where she saw this twisted ring in the ashtray. "Ah, what's this, how is it so mangled?" she asked so I explained, "It's a ring, someone broke up in a moment of temper".

So Millie took the ring and exclaimed, "I can fix this!" She took the broken ring and had it fixed then placed it on her finger and went with me to inform my mum that "We're engaged". My mum looked at me askance but said nothing. I wouldn't put anyone down; if she said she was engaged, then she's engaged.

Millie was nice, she knew I liked her but I wasn't ready for marriage though I think she felt she could change that. Then after months went by and nothing's coming from me about marriage she became irritable and just as before, she got mad, told me off and chucked the ring at me. Well! As before I took the ring off the floor and put it back into the ashtray. I didn't see her for quite a while after that; she has changed her hospital and went to work elsewhere near Birmingham. However, on one of my visits to the city we met up again and went out for dinner but the relationship was now more platonic, she realised it wasn't going anywhere, so we parted as friends. I suspect Millie must have met someone who was more ready for marriage, as she did not contact me after that. However, my Birmingham relatives were quite disappointed as they thought she would have made an ideal partner as they kept saying I was so foolish to let her go as she was such a nice girl.

So, now I'm back in my usual groove and meeting all these new and interesting people. On one occasion Mac took me and Tim to a party hosted by these African sailors, friends of his, on this boat which had docked on the Thames. For me, this was unusual, as I had never imagined a black sea captain on such a large boat in the London docks. But the reason behind the invitation was that these guys were in London for over a week and they needed to have some female companionship. Well, finding black girls who needed an adventure was not a problem at that time, particularly when we told them about the black captain, the boat and the party that was being planned. So on the night in question, we collected these girls and went off to the docks where we all had a fabulous party on that boat.

On some weekends my younger friends around Streatham and I would go to this black club off Edgware road. A black club meant mainly black people, black music and black food – "soul food". There, you would see black celebrities from music and sport: people like Muhammad Ali, Bob Marley and others going there to socialise. And this club was popular with black people from all background and professions, not only because you could feel relaxed and comfortable among your own people, but because the celebrities drew in lots of the best looking and sophisticated young ladies from all over London.

The "Q" club was located on a side street off Edgware Road and when someone famous was either performing or visiting you would get lots of groupies and that was good for us too because we would get to know the disappointed females, the ones who didn't manage to get off with one of the stars. So we would turn up at the "Q" club when we knew someone famous was going to be there. Yes, that was the sort of regime to our social lives and we didn't mind the scraps that fell from the table.

My lifestyle became more and more expensive with the constant partying and the physical and mental demands I was forced to endure, not only was I working Monday to Friday but also going to college two or three evenings every week. So in spite of that and in order to fund my expensive lifestyle I decided to get a job for the other evenings I wasn't attending college. I got some work at Lyon's Corner House opposite the House of Parliament, working in the kitchen washing dishes and clearing tables. So, straight from the Tin Council in Haymarket I would take the bus right outside the building and in ten minutes or so I would be at Lions Corner House and on time as good timekeeping was always important to me.

The great thing about that job was that I always got dinner, a nice three-course meal on those evenings I worked. And there was little chance of any of my superiors from the Tin Council seeing me working there as I was not sure about the conditions of my work contract with the Council.

Oh, my gosh! All the politicians would come over to eat, as it was right opposite the Palace of Westminster and right above Westminster tube station. But as I wasn't really into politics I wasn't a fan of any of them except possibly Prime Minister Wilson whom I never saw there.

Where girls were concerned, I learnt at an early age that there is no such thing as loyalty. The girlfriend you had was only loyal and trustworthy until someone "better" came along. Maybe it was my insecurity; I didn't want to be on my own. Maybe it was because growing up in Jamaica I didn't really have a loving and stable family existence, but it was important that I have love and maybe it's a combination of that why I had about three girlfriends on the go at any one time. So, when one said, "I have had enough of you", then number two becomes number one and I'm looking for number three. With three girlfriends I learned to be a good political person, because you know how to say "No" without actually saying no; you learned how to not tell a lie by sugar-coating the lie, if you see what I mean. You can't make mistakes when you have three steady girlfriends. It's one of those things you have to learn to manage and to remember dates, to remember when was the last time you saw A, B or C, and you cannot be with B and talk about A – you must get it right and never write anything down. So what I would do was to make up a pet name – like "Putsie", because she was small or "Bupsy" because she was bubbly, or "Cutie", because of her dimples. They loved that because it's boring saying Gloria or Marcia, so with a pet name I hardly made the mistake of calling the lady the wrong name.

I don't know if they were loyal to me, you can never tell but I assumed they weren't. One night out at the "Q" club I met this girl from some small island in the Caribbean. She was a good looker, absolutely out of this world, so I used to call her Peaches as she reminded me of a delicious dessert: peaches and ice cream.

Obviously she went to that club because she wanted to meet the male soul singers, like James Brown or whoever; or boxers like Sugar Ray Leonard or Muhammad Ali, but there was competition so she ended up with me. I was very nice to her: bought her drinks, escorted her home at the end, never would I make a move on the first night, just get the interest going. So I'd say, "Well, I'll see you", being polite and kind but never rushing anything, just taking things slowly. Let her do the chasing but show definite interest and so you play the game, which was great fun and makes the "kill" even sweeter.

I got those ideas from the novels I read. I would read lots of books, usually just before going to bed as a means of relaxation. Sometimes I would watch TV, but mainly I would read, publications like "The Readers Digest" and "The Weekend magazine" which was a favourite of mine, particularly the real life stories, which I read religiously in addition to the novels which took days to complete. Both the Weekend and the Readers Digest had great stories about people's experiences and human relationships. So my technique developed from those materials; you nurture it and allow nature to take over, and always on the first date be as polite and as sweet as possible, smile a lot as it releases tension. Be the gentleman, escort her to her home and if she says, "Would you like coffee?" take a rain check, "Well, maybe tomorrow".

But if you do go in and you do have coffee, she might think you are a complete prat* if you are oblivious to her advances. Never initiate anything on the first date, maybe all she wants is companionship and a chat because she feels safe and comfortable in your presence so at a convenient juncture you excuse yourself and leave.

So, you go and never offer to kiss her unless she really wants you to. And you don't see her the next day, maybe you don't ring her but call the day after and by now she's anxiously expecting your call, so you play that game, and it's fantastic when the plan works.

I am a nice person really but this is a game. Life is a game, isn't it? And the day you call you want to know all about her. You are not important; it's all about her. And then you may ask, "What are you doing at lunch time?" You don't want to make it the evening because of what that might imply, so you make it lunch.

A restaurant called Stock Pot off Haymarket (maybe still there) owned and run by some Italian or Spanish ladies, was a popular place for eating spaghetti and stuff like that, and the food was cheap and very tasty, so if the girl was working in the neighbourhood we would usually meet for lunch there.

The girls I wanted to woo would get first-class treatment, absolutely; she's got to feel good about herself. It's important that she gets to feel good about you too and be comfortable with you. It's not about what you want, you are just there to accommodate her needs, you influence her wishes but you don't push it; after all men are here to service the needs of the farer sex.

Every young lady should be treated perfectly like a queen and whoever I choose is the lady who becomes my queen.

I suppose I was a bit like my father as it seems he too loved having the ladies around him. I don't know how well he used to treat them, although I do know that he used to beat my stepmother. Now, I was too young to get involved in all of that but that was him. I think lots of girls were attracted to him because he was rich; he had clubs or dance halls in every large town between Portland and Kingston and he had his ladies running them (in other words, milking him dry). So that was him. In my case, I didn't have money. I was poor and struggling but I know that what I do want is success in life and I wanted to be knowledgeable, I wanted to know things and I admired girls and enjoyed their affection and companionship, unlike some guys who seem to inveigle you into doing bad things.

Now, this girl I was telling you about, the one I met in the "Q" club, I took her home to my humble abode and Marcia my new friend was absolutely wonderful. Now that's not my normal routine; I don't usually do that. Normally, I just say goodnight and play the game but, like I said, Marcia was like peaches and cream – irresistible. She said she didn't want to go back to her place, she wanted to come back to mine. I don't know why, but she came and it was nice and warm (my little valour heater was working great) and we had something to eat, played a bit of music and she ended up spending the weekend. We had a great time and the guys in the house who met her loved her, and the guys were like "Wow!" But it was pointless because I found out that too many guys outside there loved to be around her and was pitching for her attention. Marcia wanted to go off to clubs every weekend and I wouldn't say you can't do this or that. Well who am I to stop her? Although I was reluctant to let her go when she would come and spend time with me. To be close to me Marcia actually moved into a house a few streets away where she rented a small room, although she hardly spent much time there except when she wanted some space. However, one Friday night, Marcia was nagging me to go with her to the "Q" club as there was some group appearing that she wanted to see. I wasn't keen but she was overly keen to go so she said, "Well, can I go?" And I grudgingly said yes, so off she went and I didn't see her for two days. Maybe I'd got a bit too close to her (and if you ever did that you were bound to get hurt), but I hadn't seen her for two days and it was now Sunday and I thought I would pop up to her lodgings and surprise her. Bad decision.

I went to the house and rang the bell and the guy downstairs let me in because he knew me and said, "Just go up". I went up and knocked on her door Marcia opened the door and there was this "Mandingo" in her bed. I was absolutely shocked and for a moment speechless.

The thing is, you might know that this is something people do, but to actually experience it face-to-face was different. The place reeked of sex; the entire room smelled funky. He was underneath the sheets naked and there she was half-naked and suddenly a rush of blood went to my head and I was seething. Then I calmed down; she looked straight at me jerking her shoulder and said, "What did you expect?" Well there you are it's my fault.

So there, that was my first real up-close-and-personal experience of deceit. Unlike with my childhood crush where there was a question mark about whether my "love girl" had actually cheated with my best friend, there was no denying this time: the evidence was right in front of my eyes.

This experience got me thinking, well, I suppose there are good girls and there are not so good girls and these things do happen in life get used to it. I was really jealous and really disappointed with her but I should have expected that. Part of me thought that it was my fault why she did that, but anyway it shocked me that Marcia was doing those things behind my back and being so nice when we were together.

How many more? I wondered. And to think, everyone thought she was so sweet, maybe that's it every young man had designs on her, but then I thought back to Brenda when she had also cheated, and she was suppose to be a Christian woman and it did not take much temptation as she managed it in a short weekend trip to Birmingham where she'd met that guy. Then, as now, I'd found out about her infidelity on a surprise visit but nothing as frontal as this. So, for me, there was no trust or loyalty between the sexes. Trust your girl only when you can see her.

After that, I concluded that women weren't trustworthy, so this convinced me that I needed to have more than one girlfriend at any onetime. You couldn't rely on just one because she was bound to stray. Can you imagine if I didn't have a second one to pull me up when I was down? I would be on my own and even more depressed. After that let down I had to move on, and so, like a tomcat I was back on my feet and in circulation once again. I started to go out again with my mates in Streatham when I am not going out with the guys in my house. Week days I was too busy working and studying and on the evenings of Fridays, Saturdays and Sundays it was party time and some people would ring me up and tell me about parties or ring me up and asking me about parties. Or some of these young ladies would be having parties at their hall of residence and I would be invited to take some male friends along with me.

Through my regular visits to clubs in and around the west end I met some more nurses from the Chelsea Hospital but boys were not allowed to stay on the premises beyond ten at night, and they were not allowed to stay out after that time either, so having a normal relationship was very difficult. Taking them out and taking them back and finding myself home late at night was problematic, so what I used to do was take them out to the local clubs for a good time and then I would sneak back to their room and if anyone came in, I'd fly underneath the bed. Her friend might have come in and say: "Shirley, so and so" and she would reply, "I'm tired, I'm going to have a sleep, speak to you tomorrow." And she'd lock her door and I'd emerge from my hiding place. Then the next day, twelve o'clock would be the time for me to slip out of hiding, creep out the front, knock on the door and pretend I was just arriving.

Anyway, after living in Streatham for a good while, Tim decided that he was going to sell his house and so we all had to find alternative accommodations. However, just before that, my dear cousin got involved with our good friend's wife and the whole thing became embarrassing and eventually it became really nasty. Mac did the same thing with another friend's wife. These older men are setting really bad examples. Of course the husbands found out and jealousy forced them round to the house and their wives were hiding in the house and the men would come round trying to force their way in and threatening to kill them, to "chop them up".

Now our friend Oscar had a very beautiful wife but for whatever the reason he always wanted to go out with us leaving this gorgeous woman at home on her own. However, Oscar suddenly became violent when he learnt that Tim was having it off with his wife when we were out at parties when Tim was supposed to be at work. Yes, Oscar had a nice Guyanese wife, absolutely beautiful with a sharp nose, high cheek bones, long wavy hair and a figure to kill for and with a charming personality to boot; half Chinese, half Indian, but she was very nice to all of us and she always gave the impression that she loved us all; very tactile, but although tempting, I left it alone. You can't be taken in by your good friend's wife, but Tim reckoned he could not help himself.

Initially, he would pretend he was working nights or that he was ill so he was not able to go out with us boys, while all this while, unknown to us, he was having a storming affair with his friend's wife. When I found out I tried to talk to him about it: "There are millions of girls out there, you don't have to get involved with this woman", but of course Tim claimed that he couldn't help it as he was trapped by her radiance. We called him "the dog" but it was partly our friend's fault for going out with us and leaving such a desirable woman at home alone. Before long, she was bound to stray. And when the husband found out he got really nasty: "I'm gonna kill him", he would yell, and I was there trying to be neutral between my cousin and my good friend.

Eventually, this man came with a cutlass when Tim was at the house. It would all flare up into a big argument. Sometimes the woman would be there and he would let her out through the back door and then Mac would come and say, "There's no one here". Mac is like the peacemaker and the guy would be cussing terrible Jamaican swear words: "R******, I goin' kill him, that so and so".

In the end, Oscar's wife had to be taken into a battered wives home, but, despite all of that, Mac went with his friend's wife also and she was apparently very much in love with Mac. Eventually, after a lot of similar hassle, she divorced her husband, got married to Mac and went to live in Jamaica.

I had moved out by then. Tim was in the process of selling the house anyway, so I moved up the road to rent a room at this Jamaican's house. The place was clean and roomy and the wife was Ok, but despite that every time a girl came to see me Leroy would get jealous and try to interfere by chatting her up behind my back, so I could never relax in his house. Not too long after moving there I decided that I was getting out of all of that and going to live in the country on my own. That was when I decided to buy a property in Greenhithe.

* Prat – Fool

17

Ghost Town

I wanted to buy my own place and not rent because, at that time, everyone I knew was talking about house prices getting out of hand and I thought I would never be able to afford anything on my measly salary. What was it, £15 a week? I could never afford anything in London, and out of desperation, I got a place in a little Kentish village called Greenhithe, near Dartford for the main train station to London. I met this mortgage broker in Peckham who assured me that he would provide me with a property and a mortgage package to suit my needs.

He said, "I've got this place. It's not exactly kosher but it's OK and will suit your budget". I asked, "Anything illegal?" He said, "No, it's not illegal, but come and see for yourself"

So, we drove out to Kent to see this property. I thought we were driving for a long time as we motored away from the city through miles and miles of rolling fields before we eventually arrived at a quiet little village near the River Thames. I saw these strange little old terrace houses. There were no new properties in that quaint little village in those days (although these days places like Greenhithe are regarded as "outer London").

The broker showed me this quaint structure at the top of some steps "this is the train station to Dartford and London, so it was easy to get in to London". Well the village looked deserted and it was a Saturday. The house was in Charles street, it looked nice enough, bathroom on the ground floor, garden was Ok and so on, and I noticed the cement works opposite but at the time it didn't occur to me that it would be difficult to breathe, with all the dust swirling around when the machines were working, or that putting my clothes out on the line would be a problem. I didn't really think about those things, I was just pleased to be owning a property so I went for it and the broker arranged the mortgage and the purchase of the house costing about £12,000.

Once the deal was done, I moved in to take up the life of an English gentleman; suddenly I heard a rumbling noise towards the end of the garden, "Brrrrrh!" There was a train line just behind the property and when the trains came down from London in the rush hour the whole place vibrated. So, all of that I learnt after agreeing to the deal, but anyway it was my own place; I'd got my foot on the property ladder. It meant the world to me that I was a homeowner, even if my new home was in the middle of nowhere which rattled when passing trains go by, and was located in an area where I was the only black person.

In those days, Greenhithe was a quiet backwater that was little more than a stop on the train to Dartford *en route* to its destination at Gravesend. But it wasn't a complete wilderness. The cement works I saw that first day was a Blue Circle plant, but aside from that bit of industry, the area was covered in old ships and rusting metal anchors and discarded merchant vessels, a bit like a ship's graveyard littered with big anchors and abandoned, rotting old boats. In some ways, it felt a bit like a ghost town.

There was a little pub on Charles Street near to where I lived. When I ventured in there for the first time, as I opened the door and went in, to my complete surprise, everyone stopped and looked round. On seeing me they froze and there was dead silence. There was absolutely no movement, no sound, not even from the bar staff. It was like in the cowboy films when the stranger rides into town and comes into the bar and everyone stops whatever they are doing and just stares at the intruder. It felt surreal and a bit menacing.

Some people were playing with a strange object on a table with wooden balls at the ends of strings that went, "Gonk! Gonk! as they manoeuvred it. It was very odd and to this day I have no idea what the object of the game was or indeed the purpose of that game. It was weird, I couldn't understand it.

And some were also playing skittles and darts, but it was the *gonk* game that had initially grabbed my attention – that is until I saw the expression on their faces as they froze when they'd seen me in the doorway. I was quite shocked at that and suddenly felt small in the presence of this hostile-looking crowd.

How did I come to be in this remote place? What happened was that my mum had always wanted to have a house of her own, but not having a steady partner we couldn't afford it. And we definitely couldn't afford a house in London, but she didn't want to leave her friends, so there was little chance of her moving away to a less expensive area, perhaps outside of London.

I could see the advantages of owning a property of my own, even if it meant going out into the countryside on my own.

The locals used to say that pirates had lived in those little houses as they are so close to the Thames, and I always used to wonder what was in the loft. I thought that there might be some treasure or even skeletons tucked away up there, but there wasn't any access so that's the reason why I didn't go up there to investigate – although that didn't stop me wondering why there was no obvious access.

The need to own a property was the reason why I moved to Greenhithe, which couldn't have been more different to what I had been used to in south London.

Well, my mum gave me her blessings but she didn't want to live outside London away from her people and job opportunities and because the mortgage was a bit, what Jamaicans call *simi dimi**. She didn't want to get involved in that either.

Anyway just before getting the house I met a young lady, Norma. She was fair-skinned with black curly hair and was quite attractive, although shy and a bit insecure, I liked her quite a lot. Norma lived with her mother, Miss Anderson, in West Norwood, south London. Her mother was very nice to me and so I was allowed to visit without any restrictions.

It was just Norma and her mother living there as it appeared that they were very private people and it seems they had no other relatives in the UK. However, later in our relationship I discovered that Miss Anderson's cousin was Beverley Anderson, who at that time was married to Michael Manley, the then Prime

Minister of Jamaica, and apparently both Norma and her mother would spend holidays at Beverley's residence in Jamaica.

Well, I was surprised, as it didn't seem they had much contact with any relatives. However, one evening I went to visit Norma at Thamesmead where they were living at that time. As I got to the house I was greeted by Norma at the door and was told to be on my best behaviour as they had some very important visitors in the house.

In one room I met some young black political activists, including Paul Boateng, a solicitor, who would later become one of the first black Members of Parliament and a cabinet minister. However, the World Cup was on television in another room so I decided to go in there to watch the match and to my great surprise there was Mr Manley, Jamaica's Prime Minister, sitting there watching the football.

For a moment, I froze then collected my senses and introduced myself. I was surprised that he was there but more surprised to see that he was a great football fan. Later on, the other guys came in. I think they were more interested in talking politics, some of which went a little above my head, so I left them and went into the kitchen to join Norma and her mum.

Initially, Norma and I were good friends but later in the relationship she became my girlfriend. Norma was a fantastic person, but as I found out later in the relationship that my tight finances were becoming a problem for her. We got on well and went out for a while up to the time when she was in her final year of her degree at Avery Hill College but the relationship was becoming strained.

The long journey after work travelling home to Greenhithe did not help either as it was always difficult for me to see her because I had so little money. I could not afford to visit as often as I would have liked, or arrange for us to go out to nice places as frequently as she wanted. Eventually, living on a shoestring really put a strain on our relationship and possibly lead to the break-up.

* Simi dimi – Dodgy, bordering on crooked

18

The Moonlight Flit

So, I was living in this quaint village opposite the river Thames which was interesting, but the noisy, dirty cement works opposite the house and being on my own particularly in the dark winter evenings was becoming a bit depressing. After a while I decided that I couldn't afford to live there any longer, particularly because of the rising cost of commuting to my job in London and not being able to afford to visit friends as often as I wanted to. Most of my money was going on travelling and then, of course, I was only surviving by eating baked beans and rice, which, looking back, was not a proper and acceptable lifestyle for a young man in his prime, but that was how I survived.

In the end, I decided to rent out the property and move back to London. I placed an advertisement in the local paper but the only person who came to view was a lady called Meek.

Mrs Meek had just returned from Australia with her kids to settle back in England. Apparently, the husband was due to follow once they'd settled. Now, if I had thought about it then, I would have realised that anyone with a nice name like "Meek" would be exactly the opposite in terms of attitude and personality, and that's very true as I found out to my cost. I should also have been suspicious about the relationship with the so-called husband, who never did turn up to help with the rent.

Well, being the nice guy that I was, I took pity on Mrs Meek and so she and her children moved into my house in Greenhithe. As I said, this lady had come back from Australia and apparently she couldn't get a place to live, particularly as there were two or three young kids and no partner.

I subsequently learnt that sympathy or compassion doesn't exist in business and that it is only the hard-nosed business people who survive in this unfair world.

The thing was, although the social services didn't give them much time or show any genuine interest to their plight before, however, as soon as they were renting somewhere, suddenly social services got involved on their behalf. And I think the law then was totally in favour of the tenant and so after maybe only a month the rent wasn't being paid and it became clear that it was her intention to live rent free for as long as she could.

I can't believe that I was that stupid, that before offering the house I didn't assess whether or not Mrs Meek would be able to pay or that there were other motives at work. I must have just asked her questions and she was convincing, maybe she said that her husband was doing it or whatever, but anyway she moved in and she was very happy and grateful then, but soon after she settled Mrs Meek refused to pay the rent citing all sort of spurious reasons. It became clear that this was her intention all along.

Despite my reasonable approach over the months I didn't get any rent. I'd ring her and she would give all sorts of excuses, so I went to the property to speak to her personally. I knocked on the door politely and was invited in.

Obviously, she didn't have the money and was a bit embarrassed and I suppose she took umbrage at the fact that she had come back to her home country and there was this black man telling her that she's got to pay to stay in his house. I suppose that's what was going through her mind, because her body language indicated that kind of arrogance.

Her response was to go to the council and report that I had harassed her. The council contacted me and said they had heard that I was harassing Mrs Meek and her children. I couldn't believe the guile of that woman.

The thing is, when something like that happens, the authorities have no interest in what you, the landlord, had to say in your defence. They had a complaint and so it was their job to execute the duties without regard to what I had to say in my defence. So, Social Services went through some type of slow investigation which appeared to take forever. In the meantime I had to pay the mortgage and was banned from visiting my own property, and during that time she was getting free accommodation with complete disregard for my costs.

Eventually, I decided to take her to court, which took another length of time, but just before she was issued with a notice to vacate the premises and pay compensation she did "a runner" – a midnight flit. But, not only did she do a runner, she also sold off some of my furniture to people in the street. I went around the neighbourhood asking if anyone had seen her and told them that she hadn't paid her rent and that there was a court order on her; one person's conscience must have pricked her and she said, "I think this is yours," handing me an item of furniture that Mrs Meek had sold her.

And I could not believe how many people had colluded in her scam. They must have either bought or had been given those things and now felt embarrassed or guilty or whatever when I said I'd have to try and find Mrs Meek through the police. The police came, but typical of the authorities at that time, their response was a big let down: "Ah, don't bother with her". That was the impression and advice they gave me. So I said, "Well, it's stealing. She has actually stolen my furniture and I could see some of it in the neighbours' houses."

It was clear for whatever reason that they did not want to pursue this legal route much further so they went round the various houses and got some of my stuff back and said, "Here's your stuff", but they didn't seek her out to prosecute her. So I thought well, what can I do? I just put it down to a nightmarish experience.

I decided I wouldn't rent the house again so I put it on the market but there was no interest because, at the same time, Dartford Council was buying up properties in Charles Street through compulsory purchase orders because the Dartford Bridge was in the planning stages and the authorities felt the land around that area would be required. Eventually, I sold the house to them, securing just enough for a deposit on a house closer to London, in Bexleyheath.

The house at Greenhithe was my first venture into renting and I put it down to inexperience, realising that we live in a very uncompromising and opportunistic jungle full of predators waiting to pounce. I thought: "Never again!"

19

A Woman Scorned

As it happened, the house I bought in Bexleyheath, was directly opposite a pub, turned out to be very nice house with a massive garden at the back. In the summer the garden reminded me of Jamaica, with those big long trees swaying in the wind. I loved it.

Although closer to London, Bexleyheath was still regarded as Kent and was much too far from Peckham for my mother who continued to reside where she was in south London, along with my younger brother. Mum liked the idea of being within walking distance of her friends and the shops where she could buy her West Indian provisions.

Now that I was "closer" to the so-called Front Line in Brixton, all my friends from the area started coming to visit me at Bexleyheath every weekend for parties.

I was one of the few black guys of my age then who owned a house and was living on his own, so it became a bachelor pad for all my friends. It was a nicer area than Greenhithe and not too far out from London; you could take the number 89 bus from opposite my street at Lion Road into Lewisham, and from there get a connection to Brixton or Peckham.

I had some mixed-race friends from Jamaica who were then living in Streatham who, together with their beautiful sisters, used to come down to me most weekends because Bexleyheath was regarded then as on the better fringes of London, away from the hustle and bustle of the inner city.

It was around this time that I met a girl called Faye. At this same time I was thinking more about my career and my future, and I suppose being a bit more grown up, I was becoming more weary about drifting through life and reasoned more about things like work, my future and relationships: that before you commit to anything you've got to think sensibly about all the options so, I became serious about most things and then my career was the main focus at this time. I started thinking seriously in terms of where I was in my life, where I wanted to be in the future and ways of getting there. I had taken some exams and was doing some more and was making a slow progress at the Tin Council where I still worked. I started thinking about career options and the savings I needed to make in order to make some headway in life. Up to now progress was very slow, but now I am looking for openings to move up to a different level.

It was also around this time I was promoted from being the general "dog's body": the tea boy, the "mail man" and the "go for", to working in the statistics department as a statistical clerk. There, I was dealing with figures and helping to produce a monthly statistical bulletin for distribution to the Council's international members showing data on tin production and consumption, knowing that important decisions were being made by the organisation based on those figures.

So, it was during this period of self-assessment when I was stretching out a little in terms of my responsibilities at work, that I met this ambitious young lady called Faye.

While I was being introspective about the direction my career was taking, I had decided that I also needed to have a fun lifestyle as well, and as it was the same summer that I'd bought my lovely MGB GT sports car I decided to cruise around town to show-off on this beautiful and hot summer's day. It was then I noticed this very attractive young lady with very long and perfectly-formed legs walking towards East Street near the Elephant and Castle my stomping ground of South London. I was just cruising on my own, and being the charmer that I am, I had to complement her on her perfect form. I stopped, turned the car around but I couldn't park, so I called out: "Hello, you look very tired, can I give you a lift somewhere?" She looked at me but more at the car and then decided, "OK, then." So I was the perfect gentleman and politely opened the door for her to slide in while she moved about to find the perfect position for those long legs. I thought, "Yea, I'm on to something good here".

I drove very slowly to her house, enjoying the cool summer breeze caressing our faces as we talked and got to know each other.

I asked her if it was OK for us to go out on a date the following week, maybe for a drink or a meal. She didn't say no but wasn't giving much away so I decided to play it very cool; you mustn't rush things, so I gave her my phone number and told myself, "Boy, if you want something badly enough, don't rush it, just let it happen".

The next day the phone rang, it was her and usually I would string it out by saying something like "I'm busy with college work" and stuff like that to heighten the interest. However, this time I was really busy and so I told her I couldn't make it but could we arrange to meet another time.

Maybe she thought I wasn't very keen but, anyway, eventually we got together and that was a good thing actually because my on and off girlfriend at the time, was becoming a pain. Not only was she becoming a bit too selfish about most things but she was also much too demanding, so I decided that I wanted to finish with her finally so that's what happened. Faye's timing couldn't have been more perfect.

Faye was impressed with my attitude to life particularly the fact that I was still trying to better myself through education. We were getting on fine and she appreciated my resolve to succeed in the world, and probably saw a future for us. I, on the other hand, wasn't thinking that far ahead. I fancied her and thought we could have some fun together.

She would come to stay over at weekends and I did look forward to those occasions, but after some time she suggested she should move in with me since she wanted to look after me properly. I couldn't think of a good reason why she shouldn't, so she moved in.

Now, I didn't really want her to move in as I have always lived on my own. A bit of a selfish life maybe, but I felt more comfortable like that. I was a bachelor and enjoyed the freedom of living alone. I was used to coming and going when I liked, doing my own cleaning and cooking, and I certainly was not used to sharing a house with a female on what appeared to be a permanent basis. I wasn't used to that at all.

But now, you start thinking there is another person to consider. Well I didn't want her to come and live in my house, but she sort of persuaded me to let her. Anyway, I decided to move with this lady.

After a while you start seeing more than just the outside beauty; you want to see the person inside. You start seeing people from the inside, how they are with kids, your friends or would they support you in a crisis? You start observing those characteristics and start pulling these things together and building this mental picture of your perfect partner. You know, she's not self-centred, she doesn't want to go spending all the time, she doesn't want you to live in a castle; she's quite happy wherever she is. I mean, to me, that's ideal, so you start looking for these things in people you are spending time with. Anyway, Faye seemed ok and her family were lovely people. Faye was a children's dentist, and was very fit as she was always going to the gym. Sometimes we would spend time wrestling on the floor and on the bed. She loved wrestling with me and that girl was strong too, she had muscles. I liked the fact that she was my mate as well as my girlfriend. But then, of course, she didn't like it when friends of mine came down to have parties, she did not mind short visits but hated the distraction of having others around the house. It's as if she didn't want to share me with anyone. Faye was happiest when it was just us and she preferred it when we didn't go out to parties but stayed in, or had a quick meal at some restaurant and return home with a bottle of wine. That was the ideal weekend for her. However, my friends were not very happy that I could be put under such strict "manners"* by a woman and they missed the weekends we used to have as a group of lads going out and having fun and I think they resented her because of that.

The Bexleyheath area was quiet and family orientated, the houses were mainly semi-detached. The neighbours were alright apart from the occasional idiot you euphemistically bumped into on the road.

On one side of my house there were other young people, Irish, I think. They were great neighbours and we visited each other houses regularly for chats and have a few glasses of wine or coffee most evenings, and on the other side were older English people. They were pleasant and we got on with them as well. Usually, I get on with people if the attitude is right, but sometimes it's best to keep away from some people, it all rests on their attitude their views and body language. It is always pleasant to have a good relationship with neighbours whatever their race or culture, for the occasional chitchat, and so on. So there was no real tension or racial problems on my road. Occasionally, I would have a run-in with the people who went to the pub opposite because they would park in front of my drive blocking me in, so I would have to go over to the pub to get the idiot to move his car.

(Knock, knock). "Hello, who's parked in front of my drive? I mean how would you like it if I went and parked in front of your drive?" Maybe because they know who lived there and did not care whether they disrespected us. However, I had no fear about going over there and making my presence known and asking out loud "Could someone please move the car that's parked in front of my drive?"

It became so embarrassing for the landlord and eventually someone would go and move it and after that the landlord would prime his customers. He used to say, "I hope no-one has parked in front of number so and so". I don't know what else he said to his drinkers but we didn't have many people who parked there after that. I didn't think about getting a brick through my window in retaliation back then. When you're that young things don't really matter that much, you don't think about such consequences.

So, the lovely Faye moved in and that was ok for a while, but then she wanted marriage and, although she was a nice person and really physically attractive, I wasn't thinking about marriage at that stage. I just wanted to enjoy life with someone pleasant without the commitment of marriage. Maybe she wanted to get married for reasons I did not or could not know. She was young, attractive and a working professional, why would she want to get stuck with a husband at that stage? Is that the ambition of every young woman? I just didn't know. I don't know what was going on in her mind or what in her family background was making her so eager to settle down as a married woman at her age. Perhaps being the eldest of her sisters she wanted to be the first one to get married, I don't know, but I wasn't keen on the idea. I had things to do, anyway, I needed to focus on my studies, get a better job, and start saving money to become financially secure. I think I was finally growing up. My mother needed my help at times and I was not even close to being financially stable. I had a father but he did his own thing and was never going to help out my mother with her needs, so it fell to me. Anyway, by this time he'd gone to live in the United States. He had lost all his money in Jamaica when the tax man come to claim the taxes he owed but he didn't have the money so they took away a lot of his possessions and he needed to find work. He ended up in America with a new wife and a set of young kids.

His experience in Jamaica was that, although he was supposed to be running his businesses, he was a man who went to the bars with his mates, that's all they did: drank, told dirty jokes and played dominoes. He ended up lending a lot of his money to various people, including his uncle Conrad who had the bus service in Portland at that time.

When they say "lend", forget it; gave, more like. Unless you write a contract, forget about getting that money back, and he hardly ever did. He was always shelling out, and I don't think he worried much about whether or not he was ever going to get a return on his largesse or get any of the loans repaid.

I remember once these men in suits came to see us in Hector's River and they were talking with him for a long while. It transpired that they were tax people visiting to establish the outstanding taxes that my dad hadn't paid on his businesses for so many years, and therefore he owed the authorities lots and lots of back taxes. Despite that Red Man was always promising how we're going to do this and get that but he was full of promises and I could see that he was on his way down.

In the end, I think they took away a lot of his assets and the only thing he had left was the house he and Miss Inez lived in.

My dad must have found it very embarrassing and wanted to get out of the area. That's when he went to the USA to find work and ended up working in a restaurant somewhere in the Bronx and sending money to support the upkeep of the house in Jamaica.

Miss Inez stayed on in Hector's River and later on she followed him to New York but by then he had established himself with a young lady who was in her late twenties while he was in his late fifties. He moved in with this young lady and she started producing more sisters and a brother for me, four of them in total (apparently years later the boys got involved with one of the local gangs in New York and was fatally shot). Poor Miss Inez, she followed behind him like a loyal puppy, but he was too busy doing what he had been doing for all those years: loving other women.

Anyway, I am here in this house at Bexleyheath with this girl who is pressuring me into marriage and I don't want to get married. I tried to be honest with her, admitting that I was not thinking of that kind of commitment at the moment. Maybe I should have been, but I didn't want to be married until I was in my thirties. She wasn't happy about that and she tried everything to pacify herself, eventually she said, "OK, let's drop the subject".

Now I can't remember fully what I had promised, I might have got engaged to her just to keep her happy or to keep her quiet for a while. Yes, I might have done that, but later when I was being pushed into a corner to set a date for the wedding I said, "Look, Faye I'm really not ready to be married yet".

She became very upset and said she was moving out, adding that she was going to take me to court for breach of promise. In those days that was the law.

I thought, "Fine, do that", and I consulted a solicitor but really I didn't want to go through with all that nonsense and I didn't think she had any grounds for legal action. I thought she was making a mountain out of a molehill. However, the solicitor asked me how long I had been living with her and I said about two years so he said something very derogatory: describing the relationship as, "a very expensive ****", and told me that I had a choice: "You either negotiate with her and pay an amount of money to get her off your back, or you go to court".

He advised me against going to court because it would be a long, drawn out and expensive business and she would get something anyway, as that was the law in the 1970s. So I negotiated with Faye and offered her £3,000 as suggested by the solicitor (a lot of money in those days). I got an increased mortgage on the property and paid her that amount. In the event I learned a very expensive lesson: never again would I allow a woman to take up residency in my house unless I intended to marry her. I understand that the £3,000 was equivalent to the amount she had contributed towards the household over that period of time. I think she got what she wanted: "revenge and compensation".

I think the price of the houses then was about £20,000 or something close. Anyway, she got that and I said to her "Now Faye, there's no need for us to be uncivil to each other, we've both learned something from this", so at least we were on speaking terms and occasionally would meet up for a coffee and chat. However, a cousin of hers and a good friend of mine would tell me "Oh, Keith I think Faye still feel that you two will get together again, she was saying such and such about you", but I was not going to get involved again: "once bitten, twice shy". But occasionally her cousin would have a gathering and Faye would be there and out of respect I would always turn up on my own and sometimes we would talk, but I could see the disappointment and sadness in her eyes because we never were reconciled. I mean the point of this is I might have loved her but I was not ready for marriage. Why couldn't she see that?

I did not hate her despite what she did. My take on this is that one gets to a point in life where you think I've been with this person for some time and it's about time something happened by way of a commitment. I don't know whether she was telling her friends that we were thinking of getting married and they wanted to know when it would be, I don't know if she was been pressured.

After the split we'd meet at one or two parties and we'd be dancing and it would feel as though we're getting back together and she'd suddenly say, "I don't mind giving the money back to you provided we forget about the recent past and commit to each other." And she would add: "We could use the money for the wedding".

I suppose for a moment there I was tempted – we were still good friends and every time I saw her I liked her, as she was quite attractive, but it's just this one thing that I just couldn't do.

They say you can't hurry love and you shouldn't try to force it, either. It could have been a case of right girl, wrong time; or else wrong girl, wrong time, who knows? But the more she pushed, the more I rebelled. I'm thinking maybe she wasn't the one or that getting married would mean that I would have to stay home and not be able or allowed to go out with my mates. I don't know what it was that I was afraid of or apprehensive about, but I knew that I did not want to be married at that time and the more she wanted it, the more I wanted out. I realised then that it was important to make a clean break. We still had strong feelings for each other, but it had to end.

I don't think Faye ever got married but I heard that she decided to enjoy life to the full so she got in with one guy with whom she travelled a bit, promised her the world but delivered very little and got her to pay for everything, including lovely holidays abroad until all the money was gone. It was a shame really, because when I met her she was such a lovely, bright and ambitious young woman.

* Manners – Good upbringing

20

Losing My Soul Mate

After my experiences in Greenhithe and Bexleyheath, I met Pauline, the girlfriend who was my first time true love; the one girl up to that point whom I really wanted to marry and settle down with.

I was now back in Peckham living at my mum's flat as she had gone to stay with her friend Babs in Florida. One weekend I went to Birmingham to visit relatives and through my female cousin, Chubby, I met this absolutely gorgeous young lady. She was going off to study at the University of Reading, but at the time was living in digs around the East of London, an area I wasn't keen on visiting because of notorious stories about the Kray Twins and their gang in that part of London.

However, Pauline was a perfect young lady, the girl any young man would wish to settle down with in married bliss. She was smart and very calm, Christian in her outlook and got on very well with everyone around her. My friends her friends loved her and she was very good with kids, her colleagues and was great with her family. Pauline was just a fantastic girl.

Pauline had a great personality and was a person I truly admired and it was clear from the word go that we were meant for each other. So, yes this is it I thought, we are going to get married, I decided privately.

I used to go and visit with her at her digs in East London but, as those were the days of the Krays and other east end gangs, it was a relief when she eventually vacated her digs and went off to Reading University studying something to do with nuclear fusion, isotopes and things like that.

She lived on campus and I would visit with her some weekends and made it clear to the guys there that this was my lady. Anyway, I was living at my mum's place as her visit to

America lasted for some months, on alternative weekends Pauline would come down to Peckham and stay with me at the flat. On those occasions we would visit museums, clubs and cinemas, she would then return to Reading on Sunday evenings in time to prepare for her classes the next day.

Now, this time I got engaged to my girl with a serious intention of getting married as soon as it was possible. However, as she was in her critical year at university I did not want to upset her studies in any way, so we decided to wait until after her graduation. I had seen lots of my friends discourage their girlfriends from proceeding with their studies, but I didn't want to be that selfish as I realised a good education was beneficial for both of us.

For her penultimate year she left Reading and was doing a year at a lab at Radcliffe, somewhere in Oxford. On one of those weekends she came down to see me as usual and we went out clubbing, however, the Sunday afternoon I noticed these big blotches all over her upper legs. I was very alarmed and asked her, "What are these things?"

She too looked surprised herself and said with tears in her eyes, "I don't know", but she was telling me that a few weeks before they had been dealing with isotopes where they had to be dressed up in specialist outfits because the lab was very radioactive and I think she said there must have been an accident or something. Pauline also said that she was walking across a field and got hit by lightning, something like that. So now I am worried and very confused. It seems that all of these things had culminated into these strange blotches appearing on her thighs and I didn't know what to do so I started to panic. I rushed her to King's College Hospital and after examining her, the doctors asked her questions mainly to do with where she worked. When she told them they disappeared into a room and contacted someone in authority, I was now very worried by the physician's questions. Whoever it was they contacted told them that they had to get her back up to Oxford straight away. When I next saw Pauline she was in a private room at the Radcliffe Hospital being treated for leukaemia and within two weeks she was dead.

I had been there at the hospital in another room and I knew the instant she had died because I could see her in my dream going over this area of water, almost floating. It was like a stream which was surrounded by a low mist and Pauline was smiling and waving to me: "Bye, bye", and she looked so beautiful as I would imagine an angel would look.

It was just like in my boyhood days when I'd experienced those strange premonitions that turned out to be real; when I used to see things before they happened. I was dreaming this, or it felt as though I was in a trance, and then she just disappeared in the mist, I immediately jumped up from the chair and rushed into her room which was next door. When I got there she had just died. Pauline was still quite warm and I was just devastated. I felt terribly weak in the knees, I cried for days afterwards.

She had been in so much pain and had suffered so much with these tremendous headaches during the last week of her life that death was like relief from the pain and suffering she endured and I had tried everything to comfort her in those final days. But she was suffering so much that at times she was confused.

I reckon it was a scientific accident which was covered up. I mean her parents were from a council estate in a not too wonderful part of Birmingham and would be viewed by the powers that be as a soft touch. Pauline was the first one of her family to go to university and was going to get them out of poverty and their council flat into their own house as soon as she was able to; she was their hope for their future.

Pauline was an honest and hardworking person who just happened to be from a poor neighbourhood with no financial or other support mechanism to force an investigation and I think her employers must have gone and spoken to the mother: "Oh, blah, blah, these things happen." I had no say in what transpired as I was not family but I was devastated and angry. And I suppose they were the typical stereotypical West Indians, quite happy to accept everything without question and not wanting to make waves even though they were told there was an accident.

Anyway, we gave her a good funeral and I went to the cemetery in Birmingham and completely lost it. She was only about 20 and I was devastated. I didn't know I could cry, but here I was on a train coming back from the funeral and I was just looking out the window and crying in front of all these people. I didn't even care and you could see some of those white people looking as if they wanted to say something to console me perhaps but deciding that they're not getting involved, but yea, that was pretty earth-shattering and for about six months I just kept away from people. I went to work, came home, sat down and vegetate before the telly, didn't go out with anyone and didn't want to go anywhere or do anything, I felt lifeless and gutted.

Eventually, friends came round and persuaded me to go out with them so I started going to parties again but it was not the same. I had lost my soul mate and I was devastated and felt empty inside. I started thinking about life and what I was doing with mine.

I think that was the first time that I was really in love. I mean there were lots of girls that I have loved or liked a lot but not to get married to, Pauline was just the perfect match and I wanted to spend the rest of my life devoted to her. Some time after she died, I remember I was at home and I was talking to The Master (as I call the Lord God), and I said, "I know you had a good reason for taking her away. Whatever that reason was, you know, and I know that you will bring the right person to me when the time is right. I look forward to that."

So, that was it. I shut myself off for a while allowing time to heal my fractured spirit, and after some time had passed I went to some parties and did try to have fun. There were girls around trying to bring me out of myself but I wasn't really interested. Bereavement can have that effect, totally stripping you down to the most basic of emotions and forcing you to think about life in a totally different way.

Some time later, Mum had come back home from the USA and I was back with Tim and the others. I started going out with Tim to parties, and at one of those parties I met some girls through Tim who always had an antidote for problems of the heart. However, on this particular night he had a great-looking bunch of girls, all nurses. Tim suggested we all go back home earlier than usual for a private party instead of taking them all the way back to their accommodation in Surrey.

Later that night back at his place, Tim disappeared upstairs and the others went into various other rooms, leaving me with this girl in the sitting room. I went off to the kitchen for something to eat and couldn't believe what I was seeing when I got back: she'd found herself in my bedroom and had taken off her wig. She looked bald, and nothing like the hot chick she appeared to be inside that party.

Next, she took off her eyelashes and with no hair on her head she looked like a bald eagle. I almost creased myself laughing. Even the succulent-looking breasts were no longer pert; everything was deflated like a punctured tyre.

It was so embarrassing but amusing, I even managed to crack a smile, though not so that she could see. Any anxiety I may have had about whether I was ready to get involved with anyone just went whoosh! But I didn't want to be too insulting or make her feel too self-conscious so I just said, "Sorry, I'll let you have the bed, I'll go and sleep on the couch upstairs". I didn't know what to do with myself so I stood outside the room and then when enough time had passed and I thought she must finally be asleep underneath the sheets, I went back in the room and there was her hair there, her eyelashes there, and I don't know if she had stuffing in her bra to bolster her tits, but she had taken her shoes off and even the toes didn't look right, so for the first time I was shocked into becoming a perfectly polite guy and left her to get her beauty sleep, which I was sure she needed.

I thought, good god! It was damn funny, but sad. The next day I asked the guys about their girls and related my experience and they tried not to laugh but they could see the funny side.

So, after that experience whenever I went to parties and saw nice-looking girls I would think, I wonder? I'm inclined to want to pull the hair to check if it's real, but I dare not. That was one experience I did not want repeated and I think it brought me back to reality. Eventually I started to focus more on work and got through my exams and was now promoted to assistant statistician, second in charge in the department. It meant that I had more work to do but it was also more money.

Emotionally, I had hit rock bottom, but losing the love of my life had made me grow up fast. Now that work was starting to look up. Surely things could only get better from here on in.

21

Princess Maria

While I was in the employment of the Tin Council I met this African princess from the Congo called Maria. Her father was the High Commissioner in London in the late 1970s and was supposed to have been a commoner who had married her mother when she was then queen of some province of French-speaking Congo.

When I met Maria her father had re-married and the family were living in east Finchley, on the famous Bishop's Avenue, known as Millionaires Row.

Maria had just got a part-time job at the Tin Council, possibly as a favour to her father as he represented an influential tin producing member country of the Council. The ITC was of course the nerve centre where the producer and consumer diplomats from all over the world had regular meetings.

I suppose Maria got this little summer job mainly to keep her occupied and to be accessible to her father, who regularly attends ITC meetings. I think the management took her on because of her vast language skills which enable her to help out with translations.

However, Maria seemed spoilt by her dad and appeared to get whatever she wanted but she was a beauty; intelligent, sophisticated and spoke several languages and was very easy to get on with. She was actually a very nice person, much liked by the other staff but would always pronounce my name as "Kith", which was so funny to hear in her French accent.

I met Maria one day when I was going into the conference room. I think she was working in the general office with other girls helping with the translations, so I went in there to nose around and try to find out who she was.

Maria was very forward and she called me over. I introduced myself as Keith from the stats section.

"Kith, Kith", she said, "I like that name!"

"And what's your name I asked?"

"Maria Bahezie, call me Maria."

"Nice name", I said "very angelic."

As it transpired, I didn't know that she was a princess at the time as she was so normal and down to earth as anyone. She frequently went out to lunch with the girls from her department and she loved to have a good time. When she wanted money to go shopping, she would just invite her dad for lunch and he would then gave her loads of money which she then spend on shopping in Regent's Street or New Bond Street. Maria was spoilt rotten by her doting father; she was so spoilt by him; she was really his little princess.

Anyway, I got to know her and as I said she was very nice, personable and a gorgeous looker with lots of personality and oozing confidence. Wow, was she confident! We would go out to lunch and of course she was a breath of fresh air, a really fabulous girl who could communicate fluently to the staff in their own languages, which of course impressed the variety of nationals at the restaurant.

Maria then invited me to her house for dinner. "Come to us for dinner", she said one day. I was not too sure about that as her father was an important man, the ambassador of their country and the representative to the Tin Council.

I said, "Ah, I would love to but your father may not approve." She said, "Don't worry about him, it will be fine. I'll speak to him and show you what to do". I accepted, "OK, so how should I dress?" So she said, "You decide". I said, "Are you sure? She nodded her approval. So, what's the address?" I asked. "Bishop's Avenue." "What number?"

"It's so and so house. Get off the train at East Finchley station and walk up or take a taxi. It's not too far."

I said, "Fine, see you there".

So off I went and made sure I was fixed up nicely for this dinner invitation. I got out the train, as instructed, at East Finchley station and I thought, well, I don't know how to get to this place so I approached a taxi driver and asked him how far it was to this address in Bishop's Avenue and he said, "You can't walk, it's too far. If you're going there you can afford to pay for a taxi."

So I went in the taxi and he drove up to Millionaire's Row given that name because then there were all million pound houses. As he's driving up towards this flood-lit driveway I shouted, "Stop, you're going to the wrong place."

But he just kept driving, passing these massive flood lights and parked Rolls Royces and I'm thinking, "He's got the wrong address."

Suddenly, he stopped and said, "Now, it's here".

I was expecting to go to a normal house, but now I am feeling a bit nervous and overwhelmed. I got out and paid him a note, a ten or twenty, I was too confused to remember which and obviously he didn't expect to give me back any change.

He pocketed it quickly, "Thank you very much, sir", and drove off. I'm standing there thinking I'm sure I should have got some change but I didn't argue. I was too overwhelmed by all this so I gingerly went to the door and rang the bell: "*Bing bong!*" The door opened and a deep-throated man responded. "Yes, sir, can I help you?"

This large white guy dressed up like a dog's dinner opened the door and greeted me. Of course, it was the butler! I must have been frozen to the spot.

He asked again, "Can I help you?"

I thought I'm sure I've got the wrong place and I'm feeling stupid but I mention the name Maria. "Oh, Madam Maria…"

"Oh, Kith", she shouted from behind him, "how are you? Come in," she's shrieking excitedly.

She grabbed my hand and literally dragged me through the house. "This is my friend", she called out as she dragged me into a room where I am meeting these important looking individuals and some of her millionaire friends are sitting around enjoying a quiet drink. I met all of them and I met a few of the diplomatic people, her father's associates, who were snacking on finger foods.

I was taken further inside the house where others were having cocktails and so on and at the back of the house some people were playing tennis and others were swimming in the large pool at the back. We mingled awhile until we heard a loud bell: "Blerp blerp", and the butler announce: "Dinner is served!"

I thought, "I'm not going to last." I was a bit...more than overwhelmed. I felt so tiny and quite shy as a result of this overpowering experience.

We were directed to a long table where we were encouraged to help ourselves to the wide choice of labelled food and Maria is telling me, "Now, this is giraffe..." They had bush meat alongside a wide variety of other foods on that table and so I went round and packed my plate and then went with my new friend to sit by a little table outside in the garden.

It was a gorgeous summer's evening and because it was an informal gathering most people ate in the garden, some around the pool. Maria was very nice, I think she sensed my nervousness and tried to calm me down.

During the meal I met her dad. She pulled me up from my chair and said, "You must meet my dad", and she called out, "Ah, Dad come here and meet my friend, Kith."

"Oh, Mr Bahezie, pleased to meet you", I said, putting on my best accent.

And I'm thinking to myself if I put a foot wrong I might get sacked tomorrow. Anyway, it was quite OK. He was a very nice guy himself and was quite pleased that Maria had introduced me.

Mr Bahezie was married to a very pretty white woman. Apparently, this happened after he was divorced from Maria's mother. I found out that Maria herself had spent most of her life in Europe and went to finishing school in Switzerland. She spoke about seven languages with great aplomb: French, of course, which was obviously her main language, flawless English, German, Italian and I think some Swiss and Flemish.

And, of course, she had these wonderful friends, including some great-looking guys, so I am thinking, "Why me?" Of all the people she could have chosen, she wanted to be with me.

We used to go to the "Q" club in Edgware where the rich and famous black people from overseas used to hang out when they were in London. Maria said to me, "Let's go to so and so club." I was surprised she knew about "Q" club so I asked, "Do you know this club?"

She said, "Oh, yea, I go there quite a few times when I am in London."

She was quite a party girl and she loved London as a cosmopolitan city with all the places available to her.

So we went there. I mean, I'd been going to this club for years. You were pretty lucky to get in half the time. They could be selective and you had to show ID and let them search you, so it was difficult to get admission particularly if the bouncers didn't like the way you look. However, when we got there that night we were met with a shriek of excitement: "Ah, Ma-ri-a!"

As soon as she turned up there everyone recognised her and started calling out to her. The whole club seemed to know this girl, or so it seemed. I thought it is weird. They all knew Maria and so she didn't even have to pay to get in. Can you imagine? It was like, "Oh, it's a pleasure to have you here tonight. Pay? We would pay you to come here madam."

I was confused. I really was confused. I liked this girl but I was confused by her and her popularity. I knew she was a diplomat's daughter but I thought that was it, and it was weird that she should generate such a reaction. It was only after that occasion that I discovered her true identity that she was in fact a princess from the African state of the Congo that it all made sense.

So, that was Maria. She then decided she was going to take me to Belgium to meet some of her closet friends.

"But I don't speak the language", I protested.

"Ah, don't worry about it, Kith."

"But your friends might not be pleased about that", I said.

But you didn't say no to Maria; she had a persuasive way about her.

Anyway, we went to Belgium. Maria had a flat in Brussels for her to use whenever she was in town. Maybe because she was being schooled in Switzerland she got that apartment in case she wanted to hang out with her friends during the holidays. Nice place but you could see that she hardly used it, if ever.

We went there and spent the weekend visiting her friends, going out each night to the hot clubs of Brussels where I taught her the James Brown shuffle. During the day we spent time at her friends' apartments or at different restaurants having lunch and chatting, with them laughing at my accent and encouraging me to learn French.

They were all very nice people. One thing, they were always laughing and making you feel good. Of course they were well-to-do Africans, privileged and with time to have fun and enjoy their young lives. Her friends were polished and all so beautiful and I'm thinking, I'm sure the Africans I've been associated with before didn't look so good nor were they so sophisticated. Why is this lot so different? Could be selective breeding, education or possibly resulting from their affluence and being able to afford to do what was necessary to look great.

But they were so polished and flawless it fascinated me, as with Maria it was the walk: there was poise, a sophistication in the walk and how they sit, like models and you see that with all her girlfriends. Maybe it was the finishing school. I hear that girls go around at those schools with books on their heads to improve posture, whatever it was they were absolutely amazing to watch how they carry themselves.

Anyway, back at this club in Edgware Maria announced to all there that she was having a party at her home for me as it was soon to be Valentine's Day.

I said, "Maria, I don't think that's a good idea." She said, "Yes it is".

As it turned out, most of the club was invited to her house for this party.

I invited my brother Kenneth and my friend Bunny, and I said to them, "You've got to be on your best behaviour because we're going to this party at this house where this wonderful princess lives."

"Ha-ha, ha-ha!" They roared with laughter "you have been reading too many nursery books" I tried again, insisting, "She's a princess, an African princess and you've got to be on your..."

"Princess, eh? Ha-haa ha-haa!" They had a good laugh, doubling up with glee.

But, they decided they'd come to the party anyway and see this princess.

Like me, they were overwhelmed when they got to the house. "Wow!" They were both speechless. After the initial surprise they settled into to the party.

My brother went upstairs. I had never been upstairs, but he went upstairs with the French-speaking nanny and spent the night upstairs with this girl – typical of Ken. Still, the nanny was an attractive girl, she was a white Belgian and was very pretty with black flowing hair. He disappeared with her while we were having the party downstairs.

Meanwhile, Bunny was like a kid in a candy shop and introducing himself to the girls, mainly. "Oh, I am Keith's friend."

And they're quite happy to meet him and he was overjoyed with all those beautiful ladies around him. It was a fantastic party and what Maria did for me was a very, very nice gesture.

Her father didn't mind about our relationship. She used to come and stay with me at my humble abode in Streatham but every Sunday they had a family picnic out into the countryside. Maria, her dad, his wife and her two little brothers would go off somewhere into the country for this ritual. It was a regular weekend thing that they did and no matter what else happened or where ever in London they were, they would always get together for that.

Once, she stayed over with me in Streatham and she said, "I've got to tell my dad where I am, it's important he knows. It doesn't matter where I am, well, it does matter, but he needs to know who I'm with and where I am." So I nervously asked, "Are you sure he's ok with this?"

She replied, "Yea, yea, he's all right. My dad is ok, he likes you and anyway I am a big girl".

So, Sunday morning came and beep, beep! A Rolls Royce was parked outside the house and she went out through the front door and waved me goodbye:

"I'll see you, I'm off." And off she went. Her dad was so broad-minded but to me, it was very strange. Maybe he was just happy to know that Maria was happy. She had never stayed out at a guy's place before, but her father took it in his stride. However, she was a virgin all this time although he was so broad-minded, amazing, isn't it?

But the thing is the politics changed in the Congo and I think she was offered in marriage to the prince of some other part of the Congo. You've got east and west and there's some allegiance going on there and she was part of the package and it didn't matter that she was over in Europe, it was now time for her to get married to this prince, but she didn't want to.

I met a few of her friends and they drove Porsches and Ferraris and we used to meet them in the west end, maybe they were supposed to keep tabs on her. Sometimes, I felt like the odd one out. I tried to fit in but it's not normal; I felt a little intimidated by them and their wealth, although they were very nice people. It's amazing, that although they were wealthy people they were very down to earth. Maybe that was for the benefit of Maria. I don't know if that's how rich people are, I don't think so.

Anyway, as I said the politics had changed in this Africa region and Maria was supposed to go home but she didn't want to. She reckoned that we should go to Jamaica, and it seems she was hiding from whoever; ducking in and out of places and acting quite out of character. She was spooking me so I said, well, if you're so nervous and insecure then obviously it's serious and if you are hiding it's obviously going to affect someone else in their quest to find you to do what they want.

There were some royals, related to her mother, the queen, at her house in Finchley trying to persuade her to go back to the Congo. Apparently, a senior relative of the queen was actually there at her house one evening when Maria had invited me over and I didn't know that they'd come over to stay for a while, perhaps to convince Maria to go home with them.

She'd become westernised and very independent and she didn't want to be a subservient female back in Africa, being told where to go, to do this or act a certain way. She was too liberated for all that. I think that was the main reason she didn't want to go.

Maria then became very concerned because someone had apparently framed her father. Somehow, his wife had died in a boat accident in the Congo and some enemies had ceased the opportunity to frame the father for the accident. I think there were some political strings being pulled because he was the only person who had any influence over his daughter and they realised that was the only way they were going to get Maria to do what they wanted.

Maria would tell me that there were people following him and watching her also. The political intrigues were too much to comprehend. I felt for her but how could I help? This was out of my league, so I said, "Maria, I think really you should go to Africa, because if they start doing that, what else will they do? In particular, what will happen to your father?"

She wasn't happy about it but she said, with a vacant expression, "Maybe you are right."

Anyway, Maria went off to Belgium and spent sometime with friends and when I heard from her again she had made up her mind. On the phone she sounded quite resigned to her destiny. She spoke about the great time we'd had and how much she would miss me. Then she said finally, "Kith, I love you, I want you to know that but I'm going home. I'm going to the Congo and I'm going to get married and I'm going to have loads and loads of kids."

She then hung up. Maria had resigned herself to her fate and that was the last time I heard from Maria.

Initially, we had been mates who enjoyed each other's company, and then she became my girlfriend. Maria would come and spend weekends with me and she loved that because on Saturdays we would go walking and shopping in the local street markets of Tooting Broadway and Balham and she was always asking me to take her to Brixton, so I took her on the bus to Brixton to mingle with the folks. She would have a Jamaican patty and a ginger beer, which she enjoyed in fact she really enjoyed the Brixton culture. Maria liked the simple things of life which, I suppose, she'd never had. But I think the politics just got to her and going back home was the best thing for her as she loved her dad too much to risk him getting hurt.

I don't know what happened to them but from time to time I did wonder. Still, it was good while it lasted and I would never forget her. I hoped things turned out well for them after all.

So, I almost married a princess and possibly she would have made an ideal wife too, but I thought going to Jamaica would be dangerous and would possibly have aggravated things. Besides, what for? I mean, what could I offer her there? I thought about it logically: this is what she was accustomed to; this is where she's been, this is her life, this is her education; her lifestyle is like this, everything is given to her and that's what she could not have expected with me in Jamaica. How was I going to afford to keep her in the lifestyle she is used to?

So, going back to the Congo was the best thing for her and, of course, life goes on.

22

Back to Jamaica

I have been back to Jamaica several times since coming to England. In fact, after living in the UK for some time I had often thought I would like to go back home – and I used to use the word "home", but I don't anymore.

In a way it was more than a desire, it was a plan for the future so I would tell friends of my plan to return back home to enjoy a more relaxed existence and see out some of my twilight years. So after 15 years in England I decided it was time I went back home to check out family and friends and get a feel of the old country. I was a bit hesitant about going back after such a long time away, as I expected the attitudes of people I knew would have changed after such a long time away and I didn't know what to expect, except that I would be treated as a stranger.

However, my adopted cousin, who at one point had lived with us in Hector's River all those years ago, was now doing very well in her travel agency business in the north of England. She had lots of contacts in Jamaica society and elsewhere and as she was arranging to go to Jamaica for a well-deserved holiday she suggested I should tag along.

So, I made the arrangements, paid my fare and travelled with her and some of her friends to Jamaica. It seems that a lot of changes had evolved in the 15 years I was abroad or maybe because I was now a man I was seeing things differently. Perhaps it was a bit of both. Anyway, I was put up at one of Paulette's friend's place in Amour Heights, a swanky part of Kingston.

Going back to Jamaica for the first time – fantastic, I thought – I'm back home. The excitement of the home-coming, having gone through the traumas of living in a predominantly white country where prejudice was the common, everyday way of life, where black people were treated not just as second-class citizens but as lackeys, and if you were black you were not supposed to be doing anything more than sweeping the streets and other menial jobs. And where it was considered OK for the police to stop and search you, take you into the station because it's cold for them walking on the streets and the quickest way to get warm was to grab a black man on "Sus" charges and take him back to the station and get warm, maybe have a cup of tea, while writing up a trumped up charge.

So I went back to Jamaica and I almost kissed the ground when I arrived – it was fantastic. The first night, a group of us were all going out for a fish feed at a popular bar. So, off we went to Port Royal to this fish restaurant which someone had recommended. There you chose your live fish from a tank and someone cooks that for you fresh.

We got there, chose a table and sat down expectantly. However, the first thing I noticed as we were sitting there was that the waitresses were only attending to and serving the white customers, even the ones who had come in after us. So I'm thinking to myself, "What's going on here?" I thought, this is home isn't it? I'm home! I thought I would get the appreciation and privilege of being back in my own country. Besides, my money was no different to theirs. Why were they doing that? But I suppose deep in the psyche for those without knowledge or the experience of travel, is the thinking that you must give attention and preference to those who are white.

These restaurant attendants may have thought, if white they've got money to burn and you're likely to be given a big tip for good service – but if you're black the assumption is that there is nothing there to benefit them.

Suddenly I start feeling my blood boiling and then I became sad and disillusioned for what I thought was my own country and for the attitude of my own people towards me. What had I come home to, I thought? Not even in my own country was I treated as an equal or respected as a fellow human being.

I am thinking, "Why don't they come and serve us?" But I suppose I was a bit naïve about the priority so I got up, strolled

Meeting the local talent

Relaxing out in the deep blue on a friend's sailing boat

over and said to the girl, "We were here before them". Well, what a reaction they gave me for talking to them like that, they were very surprised that I dear make a comparison.

So I repeated, "We were here before those people. Why are you serving them and not serving us?" And I suppose that out of sheer embarrassment the waiters came over and took our order but the people being served were embarrassed too as they knew what I meant. There was a young lady in our group who kept saying, "Oh, leave it, leave it, let's go". But I insisted on service as we had come a long way for this meal, so we stayed to the end to enjoy our fish meal but the food took such a long time to arrive and I did wonder whether that was to spite us.

Now there was this other girl in the group who had said nothing until now, she was a bit sassy, a bit of a yardie type and had observed the confrontation with the staff without saying a word, suddenly she said to the waitress, "hey girl, I have got some money for your tip." I said, "Yea?"

She said, "Lend me some dollars, not Jamaican, I want American money. So I said, "OK", sensing that she was up to some mischief. I gave her US $20 and when we were going she put the money down on the table and then said, "Oh, I just realised that you people didn't want to serve us – look what you missed, $20 but I guess I'll have to take it back."

And she grabbed the note and walked off. She got her own back, and felt a bit better I think.

Those servers are ordinary people and maybe they're not educated and may have acted like that because they don't know better or else they're thinking they can only get a tip from white people. I suppose this sassy girl did teach them a hard lesson. I pitied them because I was disappointed but hoped that attitude was not reflected throughout the country.

Well, the experience didn't get any better. I spent most of my holiday at this guy's house. He was a nice enough person, but I felt I was spending too much of my valuable time either at his business premises or at his house, although where he lived was quite nice and comfortable up there in the hills overlooking the sprawling plains below. It was fantastic to be on the balcony at night, feeling the cool breeze over your body and looking over the expanse of the city below but on a holiday you want more time at parties.

My accommodation was in a self-contained basement apartment but the whole house had security grills and high gates to the front yard. I didn't like that, but apparently that is how things were out there.

The maid came in and was treated like a skivvy and she was not trusted. He had a cage in the kitchen with the groceries under lock and key and he would give the maid a certain amount to cook each day and the rest was locked away. The whole point is to prevent pilfering as this was said to be commonplace, so this treatment was a clear statement to his maid. And I started getting disillusioned with everything as I was really hoping to get around visiting interesting places, meeting interesting people and enjoying my holiday.

I went to his garage to arrange a car for hire and realising I needed more time out and about as a tourist he and some friends promised to take me out to some restaurant up in the Jacks hills. Ok, that sounded good and then he said to me, "Have you got any dollars? If you've got dollars or pounds give them to me and I'll give you Jamaican dollars in return."

I wasn't surprised by his suggestion because in those days there were restrictions on acquiring foreign currency and on taking foreign currency out of the country as Jamaica was going through some economic turbulence during that time.

For me, there was no problem giving him my foreign currency as I needed local currency anyway as I was there to spend and enjoy myself.

He said to me: "I'll give you Jamaican dollars at whatever rate you decide."

So of course I said, "That's fine."

He took me into a room where he opened up his safe. I had never seen so much money in one place, not even in a bank. One shelf was filled with bundles of US dollar notes. Another was thick with Jamaican dollars – mainly big notes, and another filled with pounds. And I was thinking to myself, how can he make so much money running a garage? Anyway, I wasn't going to lose sleep about it.

It appeared he was into drugs but no one knew about it because he was one of the guys who didn't touch the stuff or got too close to it – he didn't even smoke. He had nothing to do with it personally. Instead, I understand his people would go and sell the stuff and the money came back to him somehow and it seemed as if the garage was just a front for the ganga trade.

However, the surprising thing was that no one spoke about ganga and, as a group, they all seem to be well connected to people who knew people in important positions. All the people in the group of friends did favours for one another. For example getting a phone installed in your home or business premises in those days could take months but for members of that group all this entailed was a phone call to one of the members in the circle of friends and the phone would be connected within days. On the other hand I found out later that for ordinary people the normal waiting period to have a phone installed was over a year. The circle of friends would include professional people from all section of the society such as solicitors, barristers, police inspectors and politicians.

One night I went out to a gathering with some of these other people and as a first timer back in Jamaica I was very surprised and disturbed by the level of affluence I observed. We went to this man's house and as we entered the place I could smell the wood; the richness of the place was overwhelmingly intoxicating. It had wooden floors and wooden panels everywhere. It smelled rich, if you can understand that, and he happened to be something to do with the judiciary. He could not be earning that much from being a barrister or maybe he could, who knows, yet I felt it had to be coming from some additional income source. But no one talks about it. And none of those people ever got close enough to people who smoked dope, but any intelligent person could see discrepancies. I felt there must be foot soldiers out there doing what they do to make these guys so wealthy, but that was my view which could of course be completely wrong.

Enjoying a great party uptown Kingston

Relaxing on the beach with a local beauty

After drinks, we went up town Kingston for a grand party but before you were allowed in, there were these guards checking the cars and searching you before you got into this drive leading to this massive house where a party was in full swing. It was a wonderful party even though the guy who was throwing the party looked quite ordinary. "What did he do for a living?" I enquired. He was a businessman I was told.

I'm trying to work out in my head what sort of business he could do to own such luxury and be hobnobbing with such people but decided that was his business. I was there to have fun as you only got into those parties if you knew someone who was well connected. I accepted that I was lucky to be here and continued to mingle.

It was the best cars in the land turning up there, the best looking girls and a great selection of food, drinks and entertainment. It was obvious that these were people of substance and influence. They had some absolutely gorgeous women who just seemed to float about the place. They are there to make sure that these guys were looked after. So as a young man of humble means there was no chance of me getting friendly with any of those gold diggers because I was not in that category and I wasn't "one of them". However, as a young man in his prime and quite brash, I went looking and found a young girl just standing there. She was very nice-looking with a great smile and I was interested so I approached her. I thought we were hitting it off but then she found out that I was from England and not one of the clique – suddenly her interest just died and she went off elsewhere possibly to prospect in a rich vein of opportunity among those influential friends. Those guys have got influence, they've got money and they're there in Jamaica and can make good things happen to people they like. That's where she wanted to be. Can you blame her?

So I realised what this gathering was all about. I was fortunate to be invited to some of these guys' houses and the houses were massive. Opulence was everywhere and their mistresses were age about 17, if that old. And they have at least two or three of these beautiful girls to service their needs and so very young – but these guys regard themselves as sugar daddies they would jokingly call themselves "Sugar daddy". You'd see some old guy and a young lady being close, this was his mistress or one of his mistresses. Still, the girls are happy with that because they're being looked after in their career or financially.

So now I start to understand the ways of the land, or as the Jamaican would say "the Runnings" and am becoming very concerned. I am starting to think about how this could impact "my country". Then again, is it really my country or is this some foreign place?

Well, these guys we're hanging out with certainly know how to enjoy themselves and between parties we would all be invited to a country outing for a fish feed somewhere in St Thomas.

Dozens of cars turned up and we piled in and off we went to this place out of the city which had clean white sandy beach with a few cool shaded areas to relax, and as soon as we arrived there were people looking after us with food and drinks.

As I strolled down to the beach enjoying the scenery, up popped these local guys who came up to me as they do on any beach in Jamaica and asked, "What happen man? You want some of de ting?" So I asked, "What thing?"

Thinking I was refusing his offer he said, "Mek me give you someting, man."

Not knowing what they meant I asked again, "What thing?" He said, "Someting. Some herbs, man."

I was surprised that they would be so blatant. Now I have heard of ganja and had seen guys roll a spliff and smoke, so I would recognise the smell anywhere, but I had never tried it, nor wanted to. But this time I was curious. So I said, "OK".

I thought, well, I'll try this thing as I am on holiday and see what it's like. However, I felt a bit hesitant, but they say the stuff was harmless so I gave them five Jamaican dollars, at that time the equivalent of about 50 English pence and they said, "Soon come back", and off they went.

I didn't really expect to see them again but within five minutes this guy came back with so much of this bush I was flabbergasted by the amount and completely overwhelmed; you couldn't imagine it, so I blurted out, "What the hell is this?"

I thought he would come with just a little thing for me to try but he came with maybe a whole field of the stuff, so I consulted a friend in the group, "Look what this guy's brought back for me. What do I do?"

He said, "What! That's weed! You better get rid of it." And he told me there were police inspectors in our group. "You've got to get rid of it now, right now!"

What hypocrisy. But how could I get rid of it? By now the local guys had disappeared, so I tried to get rid of it every way by throwing it out into the sea, but the wind kept blowing it back in my face or coming back on shore with the wave. In fact, two of the police detectives were watching me fighting to get rid of this thing. Eventually, I just took the whole lot wade out into the sea and chucked it in the water, but of course it wasn't long before it was back on the shore with the tide. Yea, it was so funny, although I wasn't laughing. I was desperate to lose the stuff but this big piece of ganja bush kept coming back in with the tide, drifting out and coming back in and I couldn't get rid of it.

As I was keenly observed, and out of desperation I got back down to the surfs, scooped up the ganja, walked along the beach until I found a little corner and chucked it round there and quickly came back quite exhausted.

I was so embarrassed, as I could see them watching me and they didn't look too pleased either.

Well, yes, I learnt my lesson as you will never know if people are keeping tabs on you. Oh yes, they would have had something on me if ever they needed to use it. Luckily, I got rid of that dam bush, which I only wanted to investigate out of share curiosity, so I kept a very low profile afterwards.

Back at Armour Heights I tried to talk to this guy about my experience on the beach but he didn't want to get involved or acknowledge the discussion. However, a few days later when I was going to Miami with some of the group for the weekend – apparently they do this on a regular basis as most had second

On easy street uptown Kingston

homes in Miami – my host said to me "Look, I want you to take some money over for me when you came over to Miami. How much did you put down that you were coming in with?"

In fact, when I was coming to Jamaica my travelling partner had said to me they never check. "Why don't you just put down $5000 for the hell of it?" But I was thinking to myself that I could always say that I put the point in the wrong place, that I made a mistake and that it was only $500. I had my suspicions but when I was going to Miami I took the money, about $5000 dollars for him.

Now, in Jamaica they all seemed to dress down but when we landed in Miami, there was a massive car waiting for us and, suddenly, I saw a different side to the guy I was staying with. He was now well dressed and dripping with jewellery, you know, blings everywhere. Then we were driven to his house and the house was enormous. I just sat there while they were transacting business. What were they doing? I don't know nor want to know.

So that was my closest encounter with the weed and I was a bit nervous that these high-powered guys might have been concerned that I was being sucked into using this stuff by those guys who had offered it to me. I knew that I had been naïve and had made a mistake. I wasn't about to give them any more reasons to put me under surveillance.

Miami was a great place and I had a good time. I met a nice black American girl and the two of us got on like a house on fire. She took me all over Miami and I did enjoy her company. We usually had breakfast in McDonald's and I spent a whole week going around with her to just about everywhere and then at the end of the week I told her that I was going back to Jamaica later that day. She didn't want me to go back then and she also wanted to come back to Jamaica with me but I wasn't so keen on that.

"Oh, I always wanted to go to Jamaica but I've never been," she insisted. So I felt obliged and offered to take her and went to tell the guys that I was thinking of taking this girl with me to Jamaica. And then this yardie said, "Cho! leave de woman man, what you want fe tek her to Jamaica for? Whole heap o' woman in-a Jamaica, man, leave de woman yah." And he laughed out loud.

Now, I don't know if he was concerned that an American-speaking black woman in Jamaica might attract some attention to himself or to us so I said to the American, well I think I'll have to give you a call when I get to Jamaica as I am staying at this guy's house and I would need his permission.

When I left her she was very upset, and I was upset for her as well because I did want to take her. She had her passport and everything and she wanted to come but I couldn't go against these guys.

It was a clique of people who knew people; a circle of friends who stick to their own kind, visiting each other's houses to drink and play cards and that's where business is done and they always have their women and they don't want any strange women hanging around, and I just decided well, I'll stick with that; I didn't want to upset the apple cart.

Back in Jamaica, I decided there was too much restriction so I went off into the countryside on my own – I wanted to get away from those people. I didn't feel intimidated around them but I felt a bit isolated because they knew each other and I didn't know what they were thinking as I'm an outsider.

Well, after the little incident in Miami, I decided I needed my own space to make my own choices and to take the pressure off everyone I'd go off to the country and seek out some old friends.

I hired a car through the car hire service of this same guy I was staying with and went out into the country to spent a week or so with relatives and a few old friends.

However, I was very disappointed with the attitude of some of the Jamaicans I met on the way up to Portland. I was stopped three times by groups of people saying that they were "taxing" me for using the road.

I asked them, "What do you mean you're taxing me?" A few of them had shovels and other implements so they said, "Well, the government ain't doing it so we're doing it, we're fixing the potholes and we're charging people for driving on this road." So, as I was enjoying the day and the scenery I thought ok, I don't want any bother so I gave them $50, although I resented being conned into paying them money to use the road.

There were other times when I met some really nice brothers at a bar on one of my stops, sat down and enjoyed a drink and a chat about life on the "rock" and so on but there were always spoilers around, like that time in the fish restaurant at Port Royal when the staff treated us as if we were invisible.

I eventually got to my father's village in Hector's River and as the word got out relations were coming out of the woodwork. Suddenly, I got family I didn't even know I had. "Yes, Redman bwoy turn up, you know." And it spread through the district like wild fire. I'd go into this empty bar and before you know it, the place is packed with people all making their orders for drinks as they assumed I was buying.

Well, this one – she's sick; she wants to go to the doctor. She's been vomiting for two days but she hasn't got the money for doctor as the doctor a charging a $100. Everybody had their problems all needing financial solutions and some just came right out and said, "What you got fe' me?" Or, "Give me a buster", that's $500, and you find that's what happens when you come back from overseas.

So, in the bar I am having a drink with people I know and suddenly the place is full of so-called relatives and close friends I didn't know I had. The bar was empty just before I went in except for a sleepy-looking girl on the other side of the counter, and I order a drink and look behind me and everybody's in there – "Give me a drink, no man?" "I am you cousin you know. Let's drink to so and so who passed on last month." "Yea, I'll have a beer."

So now everybody's ordering and this sleepy girl is trying to cope with the orders. Everybody's talking to you about their problems and suddenly it's: "Give me sister a drink no, man?" "So where is she?" I asked, "Oh, she's at home. I will take it fe her." So now they are ordering directly from this sleepy girl who has now become animated as some other servers had come in the bar to help with the orders.

"Give me one a them rum and coke, and a Johnnie Walker whisky", specific label no less. So now everybody's drinking and having a good time, I'm thinking, yea that's cool, I suppose it is expected, and then you come to leave and so you say to the bar girl, "How much do I owe you?" And then you hear, "See you later, me gaan." And so everybody's disappearing then I heard something like, "You owe me a thousand dollars." And the session only lasted about twenty minutes.

I was quite shock at the size of the bill, "What? I only had a beer!" And she interrupts, "Yea, but you bought drinks for all you friends and relatives dem!" "But $1000 is a lot of money and I didn't tell you to give them all drinks!" "Well a you people dem"

So you pay up and that's how they welcome you back home in your district. It was my intention to spend a whole week but I didn't, although I wanted to and should have. I had my own transport so I could leave when I liked and after about two days of this and with my money running short, I decided that I would

Back in London after a great holiday

sneak out and go to explore other areas in Portie – Port Antonio. Anyway, I realised my money was running short as relatives were trying to get as much out of me as they could: aunts, uncles, cousins, and everybody else professing desperate needs and some of them even have pensions coming from America or England but if you give to one others feel they should get their share.

So I said to my friends and relatives, "I soon come back. Me just going up the road to check out this 'daata' – a young lady – and they understand that. With that ruse, I got in the car and quietly slipped away. First, to Boston, where people go to get jerk pork (a Jamaican delicacy) and then continued on to Port Antonio for the freshly made hard dough bread to go with the pork.

After that, a quick visit to the bank and then I headed towards West Portland to visit my mother's relations at Black Hill and Rodney Hall where the whole experience is repeated. That's how we "foreigners" are greeted and treated when we go back home to Jamaica.

All they want to know is, "What you bring for me?" And they want to strip you of your clothes, they want to relieve you of your cash and you start wondering about the mentality or stability of these people. Could this be desperation or is this something else?

And the thing is you hear these stories that if they think you have money and they feel you're been tight, they either try and rifle your case or get someone to come and do it to you; I sometimes wonder if this attitude is driven by destitution or just an attitude towards what they term "dem foreign" the outsiders, so where's the love? I thought, no need to hang about with these people as they all seem to have changed so I went back to Kingston and stayed in a hotel for the rest of the holiday.

One day I decided to visit Half Way Tree where I used to hang out when I was a little boy, so I went to have lunch at Tastee's Patty shop, regarded as the best in Kingston.

I drove into the parking lot and parked the car. A friend was with me to show me the "runnings", but as soon as we got out of the car some local guy came up to us as if he knew us and started talking.

"What happen, man? You no know me?"

"Excuse me boss, we just come to get a couple of patties", I said.

He insisted, "What! You no know me you no want fe talk to me?"

So I said, "Sorry boss, but we are in a hurry, what you want to talk about?"

"Give me a money, no?"

"Me no got no money to give boss."

"You don't have no money and a drive car like this?"

So I am thinking what the fuck that's got to do with him, but you don't want to enrage him as you never know how far gone these guys are and you know it's not really him speaking, maybe it's the weed, particularly when he's waving his cutlass at you as he speaks. That's what he's using to talk to you as he moves his arm in a threatening manner.

Apparently, that's the way these guys talk to you but it's a big culture shock for me having been away since I was a child and now I go back to face this man talking to me with a sharp cutlass waving in my face in such a threatening manner and I'm thinking, "He could split me open in seconds!"

I quickly moved away disappearing into the crowd leaving him so that he could molest other people who are accustomed to that sort of behaviour.

So now he starts having an argument with this other guy and there's a heap of expletives being traded: "b******** c******!" "I will chop you up, you know!"

And I'm thinking, he's got a cutlass and it's sharp and he seems high on something and you know he could snap. Then somebody calls out to him to go and find some work and he starts telling him in an animated fashion how he will chop him up, too.

Now, to an outsider, it seems the whole of Jamaica is mentally unstable. Anyway, I got to thinking, should I bother with the patty or should I just go? It's not worth the hassle. However, my friend and I got into line to queue up to pay first and get a ticket and then go somewhere else to collect our patties and drinks through this caged off area.

It's was a nice day, not too hot with a gentle breeze and clear sky, despite the tramp with his cutlass demanding "a money". I was thinking we could just sit and have our lunch and watch the crowds – but that mad man hadn't gone away, he was still lurking there, and he came over again and accosted us. "So what happen, me no eat too? Me no have mouth too"? Are you going to give me a patty? Are you going to give me a money?"

So we got in the car and drove off to a safer place and I thought – Jamaica is mad!

Another day I tried using the bus and unlike in England, they don't queue, so when the bus comes people start pushing and fighting at the bus stop and I am there being shocked by the experience.

I was going to catch the bus for the first time to go to this particular place downtown, so I went to Half Way Tree at the main bus stop from where there are buses going to various parts of Kingston. Now, everybody would crowd around the bus stops and when a bus comes all hell break loose. There was a big fight at the bus stop, with people pushing, shoving and swearing to get on the bus, man, woman and children alike and some of those big women can really hold their own. It was quite a spectacle but I'm thinking, why don't they just line up and get on in an orderly fashion; but it is in a way amusing to see two grown men stuck in the door each wanting to get in first and nobody's making progress. So I am thinking "Jamaica is mad!" and with all this carrying on, I saw this guy walk pass the bus stop stark naked and singing to himself with his privates swinging from side to side. Would you believe it, stark naked and nobody's looking surprised? Then somebody shouts, "Is mad him mad, you know." And apart from the smiles on some of those faces no one really bothers and I'm thinking, what a country this is. If it was any other place he would be arrested.

So, eventually, after the pushing and shoving, most people managed to get on the bus. There was a bit of space left near the entrance so I got on sandwiched between a number of smelly people and am thinking, "What a day" but I can't understand why they have to have a big fight every time; it makes no sense. I'd gone to Jamaica and I didn't expect that but maybe I have become too Anglosised.

So, that was my first experience back in the old land. I came back to England and thought, well, this is the culture I know. I have fought with skinheads and threatened by teddy boys and I have survived. I have earned my right to be in this country now; this is where I know and this is where I will die because I don't see anything for me in Jamaica. I have indeed become a foreigner not only in England but also in Jamaica, the land of my birth.

23

Future Wife

One day I was entering the building at the back of Haymarket House to ride the lift to the ITC on the fourth floor, when I noticed a black female figure disappearing into the lift, I quickened my steps to catch up with her.

Now, working on the fourth floor at the Tin Council you were fortunate to see another young black person, so I was relieved by this discovery because there were all white people in the whole building and no-one to open up to, except this one black guy who worked as a porter down in the basement. I hardly ever saw Paul, except when he was transporting things about the place and we bumped into each other. We became friends but he was sometimes a pain, always borrowing money to maintain his Casanova lifestyle.

However, on this particular day I was waiting for the lift to open and there she was this black girl, so I thought could she be working here or just visiting? Wow! I started the conversation by asking her, "Where are you going, up or down"? She said "up". So I said, "Ok, so am I", and I got in the lift. I asked her, where she worked and she told me "On the fifth floor". I remarked that I hadn't seen her there before but hoped I would see her again. And just before the door closed at my stop I told her maybe we could meet up for a drink and a chat. She said, "Maybe" and that was it, the lift door closed and she was gone. I didn't see her again. I would go to the lift at that time; at different times and "accidentally" take the lift up to the Sugar Council on the fifth floor, although I worked on the fourth, but I was too shy to go and ask anyone about her. Worse still, I didn't even know her name. I couldn't go and say, "Is there a black girl working here?" I don't know what they would have said or think.

La Spada, the chief statistician who was my immediate boss, was very Italian and very dramatic. He spoke about six languages and was very meticulous with his numbers and we had to be like that as well as he was a perfectionist. Anyway, my boss was a very strange or unusual chap. For example, he would go for a long jog followed by a very hot bath to shake off the flu but apart from his idiosyncrasies, he was a good guy.

One day, I was going into the library for a book and as I opened the door and entered I stopped suddenly in my tracks as I was confronted by this absolutely gorgeous black girl and I was quite awkward and a bit nervous in her presence. It was like being confronted with an unusually rare bird that I did not want to frighten away. She had come to do a test for a summer job at the Tin Council as she was hoping to work in the Stats department all summer if she got the job. Mr La Spada had been giving the applicants aptitude tests all morning and I just happened to enter while she was being tested, so I went out again, quickly closing the door. I went over to my Italian boss and whispered, "Is she joining us?" He replied, "Possibly". I asked, "Are there any other candidates?" He answered, "Possibly". Boring, why the suspense I thought.

So I said, "I think she looks like the right person for the job". And I suspected Las Spada wanted her to work there too and I think he realised she was my first and only choice. Anyway, we didn't discuss it any further but the next week, who turned up? She did. I said, "Oh, hello, how are you, how was the test? It was good, obviously, 'cause you're here right?" She smiled.

Later on I found out that she attends Imperial College and she goes to church at Kensington Temple some evenings and at weekends. "If you've got to go to the temple after work," I said, "I'll go with you." Getting to know each other but really wanting to be always with her as her protector; she looked as if she needed protection, so petite and vulnerable. She was so calm, stylish, selfless and humble, so I looked to the heavens and thanked the Almighty for sending me my life partner.

She said to me, you've got a nice boss in La Spada, haven't you?

"Yea, he's ok," I replied. "I'm sure I didn't pass the test, I was distracted and wasn't really focusing", she told me.

"But you are a maths student so then it's no problem, you should be able to do that job". Anyway, we became good friends. I said to myself, I've got to get this girl on my side, she's my girl. She was quietly sophisticated with a calmness to match; and she was just right for me.

One day I decided to drive into town and park as close as possible to work leaving the car just behind East Street on the south side of the river Thames. After work I persuaded her to travel with me by telling her, "I will take you home so we could have a longer talk as you seem to be an interesting person and I have never met anyone from Trinidad before".

She asked, "where did you park and how are we going to get there?" "By bus" I said. As it transpired later on in the relationship she told me that she would never have gone off with a guy just like that: "It was very odd that I went off with you, I trusted you and just accepted all you said".

So, we drove to her lodgings in Mitcham, on the borders of Surrey, we had a long chat on the way and as promised I drove her straight to where she was living and dropped her off. Bev was living in rented accommodation with an older sister and another sister about a year or two her senior. On the top floor, in the loft, was a guy, the elder sister's boyfriend. The sister and her boyfriend were quite friendly and so they invited us into the kitchen to make coffee, and there was all these mugs in the sink with coffee stains, thick brown stuff which the other students inside the house would just drink from and walk off leaving the mugs there and then come back a few days' later and just make more coffee in those same stained mugs. I could not believe the condition of the place. I looked at the floor and it was centimetres thick with dirt so instead we went into her room which she shared with the other sister. I looked around the room and there was cotton wool covering up the holes in the side of the outside wall. I thought, how could a landlord be so callous and uncaring? There was cotton wool around the window frames being used as draft excluders as there were wide gaps letting the cold air into the room and I am wondering how could this landlord's conscience allow him to collect rent with the place in that condition?

Bev got me a can of coke from the fridge, I remember, she could not drink her tin of coke because one can of coke would last her about three helpings and could take a whole day to finish. Well, she was a tiny girl although perfectly formed, her stomach could not take that much gas at one go, and even now I rib her about it: the girl who couldn't drink a full can of coke.

So, anyway, I went and told all my friends about my future wife. They wanted to know if she knew this so I told them not yet.

The thing is this lady was very thrifty. She had a certain amount to spend each week and she would spend that much to the last penny and not a penny more. I suppose that's what we call budgeting, that was never part of my routine.

So Bev was prudent, thrifty with a responsible attitude to life. She did not bother about fashion, make-up or trivial things that young ladies of her age would worry about spending money on. I realised that she did not need these as she would look just as good first thing in the morning as at any other time of the day and I don't think she had a make-up bag. Bev didn't give the impression that she was brainy, she was possibly shy but nice; she mixes well with people, down to earth and definitely not full of herself. I thought "she would make a perfect mother" caring and so on. I told some of my mates that I was now going see her, so they insisted they should come along to meet this future wife of mine. My Nigerian friend Victor, from college whose wife had just given birth, came along with another mate. We took a bottle of whisky to celebrate the birth of his son. So, after visiting his wife in hospital we started drinking this whisky straight from the bottle and after the bottle finished we jumped into my car to go and show them my princess. Although I was drinking, I was able to drive and anyway, it was my car, so I had to drive. We got to Mitcham, parked and knocked on the door, when Beverly came out and I introduced her to Victor and the other friend, they all got on well and of course the guys loved her. After a while they left and I spent the whole night in the car with Bev just chatting. Luckily it was summer and then the next morning we went into the house to get a coffee. Just as we got into the house, who did I see? The black girl that I'd briefly met in the lift at Haymarket, who presumably worked at the Sugar Council!

She said, "I know you, you are the boy who works in Haymarket house. What are you doing here?" And then she looked at us in surprise, "That's my sister!"

I said, "Yah?" She said, "I thought you were going to have a drink with me!"

And I thought, oh! But we never arrange anything and anyway I had prayed that I would find the right person, who was at least comparable with Pauline my deceased fiancée, so I knew that I was going to meet this young lady and that's how that happened. I met these two sisters but it was obviously meant to be Beverly, who I became smitten with and eventually married.

Now Beverly had a few guys chasing her but she wasn't really keen. Most of them were from the halls of residence for students somewhere in Chelsea or from Imperial College and a lot of them were Nigerians and you know how persistent they can be, so I am thinking I got there at the right time.

There was no pressure, no cajoling, and no forced engagements. Like before with Pauline, my beautiful, tragic sweetheart, this was the real thing. Love had come at last and I wasn't resisting it in the slightest.

* Bolshie – Arrogant, cocky

24

Love and Marriage

Beverly was in her first year at college, and with me working and her studying, we could not spend much time together, but we talked on the phone a lot. I'd see her when I could and I enjoyed her company every time. We went to the cinema, visited various museums, towns, parks, and we'd go and eat at the Stockpot restaurant off Haymarket.

Occasionally we would go and see her older sister, who was very enthusiastic about everything. She had an Aunt in Dartford, where they'd lived for a while but they decided to move to London either for work or to be close to the university, so they all ended up at this little place in Mitcham.

So, with the change in my life and other considerations I decided to buy a new house as I had sold the one in Bexleyheath and I didn't want to be out of the property market for too long so I bought a semi in Slade Green on probably the best street in not such a brilliant area. The neighbours were great and sometimes I would go away on holiday and leave Beverly behind swotting for exams. She would stay at the house so that she could work undisturbed.

Now, at this stage of my life I was headhunted by the Buffer Stock department within the Tin Council, the trading arm of the organisation. Everyone wanted to be in that department because the Tin business revolves around that section. This Dutch man, who was the director of Buffer Stock, requested an interview with me, and told me he wanted me to work in his department to help with their stats and some trading. Here you buy and sell tin ingots to regulate the tin price on the world markets.

I learnt the trade pretty quickly and before long I was trading thousands of tons of tin metal daily on the LME and Penang stock markets; equivalent to millions of English pounds. After a while I was earning lots of money and, most reassuringly, I could then afford my house and my lifestyle suddenly changed. I was going away on holiday quite often and would disappear to Jamaica or to the United States to visit relatives I had not seen for years.

My younger brother at this time was a London bus driver and my mum was coming and going between the USA and England. She got a new place in Peckham, one of the new builds for people who always paid their rent on time and had a good record with the council.

At around this time my friends were starting to get married. I am now going regularly to weddings and I would always be proud to take Beverly with me. She was always so fit and petite and I always used to say that the girl you start off with must look like that as she would eventually end up being twice the woman she used to be. (Smile).

So, we used to go to these various weddings and maybe she was thinking that way but she never mentioned it to me, she just focused on what she was doing and so eventually we got engaged. I can't remember how I proposed but knowing me I probably said something like, "You know, I think we should spend the rest of our lives together." I remember when I proposed to her she said, "I'm a good Catholic girl we take marriage seriously; we don't get divorced, it doesn't happen in my family. When you get married to a guy it's for keeps."

So I said, "I can handle that."

Anyway, she agreed to marry me. Was it a new ring or the same old ring? It must have been a new ring as it was a new start, and we chose it together. By then the old ring had disappeared and I don't think I ever saw it again.

Just before we got married Beverly graduated from university as a mathematician and decided she would follow in her mother's footsteps and become a schoolteacher. She was going to do her teacher training for another one year at Avery Hill, a reputable teacher training college in Kent, and I thought well, maybe I should teach her to drive.

We spoke a lot about actually getting married and setting a date for that. Initially, her people, mainly her aunts, didn't like me much. The reaction was, "A Jamaican! How come you're getting married to a Jamaican?"

Later, I would understand that during their early years in England one of the aunts had met and got pregnant by a Jamaican guy and then he disappeared, so they hated Jamaican men from that point. "Fair cop", I thought. After all, we do have different experiences in life which formulate our views about things.

The Aunts were very suspicious of my intentions and so dislike the idea of me getting married to their lovely niece, they didn't want to know. But Beverly didn't care nor was she influenced by them. She said, "Well, whatever will happen, will happen." We were blindly in love and committed to this relationship so the aunts sort of relented and went along with our wishes. They must have decided, well, she's not going to change her mind and she's now moved in with him.

And it's strange about the financial arrangements, I can remember on one occasion I was asked to write down a memorable event in my life for some security system and I put that I had sold my car, my cherished BMW, to get married and the female assistant thought that was such a wonderful and sweet thing to have done.

What happened was I had this BMW, SXE1 – Sexy One. That's me. It was my pride and joy, a second hand BMW which I enjoyed driving around town. My Black Man's Wheels, as we used to call BMWs, but I didn't notice the registration at the time until a friend said to me, "Typical, isn't it? Look at him; look at the registration of that car, sexy one! Who do you think you are?"

So, that was the first time I'd noticed it. Anyway, I decided that I was going to sell my car to fund my wedding as my fiancée was only a student and couldn't help with the finances.

As I said, around this time quite a few of my friends were getting out of the bachelor stage and getting into stable relationships and I knew it was just about my time for that.

We got married in a catholic church in Dartford but the thing was before the wedding not only did I have to battle with the

At the engagement party with fiancee and friends

her relatives but the priest also wanted to put me through my paces. He insisted that I had to have a session with him because I was marrying a catholic girl. We had to have a one to one in his office, so he sat me down in this room and decided to quiz me about my lifestyle and what I intended to do after and why I was getting married and so on. What about my kids, would I bring them up as good Catholics? So I said, "Well, yes I think so, if their mother thinks it's the right thing to do."

He expected that if I marry a Catholic girl, that's how it should be, so I basically told him what I thought he wanted to hear. I never expected such a detail interrogation from a man that I didn't know nor had any close relationship with, but I accepted everything for her sake. I must admit I was a bit taken aback by the process. I suppose in those days I was a bit bolshie*, and I became a bit annoyed with him because I didn't see why I should have to go and see him and explain myself. I wasn't getting married to his relations nor anyone that he has a family connection with so why does he want to probe me? After all, he was just a man who had a position in a church, so why is it so different? I was a bit hesitant about an audience with the priest, but I thought, well, you know, this is the girl I am going to marry so I suppose I might as well go through with the interrogation. I sat down with a lot of humility and listened to what the priest had to say; shook my head in the right places, nodded in the right places and actually accepted everything that was proposed.

If I did have a religion I suppose I was Church of England, but that was not my doing. It was my mother who decided that I should be baptised in whatever church it was, but I had gone to the Seventh Day Adventist, Pentecostal, different churches, and experienced different influences. Anyway, I mentioned that to the priest and I suppose he gave his blessing.

We got married in the Catholic church opposite Dartford Grammar School and after that we all went to a hall close to our home to have the reception where we had a great feast of West Indian delights, speeches, dancing and merry-making into the late evening, after which a lot of our friends came back to the house in Slade Green for more celebrations. My close relatives and friends came down from Birmingham for the joyous occasion and everyone had a good time.

It is the Jamaican way to get involved in the preparation of the reception hall, the cooking and serving was their way of showing appreciation but on this occasion I insisted that no guests should get involved in the cooking or serving side of things; they were to come and enjoy themselves, so we had caterers.

Of course, there was a lot of resistance but the relatives eventually gave in. After we got back from the church everyone was greeted with champagne and light snacks to start off with and then the speeches and after that we had exhausted those they served the main course. Our guests danced into the night and both sides of the family got to know each other and had a great time.

Next morning, my wife and I jumped in our newly acquired second hand Volkswagen (the love bug design) and off we went to our honeymoon. I had booked a week in Braunton, north Devon, in a hotel where I had stayed when I was an actor earlier in my life.

We had done some filming close by and the hotel we stayed in was absolutely fantastic so I promised myself that I would return there sometime in the future for a romantic week, so here we were.

Acting is one of the things I did when I was trying to find my niche in life.

In the early days when I was at the Tin Council doing the rounds of being more or less the tea boy or office clerk, I had lots of time on my hands. I wasn't thinking I would amount to much in this firm so I thought about going into modelling and acting. Acting was good fun and it got me some recognition and extra cash.

I was sent somewhere in the west end where I did modelling classes, learned to walk on the catwalk and so on, and then I graduated and got a modelling certificate which I still have. Life as a model was interesting and the Royal College of Art in Kensington was where I got my first break.

I was modelling for one of the college designers and the clothes she asked me to wear were made of newspaper; they had cut out this newspaper into an outfit and I was modelling it. It looked good provided you didn't move around much so I put this thing on and walked onto the catwalk, strutting my stuff although I did feel a bit foolish.

I learned to pose and had pictures done in different situations. I did quite a bit of modelling for television and poster advertisements, and assignments for national newspapers and some magazines. I remember the News of The World newspaper did a trailer for a story about gun running in Africa. They took us out into Sherwood Forest and we were dressed in these combat uniforms with big imitation machine guns. We were rushing around pretending that we were in the heart of Africa, shooting and carrying on. It was fun and I enjoyed messing about in all that mud. Of all the modelling and acting roles I've done, that's the one I enjoyed the most. It was a chance to have a laugh, meet new people and do a bit of travelling – and of course we were getting paid for it, so that was like the cherry on the cake.

At the end of filming we were going for lunch at a local pub and the director got a couple of white guys to go in front of us and me and the other black guys were going to push them into this pub creating a commotion as if we were holding them hostage to get the customers' reaction. So we burst in with these imitation sub-machine guns and suddenly everyone froze with the beer in their hands and then we all started laughing when they got the joke – that was so funny. You couldn't do that now, but at the time it was a great laugh.

I also remember doing an advert for Nescafe and one or two commercials for the American market, and when I did that I used to tell my friends and we would wait up to see what was shown here on the television. And then they would go, "Yea, look at him, he's good man!"

I had two agents, Oriental Casting and another agency called Black Boys.

I used to enjoy the whole business of the filming because we would go early in the morning or late at night to interesting locations and I would be playing a part where I am a representative of some African country to the United Nations. The director would say something like, "You're the President of Ungowara", but before we did all that we would just sit around doing absolutely nothing for hours. Some people would smoke weed or drink whisky during the long wait, trying to keep warm or to lessen the boredom and, yea, it was fun but at times it was mind-numbingly boring.

Most of my assignments were to promote an event that was coming up on the TV or in some magazine. However, I was troubled about the future because at those auditions I would see the same guys, the same faces turning up time and time again and they were getting walk on parts like extras in a crowd scene, but nothing major and it got me thinking, "Do I want this as a career"?

I mean, am I really going to be a star in a film earning lots of money? I didn't think so, so it was from then that I started to lose interest, although whenever they'd ring me about an audition I would go, but I didn't go ringing up my agent asking if any parts had come in.

Family man with kids on holiday

Man, wife and son

But what really turned me off was when I was sent by this casting Agency to Soho to audition for a film and I was really excited at the prospect. When I got to the location there was this narrow staircase leading up to a seedy little flat and at the top it led into a small room where there was a guy and these beautiful blonde girls, who were skimpily dressed sitting at a table. They asked me straight out, "Can you act?" "Ah, yea." "So what have you been doing?"

The long and short of it was that they wanted me to be in a pornographic film. It sounded a lot of money but I knew my friends watched these things and I thought about it and said thanks very much and left. There was no script but they just asked me "how do you feel about making love on film?"

(I suppose he used the words, "making love", although of course love had nothing to do with it; this was all about sex and what's more, doing it on film so other people could get their kicks).

I said, "I don't know, I've never done this before. It depends what the girl looks like", but really I knew that was not me. He said, "It's these girls". They were pretty up front about their intentions: I was supposed to have sex with the two blonde girls while the cameras were rolling. I went away, thought about it and rang the agent. He was really excited and said, "You're in buddy", but I said I was ringing to tell him that I didn't want to do this any more – I was quitting acting.

"What! It's work for about three months and it's not going to be shown in England," he replied, "It will be shown abroad."

The agents always said that because, obviously, they wanted to secure their 20 per cent commission and that is what really put me off. I thought, "Nah!"

It was the same with the TV, I'd seen these guys, full-time actors but not really doing much as they would only have walk on parts, standing like a statue and not getting to say a word. Occasionally, they might get a line, something like: "What was that you said?" Five words and I'm thinking if that's all I've got to look forward to I better find myself a respectable job. That's when I decided to turn my back on the acting and modelling and focus on finishing off my Diplomas, get serious with work and eventually get married.

So far I had fulfilled all three goals, and here I was about to start my honeymoon with the woman of my dreams. We arrived at the hotel in Braunton where my interest in acting had begun all those years before. The location was just as beautiful as I remembered it and my bride was also really captivating. The hotel was up on a hill overlooking the sea and I remember that on the previous occasion when I was acting there the weather was very cold so we had to have lots of hot alcoholic drinks to keep us warm. The people at the hotel had said to me that when I became famous not to forget to come and visit them. I am not famous but the place had lots of great facilities: saunas, swimming pool, beautiful hilltop views and sandy beaches which made this the ideal spot for a honeymoon. When we got to the hotel they had a Caribbean scene for a film that was being made. There were huts along the beach and we even saw Black Beauty being filmed on the shores later that week.

Getting to the hotel was an adventure. We were driving our VW beetle but there was a hole in the floor, a bit like in the Flintstones, and I had put a piece of carpet over the hole but what was worse, the car could not overtake anything on the motorway. The maximum speed was 50 miles an hour and most of that was down hill.

I had never tried out the car on the motorway before, and as we were going along the windscreen smashed as we were driving at our top speed in the rain. I think what happened was that a lorry was going past at some speed and something was thrown back from the wheels which hit our windscreen with force and it shattered, but being an old car, when it smashed it went right across the whole screen. I had to think fast, so I put my fist through the glass so that I could see ahead then eased over to the hard shoulder and because the car top speed was only 50 miles an hour, I was mainly travelling in the slow lane.

I suddenly remembered that I had just past a petrol station a few metres back so I got on the hard shoulder and reversed slowly, almost at a crawl until eventually we got to the petrol station where we recovered our senses, got the breakdown service to do a quick windscreen replacement, and then we were off again on our journey to Braunton.

We took the scenic route over the mountains and by now it was way pass midday. The scenic route took us over the mountains where we encountered snow, hail storm, rain and mud on the roads. Looking down from on top of those hills we could see the sea some distance away at the foot of the mountain, we were crawling up those slopes and hoping and praying that the car would not fail us and thank God it didn't. We eventually got to the top of the mountain and although there were low clouds causing poor visibility, we had good roads and finally got to Braunton on the other side of those hills and reached our hotel destination safely.

It was quite a relaxing and enjoyable week, although it rained most of the time but being typical newly weds, we did not mind. We spent most of the time in the hotel enjoying the facilities or strolling along the beach in the cold autumn air.

So that was the honeymoon. We enjoyed everything about the place but what was especially memorable for me, apart from having such a blissful time with my beautiful wife, were the freshly picked and cooked mushrooms we had with every meal; I loved mushrooms and these came straight out of the ground from the hills close by.

25

Domestic Bliss

So we are now man and wife. I became a responsible married man; went out to work as normal while the wife went off to the teacher training college and then now of course she's a new wife and still coming to terms with what that meant.

I found myself rushing off to work and rushing straight back home. I suppose that's the honeymoon period; you don't want to go with the guys anymore you want to go home for your wife to meet you in the passage with a kiss and a cuddle.

For my sins, I decided to try to teach her to drive. You should see her driving all over the road like a drunken beetle. And she would exclaim, "I don't know what's the matter with this car, it's not going where I'm pointing it!"

And I would say, "It's not the car, love, but it could be the way you're controlling it."

Before long she had knocked down the gatepost at Avery Hill College. That's when I decided she needed to have some lessons from a professional instructor and signed her up with a local driving school. However, she still managed to topple the fence in front of our house and got stuck on one of the posts.

I'd got back from work one evening and these guys who were always sitting on the wall in front of their house opposite our house were sitting there having a good laugh about something.

They looked like gypsies and I think maybe they were. I called them greasers because they were mechanics and there were always groups of long hair guys turning up to have their cars repaired. In the greasers' garage you could always see lots of broken down, greasy engines and other piles of junk, and inside the house was filthy as well because it was only the father and his three sons living there, and, like the engines, they were also very greasy-looking.

Anyway, I got back from work this evening and as always there they were sitting on the wall but this time in stitches of laughter, I was confused by this strange carrying on so I approach them and asked what was so funny. They said that they'd had to lift my wife's car off the fence. "She'd knocked down the fence with the car ending up stuck on one of the posts". Boy, did they laugh!

I had to endure all the usual jokes about women drivers and it was embarrassing because it was my wife they were making fun of. When we spoke about it she started blaming the car saying she'd crashed because the steering wheel was too tight and so on. Of course, she had recently passed her test and I thought that when you passed your test it meant that you could drive – so there you are, she obviously needed more lessons or a bit more confidence behind the wheel.

Anyway, the drama of her driving escapades aside, our lives as newly weds was going along swimmingly, as they say, and eventually, she got pregnant. Of course we were happy and excited at the prospect of becoming a family, but unfortunately she had a miscarriage. That was devastating, but fortunately she got pregnant again not too long after, which we agreed was a blessing, although the timing could have been better: I was having work done on the house at the time and I remember thinking that the refurbishment would be completed way before the birth. In fact, that was an incentive to get the work done faster.

I had contacted a building company called The Ark, they came to the house to demonstrate what they could do and explained how it was a very straightforward job which they would complete within a set timescale. The representatives seemed trustworthy and we needed to have the work done so I agreed for them to go ahead.

However, alarm bells started to ring when Ark's builders came and removed bricks from the back of the house and put in some metal posts to prevent the house from collapsing. It was a good thing too because the house did shift slightly and it was actually subsiding. This was noticeable from the cracks on the wall in the bedroom above, so they put further reinforcement in place and then started digging up the drains at the back of the house which linked all the properties on our side of the road.

I thought maybe they should have completed the groundwork first, but, obviously, I assumed they knew what they were doing and didn't worry too much until they dug up the garden, exposing all the outside drainage, and then proceeded to dig up inside the garage and remove the waste pipes.

For weeks we didn't have a toilet and there was no kitchen as they had moved that too. So, there's no access to the bathroom, no kitchen, no water and no heating, and my wife is there, pregnant with no facilities to rely on.

We decided we'd move everything we needed into the lounge/sitting room, and everything was in there for comfort: she had a kettle, toaster, a microwave, crockery and utensils, stuff to eat, plus a TV and the radio. And because there was no bathroom, I would come in the evenings and drive her about three miles to her aunt's house in Dartford to do her toilet, bath and so on.

The building company had promised that the work would be finished in two months, but it took them about two months before they actually *started* the work, then disappear and we didn't see them for a while after that, by which time the rats were coming out of the exposed drains and into the house. It was a shocking experience and we didn't know what to do but tried to shut off the living room as best we could from the rats at the back of the house.

If we wanted to urinate we had a little pee pot and if we wanted to do a "big job" we would get in the car and drive the three miles to her aunt's house or, if our friend Jennifer who lived a few blocks away was at home, we would go there instead. It was terribly inconvenient!

We tried to contact the company or find the guys who were supposed to be doing the work but we couldn't locate them. Eventually I found some people who were also trying to contact the Ark. It transpired that the company had taken their money, opened up their place and disappeared just as they'd done to us.

Some were at different stages of completion or they'd not even started the work. Eventually, working together, we found out where the company was and what had actually happened: they'd gone bankrupt a long time before and so the workmen just did not bother to come back because they weren't being paid.

Thankfully, I'd only given the company a small deposit for the materials which they'd deposited in our drive. It took us ages to see if we could get our money back but there was no hope of that.

All the stuff, which had been pre-made at their factory, was piled up in front of our garage. It was the kind of composite material that was supposed to be put together like a jigsaw puzzle. Apparently, another builder would be able to complete the work once they'd completed the groundwork and make the structure safe. However, we soon discovered that no builder was prepared to complete the work started by another builder. I suppose there was too much work around at the time or maybe it was an insurance issue or something, but we were stuck. *What the hell were we supposed to do now?*

I contacted one of my relatives in the industry who told me he didn't like doing work that someone else had started but I explained my position and told him that my wife was going to have the baby soon and how appalling our living conditions were. So he relented and agreed to do the work. He came with his team and I became the skivvy, working with him and his crew while they set about putting our house back together.

I got them their food, drinks, cleaned up after them, and did everything that was needed to keep them there doing the work until it was completed. And, would you believe it, the day they finished and I was sweeping up to putting down some linoleum, Beverly's waters broke and I had to rush her to Queen Mary Hospital in Sidcup.

I stayed with her at the hospital until she had settled in and then went back home, where I tried to clean up as best I could. By then the builders had gone but at least the place was liveable. The drains had been re-connected, the windows were all refitted, and the walls re-erected where they'd been knocked down. In the garage, where they had dug a big hole, this was now concreted over and a manhole put in place. The downstairs toilet was finished off, ready for use, and everything else was more or less completed. Later that evening the hospital called me to advise that my wife was ready to go into delivery, so I went and experienced the birth of my first child – a son. The next morning, I rushed home but didn't get much sleep as there were still too much left to do to prepare the house for Bev and the baby. I completed the painting, got some linoleum to finish off the kitchen and dining room floors, cleaned up the best I could and In the evening I would rush back to the hospital for the visiting period to spend some time with her and the new arrival.

As a new mum she was kept in the hospital for a week so I would visit every day and reassured her that everything would be alright when she got out, talked to her about the day's events and then rushed back and do a bit more work on the property.

On the day she was scheduled to come back home, I managed to complete all the painting and made the place clean and welcoming with fresh flowers. I drove to collect them and when the wife got home she was pleasantly surprised, comparing what she'd left and what she has now came back to I was chuffed.

As a father you start getting involved in things that you haven't experienced before and understanding how having a baby in your life can change everything.

The thing with this baby was he would drink his milk from one breast until that was absolutely empty and then he would go to sleep. He then wakes up in the middle of the night and bawled so loudly that everyone within earshot would jump up, and then he would drink from the other breast until that too was absolutely empty and then he would go back to sleep.

After he had his milk he was happy and you wouldn't hear a peep out of him after that. So, as a parent you got involved with all of that stuff: washing, changing the poo and all that business, but after a while it became second nature and it was a humbling experience being a father; you're a different man, a changed person.

It's amazing what this experience does to people, isn't it? You have a lot more humility; you understand what your role is, you get involved and you actually feel a strong bond growing within this family unit you've created.

So I am now feeling like I'm part of a complete family and decisions have to be made. Here I am settled into my new life and my new home in Slade Green and getting to know the neighbours some of whom were Middle Eastern but a lot of English also. Most were middle-aged and a few young couples like ourselves.

We became very close with the Assyrian family next door and with a Scottish couple a few doors down on the opposite side of the road; as the wife was also in teaching she would trade stories about their teaching experiences with my wife.

So, Alderney Road was a friendly place and a good place to bring up a young family. However, one night, in April 1981, the atmosphere suddenly changed.

Riots had kicked off in Brixton and as I watched the events unfolding on TV, I knew that there would be a knock-on effect all over the southeast and there would possibly be some riots in Lewisham and Woolwich which had large concentrations of black people. But I thought that out where we lived "in the sticks" – the suburbs – things would be different.

The next morning I sensed a kind of coolness towards us from the English people living in the street: people we always greeted were now closing their doors and avoiding personal contact.

Of course, I expected that some residents would be a bit awkward towards us but never did I imagine such a sudden change amongst those we had a fairly close relationship with. After all, these were people we knew and who had only recently been in our home to talk and drink wine, some of whom we regarded as friends.

I hadn't been in Brixton throwing bricks nor setting fire to buildings but despite that, we were regarded as the enemy. Even the Middle Eastern next door avoided us fearing perhaps that they too would be alienated if they showed any loyalty towards us.

In the evenings or if we were going out I would close the heavy velvet curtains as a protection in case bricks were thrown through the windows and when we were at home we sat on the floor in case people passing by the house became nasty.

Although we were not involved in the riots I could sympathise with the people in Brixton. There, black people were constantly hassled and were regularly searched using the "Sus laws", which meant the police could stop and search you on the suspicion that you were going to commit a crime.

Black people, especially men and male youths, were frequently dragged off the streets and taken into the police station were I understand they were subjected to all types of abuse. These excesses, coupled with high employment among black youths, culminated in the riots which apparently started on the "Front Line" in Railton Road.

The front line was where black youths could meet to socialise and have an outlet for their frustrations: playing reggae music and smoking "weed" or marijuana. However, even here they were still being persecuted and so the tensions exploded into a full-blown riot.

We weren't involved but of course we felt the reverberations all the way out there in our almost lily-white neighbourhood. That's when some people started to show their true colours and sometimes their looks or quiet hostility said it all: we were enemies and didn't belong.

26

Head Hunted

Around that same time there were also some conflicts at work in the sense that I was in the statistics department and, well, people take advantage, don't they?

Once they knew that I used to be the general dogsbody, they developed the mindset that I was always going to be the general dogsbody. So they'd come looking for me and somehow managed to persuade the head of statistics that my services were more urgently needed in the post room.

Naturally, after a while I was getting frustrated. I tried not to be too difficult but I try telling them, "Look, I'm not doing that any more, this is my job now. Why don't you get somebody else to help out?"

But it's always like that, isn't it? The guy who was supposed to be the new "go-for" or dogsbody hadn't turned up so they'd say to me, "Oh, you can do the post can't you? And I would have to protest, "But I've got my job to do!"

Anyway, eventually, they understood that and left me alone to get on with my work in the Stats department, although from time to time they would still come asking for my assistance.

My head of department was a bit soft or did not want to upset the other managers and, the accountant and joint manager with La Spada kept his job by making sure that the senior staff were happy. Mr Coombes went out of his way to ensure that he did the right thing to the right people so that he kept his job and remained in senior managers' favour so he was only too happy to offer my services when required.

That same accountant employed a guy called Norman as his assistant. Poor Norman did all the work without any appreciation from his bosses and was never made assistant accountant because, they claimed, he wasn't qualified and that was the only

Reading the daily paper during those void periods

thing that his boss had against him, although it was clear that Norman could do the job, which of course he did single-handedly.

Norman was very knowledgeable, but he had not completed his accountancy qualifications. And, although Mr Coombs the accountant was qualified, he did not give the impression that he was capable, so he used Norman as his lackey. Every time Norman asked for more money his boss would refuse to recommend it and then go to the senior managers and tell them that his assistant was ok, but he didn't deserve a pay rise. He kept him down. And that was to keep his own position because if he elevated his assistant he feared that might have exposed his own shortcomings. So, Mr Coombes was using this other guy to maintain his own status in the organisation. And Norman knew that, but he needed the job.

Norman was a great person; I liked him and felt his pain. One of the things that was interesting about Norman was his involvement into other activities outside of work, such as ballroom dancing, which he took very seriously and was more than a hubby. He obviously didn't want to have to go looking for

Pausing for thought during those busy days at the ITC

At an office party with a colleague and wife looking on

another job which would give him the freedom to pursue his outside interests in the same way. And, besides, the company was fine apart from this accountant – his boss.

Meanwhile I'm looking at that situation and thinking, "And these two are both white guys. Look at what people do to each other out of spite." It's making me realise that injustice and antagonisms occur not just between different races but also between people of the same race.

So, anyway, I was also helping out in the accounts department, building up my skills and becoming a valued member of the organisation. I never said no, as I always set out to please everyone, that's my nature. Eventually, I was head

At the ITC with my international colleagues

hunted by the director of Buffer Stock and that was fantastic as it turned out to be a great job.

This director was quite a senior figure and a strong individual; no one in the organisation would ever undermine his authority. Furthermore, Buffer Stock worked independently within the Tin Council, even operating its own budget.

It was widely considered to be the best department in the organisation and everyone wanted to work there. You get to meet all the brokers in the city and had a good personal relationship with the traders on the London Metal exchange.

We were regularly taken out by the traders for expensive lunches and to champagne bars after work: feasting on champagne and lobsters at Greens in Jermain Street in the west end was a regular event. Every other night the traders would come up from the City to meet us in the west end and we would end up at Greens or another similar bar in town, to drink white wine and champagne and scuff caviar.

So it was a great life and a few of us from the Buffer Stock department would go for lunches down in the City where the girls wore hardly anything as they flitted around taking orders. These girls were serving you with not much on, most of them with legs all the way up to there elbows and their cleavage on display, which made it difficult to focus on lunch. Yes, I think they were dressed like playgirls or bunny girls.

I think it was a restaurant called the City Circle, something like that. The girls would make you feel at ease and, I suppose, happy to be alive and they always greeted you with a broad welcoming smile (I guess they were well paid), and the food would be OK but never filling.

On the other hand, there was enough booze to get drunk if you wanted – which was one of the perks of the job. In fact, it was work! That was what was known as "networking", and the location was the kind of setting where some of the most important business deals were made.

I had never seen or been to places like those before; I didn't even know such places existed for businessmen. So, it was a good job with some fantastic perks, all on expenses, but you worked hard and were expected to be accurate in all you did at all times because inaccuracy is expensive.

As a result, I spent all my time racking my brain to get my calculations done quickly and accurately. Luckily, I had a wife who was a mathematician providing me with a formula to help speed things up, as we didn't have computers doing the work for us in those days. So, instead of going through acres of laborious calculations, I would use her formula, which made it a lot easier.

This dexterity led to a certain amount of trust among the senior managers in my ability to do the work. Now, there were regular meetings held in various cities around the world, like Bangkok, New York, La Paz, and so forth, and the senior officers would go off to these meetings leaving me with certain trading responsibility in their absence.

The chairman, special adviser, director of Buffer Stock and my immediate boss, the deputy director, would travel the world to these tin conferences – to the United Nations in New York or the mines in Malaysia, or perhaps a meeting down in Rio de Janeiro. And when they went, I would be asked to continue running the office as usual, administering tin sales and satisfying requests for payments against available tin stocks. In order to do this, blank letters would be signed by the three signatories and left for me to fill in the instructions.

We had a Spanish girl called Sanchez in the department. She would do the typing, filing and other clerical duties, and then we had Sabeeha who helped with the dealing: the buying and selling on the London Metal Exchange.

I thought she was such an untypical Indian girl because she smoked like a chimney, drank like a fish and swore like a sailor, and I understood that she was very popular down in the City with the traders. They would treat her like one of the guys, like a mate and of course they took her off to various watering holes to do the PR bit. She was also very popular with the boss and was a very sharp trader.

Sabeeha was a nice enough girl but she swore too much, drank and would constantly talk about this colour thing, like when she'd get back from one of her trips to India she was always talking about the caste differences and about when she and her friends would go to the tennis clubs in India they didn't sit in the sun because they don't want to get too dark! She said her friends all make the effort to sit in the shade because none of them wanted to be black, and the only time they went out was at night. During the daytime they were in doors avoiding the sun or they'd be in the member's clubs with air-conditioning keeping their skin fresh looking. It's amazing, isn't it? They are so brainwashed some of these Indians, so culturally damaged, and I think it's because of the time of the Raj when they were ruled by the British. Still, she was quite OK as a person and I liked her. Then, there was this good looking English guy who was still at university, was very good at what he did when he worked with us during the holidays. The Buffer Stock director was Dutch and his deputy was English and a lay preacher in his spare time. There was also Miss Lucy Vandamolen from Holland. Lucy had good contacts and the name was well known in Dutch circles and I think she got her job because of her connections.

So, there we were: one happy family of different nationalities, races and, I suppose, different classes. I am now establishing myself in the Buffer Stock department, trusted with a certain amount of responsibility while my bosses had gone across the world leaving lots of signed letters for me to fill in the details regarding money transfers, tin trades and remittances.

I suppose the company was like family to me. I had been with them for years through good and bad times, through college while I was studying part-time and working there; earning just enough to survive, still it didn't make my life too difficult.

I suppose, generally speaking, most people in the organisation treated me decently, with respect and with a great deal of trust, apart from one very racist guy from the colonial past who I had dealings with when I was the office boy. The things this racist came out with were at best irritating. And I suppose revenge is something you thought of at those times, but after a while I just ignored the sad fellow and I think he just grew old, withered away and died. That's it; he may never have existed for all I care.

I did my work and I had no problems. I worked very hard. I mean, on occasions I would wake up at four o'clock in the morning to finalise a deal which I had to complete before the Malaysian market closed that day.

So, yes, I had been there all that time and I suppose they were happy with my initiative and application hence their trust, otherwise they would not have left those signed letters for me to complete transactions with. Maybe it was quite likely they were testing or watching me, but I doubt it. Maybe they'd just decided, "He seems honest enough or maybe not smart enough to be that cunning".

I don't know what they were thinking but I wasn't that concerned. I just got on with my job to the best of my ability. As a reward, I used to have fantastic holidays to relax and gather my thoughts. I regularly had three or four fantastic holidays a year work permitting.

The reason I had so many stored-up holidays was because I wasn't allowed to have the six weeks holiday allowance in one go. Some years they would pay me for four weeks so I could only have two weeks' leave that year, because we were so busy, and at other times I would have only a week off, the most I could have in one stretch. The bosses were reliant on me so much so that Mr Engels (the Deputy director) would panic when he realised I was about to be away from the office for more than a few days.

There were times when I couldn't have any holidays because there were important meetings going on which meant all hands were required so they would pay me for the whole six weeks. I didn't mind because it meant that I was getting more money in my pocket to shore up my bank account, make a better life for my family and to go on better and more exciting holidays later on.

As a result, I've been all over the world. Of those places I haven't visited, China is maybe the only country I really wanted to experience, possibly because of my purported Chinese connections but more likely because of their history and culture and I hope one day to be walking the great wall of that great land.

27

Redundant

After living in the fast lane and enjoying a very good period of economic growth, things started to take a downturn in my sector. What happened was there were a lot of people in the stock market making too much money as prices were going through the roof.

They were buying tin and holding it, but in fact they were buying warrants that represented tin stocks, but half the time the tin stocks weren't there or did not turn out to be the quality that was originally purchased: when it should have been high grade stock only standard quality tin was available.

When the tin is dug up, smelted and graded into ingots we at the ITC are asked to make payment to the smelters. We then get about a week's notice to buy the ringgits and send it over to the smelters in Malaysia so that they can release the tin, backed by the relevant warrants.

The tin is then put on ships and arrives in Rotterdam and Antwerp within a week, where the tin ingots are put into storage while the appropriate tin warrants are released to the purchaser. We also had British tin from the Cornish mines, which were usually stored in the UK.

So what was happening was that some traders and their companies were driving the prices up by creating a shortage of tin. The long and short of it was that warrants were being sold for stocks which were not available. It was corrupt but difficult to prove. I found anomalies in the figures and pointed that out to the bosses but nothing came of it. Sometimes it's best to look the other way and say very little because the alternative would be difficult to comprehend.

Well, we started calling in the tin stocks stated on the contracts and some traders could not deliver so prices just got out of hand. You've got the spot price and the forward price.

Suddenly, the spot price is sky high because they haven't got the tin, so they're trying to buy it from somewhere and that's creating panic.

There were some people who should have delivered a particular brand, for which there was a premium, but only had an inferior brand which was acquired at a discount. So effectively the wrong brand was sold or the warrants did not match the stocks available.

I think there was a lot of dishonesty and there were more warrants floating around than there was tin available in the warehouses. There must have been a lot of corruption going on and people making a lot of money on the back of that so the whole thing then started collapsing.

I started seeing all these discrepancies when I was doing the statistics. For example, we've bought so many tons of STC brand, which was high grade, but the report we get from the warehouses showed that they've got so much less STC brand and that's completely at odds with what the traders said, so it doesn't match up with the amount of tin as represented by the warrants.

Then when it comes to the spot market they're offering you stuff that isn't even available at the warehouses shown on the warrants. Maybe it's on the seas, expecting to arrive that day or a few days later but it doesn't arrive and is not available as represented by the contract or tin warrants in that warehouse. There were all sorts of anomalies.

Well, eventually, the whole thing came to a head and the banks had the worse of it. They had warrants for thousands of tons of tin as collateral against loans and they couldn't find the tin nor did they have the right tin brand and that created a lot of problems and the banks who lent us money against the collateral now wanted to take legal action to secure their assets as prices had now starting to fall, devaluing their stock holdings.

Hence, all sorts of meetings were convened with ITC delegates, representatives of banks, international lawyers and politicians. At one stage I think the Council owed about £950 million (a lot of money in those days) to banks and brokers. They'd never had a situation like that before and it took years to unravel.

So there I was threatened with redundancy from the company I had worked for all of my adult life. It is about to fold so I am thinking where do I go next to get a regular income and maintain the lifestyle I am now accustomed to? I am about to leave the International Tin Council after years of devotion doing my part to ensure that tin consumers had a fair price and that the producers had a reasonable living from the mines so that they could look after their families and have a decent life themselves in areas such as Bolivia, Malaysia and Zaire.

Basically that's what we did, we supported both sides so that when the price got too high for the consumers we intervened to stabilise things. We then sell tin stocks, usually in the London Metal Market, to bring prices down to the middle range. If prices are too low we buy stocks to raise the price back to the middle range.

However, with the threat of redundancy I was forced to be more business-focused and so I started looking around for workable ideas. I started seeing most of my friends and colleagues at the council being made redundant and office space being reduced until it was just a couple of offices left together with the conference room on one floor, with the accounts, statistics and the general reception squeezed into one reduced area serviced by only one or two office secretaries.

In my department there was Sabeeha, me and the two buffer stock directors. As redundancy got closer I would get to the office the usual time but have time to read the news papers until about 11 o'clock when I would be asked to produce some statistics for a couple of hours and then go back to some other reading until it was time to go home. For me, who had become accustomed to roller coaster days in the office, this was soul destroying.

When eventually I was made redundant and left the Council they were still having regular meetings with the stakeholders and solicitors which I understood went on for months after. Some brokerage was trying to cease or freeze the Council's administration account and that made me very nervous because that's what paid our salaries, so I was reasonably happy to be made redundant with a few months' salary as a lump sum together with what was available to me from the provident fund. We didn't have a proper pension scheme. Instead, we had something called a provident scheme with four times our income payable to the member's dependant at death, which was not transferable, so that was lost also. We found out too late that the accountant who sorted this "pension" wasn't even competent at doing that. This providence scheme we were paying our hard earned money into was mainly going towards insurance cover so when the chairman, originally from Australia, retired just before I left, there wasn't enough money in the fund to pay his pension.

It was embarrassing but somehow the directors found money for him to retire. Yes we had life cover; four times our income if we died but there wasn't enough money to cover early retirement or indeed any retirement. I remember I ended up with only six thousand pounds after so many years of working in that organisation.

However, just before I was made redundant I met up with three of my old trading associates, with whom I did lots of business over the many years before this debacle, for a farewell drink and a chat about the good days.

One was from Algeame Bank, one from Malayan bank and from Standard Chartered all prominent eastern Trading banks during those days. So here we were just having a few drinks at one of those watering holes and discussing the roller coaster past after everything went belly up as the recession of the late 1980s began to kick in.

We were all pretty much tanked up when one of the guys suddenly said to me, "You realise that we could have been rich people and we wouldn't have harmed the company and without too much effort at that?"

I was intrigued, was this the booze kicking in, so I asked how? "Well", one of them said, "you know how many ringgits you needed to acquire each week to pay the smelters out in Malaysia and of course we were usually dealing in a thin market where your intervention could cause large ripples and sharp changes in price. "I am listening!"

"Your intervention on any day can be upwards of £20 million, and you didn't have to spend many millions to affect the price. We were the dealers you traded with most, particularly in ringgits. All we had to do was this: if you were going to spend a £100 million or £20 million or whatever figure to buy ringgits in the Malaysian currency market, we would take up a long position of say £5 million pounds in ringgits and then once we'd bought that, you could then come in with your hundred million pounds purchase, the price would go up, we would then sell and take the profit without spending any money: so simple. We would then put this gain into a Swiss bank account until it was needed."

"Like now, for example", the others nodded their approval and said,

"Yea, we wouldn't be worrying about bloody pensions now", the first guy replied. "We could have retired and split the money four ways. It would have been a win-win situation and nobody would get hurt financially or otherwise."

So I said, "Hmmm! Well, it did cross my mind but that's as far as it went; just a fleeting thought."

Of course, in those days, insider trading was quite commonplace and not illegal, and I admit it had crossed my mind because it would have been so easy. But I'd thought about it and, well, what's the point? The reason why I was doing what I was doing at the company was because of trust; they trusted me and the next thing is would I be happy if I committed what would feel like fraud? If the trust is lost you lose credibility, but I suppose if you had enough money you wouldn't worry much about that at all if you were naturally that type.

At the same time I remember thinking would my conscience be OK with that? And, besides, what if my accomplices shopped me? You don't know what really goes on in people's minds as there's never any secrecy or real trust between people, especially where large amounts of money is involved.

So I thought, forget it, but obviously they were thinking the same thoughts themselves.

That was the easy way we could have become rich quick. The other way was to just fill in one of the pre-signed letters to transfer millions of pounds to an offshore account that I could access whenever I needed to.

All I had to do was just send the instruction over by telex or fax and confirm it by letter, and then disappeared to Rio de Janeiro or some place like that. What were they going to do? Nothing, I suspect.

The embarrassment for an organisation like that would be enough for them to keep it quiet and put it down to experience. They weren't going to make it known that a little Jamaican guy had all of this power to do all of those things, it would have been too embarrassing, so they would just keep it quiet.

I could have got rich with these other guys or just do it on my own. If I did it on my own, the crude way, then everyone would know that I had done it, but what the hell, I wouldn't care because with the money in my account, and me in Rio, I could have whatever life I pleased. So that would be that.

These things would cross my mind as I am sure it did to other people with such access and influence, but I am too honest and was never that desperate to do any of those things. Besides, it's not worth it in the end. How would that have impacted on my family and friends if I had been found out? The only black person in this organisation gets a responsible position and turns out to be a thief! It is just the sort of thing that the racists would have loved, and the newspapers would have had a field day with.

But, looking back, Ronnie Biggs was in Brazil for years and years having a great time after committing that big train robbery and getting away with it, but I am sure he had regrets.

Life is full of risks, you take chances and sometimes you succeed and sometimes you don't but, yea, I didn't commit fraud to make myself rich at the company's expense. Instead, I just got on with my normal life: worked hard, did my job, got a salary and if I wanted more I would put in some over time and that would be enough for me; that would be my rainy day money or cash to put towards a new car.

But, now, not only were we faced with redundancy, but "the chickens had come home to roost". Suddenly, everyone started realising that they had no provision for their retirement. I was walking around the office scratching my head thinking I've got this money and it's only a few months' income and after that, what's next? I could use it to pay off my mortgage but that was so final, then what?

At this stage, I was starting to think about going into business and after kicking a lot of ideas around in my head, I came up with the idea for a company called Exotic Fruit Juice Ltd.

I decided there must be more to life than just working for other people. I wanted to do something that I would enjoy doing so this new company from Sweden came up with a packaging system called "Tetra Pak". They were pretty new in the UK and so they were prepared to fund any good business idea up front if it involved using the Tetra Pak system and they would allow you to pay the £70,000 cost for the packaging machine over an extended period of time but they wouldn't start charging anything until your business started making money.

From my research it seemed like a great plan, so I decided that what's needed was something that wasn't already in the shops but with a latent need. I discovered that was exotic juices being sold in Jamaica and I thought that would sell here in the UK, as there were established communities of West Indians who were accustomed to these drinks. You know why Marks and Spencer is selling those juices? It's because of me.

I was woefully stupid in my supplier choice. I felt a certain loyalty to the country where I'm from and this turned out to be a disaster. I had the idea that I would blend juices from tropical fruits like mangoes, Iteote apples, pears, guavas, all these lovely fruits that we have in Jamaica and make an exotic juice blend for the British market.

I did some research and it seemed possible. I found out from a company in Jamaica how to get the product from Jamaica to England. What the juice company in Jamaica would do was to concentrate the blend to 1 in 10 or something of that ratio, and then freeze the concentrates as this made the product easy to transport and remain fresh.

I made the arrangements with this Graces company in Jamaica but didn't actually meet the directors in person, although we did a lot of communication by 'phone and by telex as it was then. I relied on them totally so did not source alternatives; they would be my sole supplier, at least until the business took off.

They told me that they had all the resources to supply my requirement as they were a big drinks company in Jamaica so I thought one should be able to rely on them but they let me down.

I had told them what I wanted and they reassured me that the juice concentrates was something that they could provide. I asked what quantity they could supply on a regular basis and they told me, "All I needed, no problem".

So with that in mind I went off to acquire these juices locally in Jamaican food shops in London and mixed them together to find the right recipe, then put them in plastic containers and went to see Marks and Spencer.

I set up a limited company, Exotic Fruit Juice Ltd with the logos, a fresh brand look and everything; it was fantastic and I was exhilarated. The management at M&S said yes, it sounded interesting. They had a few Jamaicans working there and said we'd test the juice with them. If they liked it, the company might run with it and then we will test it in areas with West Indians concentration, like Brixton and other places like that.

To me that was a very positive response. I then went up to the north of England and found a processing company in Yorkshire. They would collect the concentrates off the boat and take it to their factory where they had their Tetra Pak machine. They would then reconstitute the juices, put in the Tetra Packs placed on pallets of so many and then distribute to my outlets.

It seemed quite straightforward, I thought. So, everything was ready to go and of course the General Manager at the Yorkshire factory was very enthusiastic. He said he liked the idea and was prepared to help as much as he could. With all that in place I got back on the phone to Jamaica, when the process was supposed to grow legs and start moving. In other words, by now they were supposed to have the product ready to ship and I've arranged funds to transfer for the job. So now I am on the phone to Jamaica to make sure all was in place and ready to go and to my surprise this lady was on the phone instead. "Well, the guys, the directors have gone to New York, you know, and they should have come back by now but I think they were delayed so they won't be coming back for another couple of weeks." I shouted, "You're joking! Is there anybody there who can help me?"

"I don't think so, you will have to wait 'till they come back."

"But this is a business which we agreed on and have put together over months. I have been constantly communicating with your guys and I came to an agreement with them. They're supposed to supply these products and the first lot is due to be shipped this week and it's got to be at Liverpool on whatever date as the firm who is going to receive the product are waiting for your instructions and details of the ship."

I realised I was up against a brick wall when she said, "Well, me no know what fe tell you, you know, because a dem man deh run dem tings and dem no come back yet, so you betta ring back in two weeks."

Anyway, the long and short of it was I lost out, big time. I was panicking and trying to find places in South America, Africa, although in Africa they didn't have the infrastructure, but by then it was too late anyway. I was so convinced that Jamaica was going to deliver, but instead I was let down by a bunch of unprofessional bastards.

In the end, the business didn't happen. Not for me, anyway. However, it did happen for those guys in Yorkshire. Well I can't really blame them, they realised it was a good idea and of course having invested a certain amount of their time in supporting my plans and seeing that I was not able to deliver, eventually I think the General Manager approached M&S with the idea and the rest is history.

It was my fault and I have learned from that experience but I could not believe that supposedly responsible professional senior management of such an established company in any country could be so lackadaisical and unprofessional in business.

"Well, yu know de man gaan abroad and them not coming back." This statement is what you would expect to hear in the schoolyards of the ghettoes of Kingston, not from a secretary of an established organisation.

Crazy, it made no sense but once again my countrymen came up short.

The benefits to them would have been enormous, as I was convinced that it would end up not just in Marks and Spencer but lots of other outlets and become a success. I was convinced I had a reliable source. So you can understand my lack of faith in the Jamaican attitude towards business. Lots of people said they couldn't understand how the company could have behaved so irresponsibly, well you are as good as your weakest link and that's how they were. What I didn't do was to get other suppliers on board from the very start.

Six months later, I went to Marks and there it was exotic fruit juice being sold there. Even now my daughter's using the letterhead I produced, as there are reams of it still around the house. Maybe if I had been more business like at the onset and sourced areas in the Far East or South America, I might have been Mr Juicy today.

So, that was my first venture into business. The next one was a game I invented called Business Time. It has been tested in a couple of schools and the students enjoyed playing it. Anyway, it is in my garage still waiting to be massed produced. The game has got to the stage where it can be mass-produced tomorrow but I think I have lost the enthusiasm.

In early 1990s some girls at Cobham Hall School in Kent tested business time and they loved it. Cobham Hall is a private school for girls and as the wife taught there for a number of years she had the access. Cobham Hall itself was an interesting place: old castle-type building in acres of grounds. Bev offered the game to the girls to play with and they were hooked even though it could take hours to go bankrupt thus ending the game.

One year I took "Business Time" to the toy show at Earls Court exhibition centre and exhibit it to a mass audience but although people were interested in the game, I didn't actually

Promoting Business Time at the Toy Fare in Earls Court

get any large orders. However, some individuals wanted to buy the odd one but I was not prepared to do that. So I thought I can't be bothered spending any more time or money. It's complete, patented and lives in the garage. So, if any of my children decides they would like to take it further, fine. The BT trademark existed long before British Telecom became BT, I'd given that name to the game I invented, and I've got all the documents to prove it. So that's as far as I want to take it.

You have a banker, four players and you have a couple of dice and there are questions and you move forward with every right answer and you can go bankrupt, can make money and so on. I haven't taken it out for over ten years but it's a game I will keep like people keep paintings.

So, that was my second business venture. I may have wasted some money but only time will tell. Later on I decided to follow my instinct and take a giant step into the restaurant business.

I wanted something that would generate an income stream for the immediate future and to fill the void after the ITC, so I started thinking about starting a Caribbean restaurant (you fool!).

I had been to some fantastic restaurants in the past and I always saw it from the business end as a customer and although I did not see what happened behind the scenes in the kitchen, nevertheless, I could see lots of money passing hands so I thought, that's what I want to do. After my first unhappy experience with the useless Jamaican juice suppliers, the only question I asked myself was do I really want to do a business which depended on Jamaicans?

I disregarded any apprehension and eventually found a place I liked in Camberwell Green, south London. This was a big freehold building on three floors and in a prominent position on the high street.

I used to think that if I ever went into business which involved premises, I would be sure to acquire the freehold interest. Don't just buy the business because if the business fails you've still got the freehold interest as a safety net which you could make liquid.

So I bought the building which needed work, and it took a lot of money to make it perfect; to refurbish and fit out the restaurant and the two flats above, one of which was rented to generate extra cash.

And so, in 1987, the Arawak Inn was born. Little did I know that eighteen months later, things would start going downhill and once again I would have to think fast to save the business, my home and the family's future.

28

The Arawak Inn

The Arawak Inn was a comfortable and attractive restaurant, as I wanted it to be of similar quality to the better ones I had visited in the city. Doing it that way cost me a lot of money, but I saw it as a necessary investment for a place that people would be proud to recommend to friends and colleagues.

The restaurant was named after the first inhabitants of Jamaica, the Arawak Indians, nature-loving people who were living on the island before Columbus made his infamous journey of discovery.

No expense was spared to make the restaurant attractive, eye-catching and comfortable. I also converted the two flats above the restaurant and rented one of them, which provided extra revenue and used the other to store provisions and as my crash pad whenever I had to work late. I installed a camera so that whenever I was upstairs in the flat I could still keep on eye on what was going on in the restaurant's dining room.

The restaurant cocktail bar had a bamboo thatch roof to give that Caribbean theme. There was a piano opposite the bar and a mezzanine level where guests would sit and enjoy the performances around the piano and the activities going on around the bar area. There was a lower ground floor situated below the mezzanine and a patio section at the back which was seductively lit and was favoured by the younger guys particularly at weekends when they visited with their lady partners for a romantic evening out. The kitchen was kitted out with the latest equipment to enable the kitchen to run smoothly, with a dumb waiter to each floor of the restaurant linking to the kitchen.

I had no experience of running a restaurant and I didn't do any training before opening the Arawak Inn. However, I had a lot of experience from the various visits to the dining rooms of well-run restaurants and I figured that it couldn't be too difficult. You simply put some food on the plate and take it out to people, and that's it. It can't be that difficult, or so I thought.

I sat down and worked out the menu for the food and a menu for the cocktails, also created a few cocktails relevant to the Arawak Inn and its target customers. I had an Arawak moment – I just put things together and made use of every drink I could think of, put them into a cocktail shaker and had some tasters to sample the results. When people said yes, it has a particular taste I said OK, I'll call it so or so. But, then, of course the more popular ones were there as well and that became part of the cocktail menu. So I established that menu and moved on to the next thing. I mean, West Indian food is not too difficult to cook if you grew up in the Caribbean. Plain rice, rice and peas, fried plantain, boil bananas, dumplings, yam, and stuff like that. Curry goat, this sort of fish, this sort of chicken, this sort of beef, this sort of the pork, some interesting vegetables and Creole recipes which I picked up along the way to complete this menu.

At the end of every meal patrons were given chocolates with their bill. And considering I didn't know anything about running a restaurant before I felt that it went very well for a time.

For the opening night I had a very sharp chef, four waitresses and a barman, everything was ship shape in the kitchen for the opening night. A large banner stood proudly above the shop front announcing the opening and all the people passing would have seen that for weeks, so I didn't have to put advertisements in the newspapers, thus saving me lots of money as I relied on people seeing the banner and using word of mouth to spread the news, which guaranteed us a great turn out on the night. Things had to be perfect on the first night. A lot of work had gone onto the preparation but something went wrong. Everyone worked hard that day to ensure everything was ready for the opening that evening. Food was put into the coolers, all the meat was nicely seasoned and left to marinate, salads were made and put into containers in readiness for the big night. Oh my gosh, as luck would have it the electricity failed and as a result everything was messed up.

We called out an emergency electrician but by the time power was restored a lot of things had gone off as it was summer time, so I got the staff to clear out all the perishables and put the spoiled foodstuffs in dustbins.

On the night the customers were given the actual menus to take away and free drinks were offered to everyone. We explained that because we had a power failure during the preparation most foods had to be discarded so the full menu would not be available to choose from and instead we will only offer a restricted choice of food like curry goat and rice, stewed chicken, and rice and peas, along with all the drinks and, of course, the cocktails.

On reflection, giving the menus to customers was a master stroke of advertising genius. We handled that quite well I thought and a lot of guests stayed back after closing to have samples of cocktails.

On subsequent nights group of ladies would turn up mainly to sit around the bar and sample the cocktails while listening to the pianist strumping away in the background, people loved sitting on the high stools by the bar and soaking up the atmosphere. One night a group of Australian girls just sat at the bar and tried out all the cocktails after they had ordered a light snack of fried plantain wrapped with fried bacon so as to make it legal for those who mainly wanted to drink cocktails.

However, as a result of the set back on the first night I didn't make any money that night, but it promoted the restaurant, and after what could have been a disastrous opening night lots of people started booking to come in groups.

The problem, however, was the chef I had. He was recommended to me by someone I knew who was a chef himself but this guy was not very organised nor very professional so before long he was showing his true colours. He would turn up late and always with an excuse, for me this was not acceptable as good time keeping was always essential and I expected at least that from such a key staff. If I was not at the restaurant he would turn up late, spend a lot of time chasing the waitresses and didn't work as hard as he should, so I made it clear to him that if he didn't buckle down he would be looking for another job and he didn't so he got sacked.

However we had many bookings, people would ring up and book most tables for the August opening period through to December – December was always going to be busy, you knew that as people were coming in and booking for groups of four, six and for larger groups for the Christmas parties.

So my Jamaican chef seeing the large number of bookings decided he was sick and wouldn't turn up for work. I could see the pattern, as he was always sick when the restaurant was booked out. This meant that a lot of money was spent on emergency cover and I had to go into the kitchen myself to help out and get one of the waitresses from the dining room to assist in the kitchen also.

Eventually, I got fed up with his malingering so I sacked him and told him to leave the premises immediately. He said he was going to do this that and the other to me, so I told him to do whatever he damn well liked but he was fired. I warned him, "Don't come back here not even as customer as you will not be welcome." So off he went in a huff. In desperation I got an agency to send me a cover chef. As it turned out, a white guy who swore on somebody's grave that he could do the job, give me a try he said, "I can cook West Indian food", but that wasn't his main problem. His problem was that he was a homosexual who liked to broadcast his sexuality and the staff found out – you know what Jamaicans are like – they found out and started to band it around the restaurant that the chef was gay. There was a big commotion and it created a huge problem, as during that time there was a lot of ignorance about homosexuality and AIDS were considered synonymous.

His cooking was OK, he wasn't worse than the other guy and it was not too difficult as he had a Jamaican cook to help him. That Jamaican cook did all the essential Jamaican stuff like the rice and peas, ackee and saltfish, and so on. So the Jamaican cook would come in, cook up the rice and peas, do the plain rice and it was just left for the chef to do the fish and the other main dishes and plate up. If you wanted brown-stew chicken, it's the sauce that makes the dish, and that was his job.

Anyway, this obsession with his personal life was hurting the business so eventually I had to sack him as well. I said to the agency look, I really don't want someone who's a time-waster as I had to sack two chefs because one was a malingering, woman-chasing-time waster and the other was not pulling his weight, and the constant promotion of his sexual orientation was too much of a distraction. So, the agency sent me a French Creole chef, who was pretty dam good and hard working. He was a French black guy who was in this country to learn the language and gain further cooking experience. Well, he didn't need it; he was an absolutely fantastic chef and fitted in perfectly. He did wonderful things with tomatoes, making flowers and so on as garnishes, and cooking nouvelle cuisine and all that stuff that customers love and he did lovely things with the desserts and with the soups at the start of the meal. His presentation was exceptional. People were happy with the chef; they were coming back to the restaurant in large numbers. But, as it turned out, he had to go back to France and so I was with this Jamaican cook in the kitchen for a couple weeks while we looked for his replacement.

I also had a Vietnamese guy, Wang, working in the kitchen supporting the chef: washing the plates, cleaning up, basically assisting the French chef so when he left Wang approached me and said, "Mr Walker, I can do good work as chef, I can do that easy. I watch the chef and I can do what he did."

So I asked, "Are you sure about that Wang?"

He said yes, it's easy. Now I am always prepared to give anyone willing to work the chance so I said, "OK, Wang, let's see how you get on. We have a couple of big parties coming tonight, crack that and you are the chef."

So, he washed his hands, put on the chef's uniform and proved to be an excellent replacement for the French chef. Wang was good at what he did so he was officially employed as the chef and was paid accordingly.

However, by then I was having trouble balancing the books as more was going out than coming in and coupled with the problems I was having with the previous chefs and other staff was hurting the business. I would hire and probably sack the same people the following week. I was starting to worry about the survival of the business and the people I was supposed to rely on were irritating me. For example, this guy hired to clean the front of the restaurant kept saying to me, "I don't want anybody to see me cleaning the front of the shop." So I just said, OK, forget it, you can go and don't bother coming back," And I just did the cleaning myself.

At the beginning I was employing all black people in the kitchen and as waitresses in the dining areas until I got so fed up with them that I got rid of all of them and employed a whole set of new waitresses, all blondes.

One evening, this Jamaican guy came into the restaurant with his "Daata" (girlfriend) on his arm. After his meal he looked around at the waitresses and said to me, "A West Indian restaurant this?" "Yes sir, that's what it says!"

"So how come you no have no black people a serve?"

So I asked him, "You happy with the food and the atmosphere, sir?"

He said, "Yea, man, food nice, place nice!" So I asked, "What about the service?"

He said, "Service good, man." So I said, "That's all that matters then, isn't it?"

You used to have that sort of thing from the women too. I think they were genuinely upset not to have any black sisters about for a good natter. But I was trying to run a restaurant not a charity convention.

However, Wang was reliable, competent and hard working. He would even get in two hours before opening and within an hour all the meal preparations were ready: all the onions and garlic were chopped, and when he was ready to start everything was prepared and ready to go.

Wang used to say, "Ready boss! No problem, anything else let me know boss."

Unfortunately, apart from the barman the others were a complete waste of space. The first night, Wang had one of the girls helping him and she was quite happy to do that, as she preferred to be in the kitchen rather than in the dining area. Wang was fantastic with his assistants until I was able to find a replacement for her.

But, it became clear that the business was becoming very challenging and I worked out that within six months the business would fold and leave us bankrupt if I did not take action immediately, so I put into action steps which eventually enabled me to sell up without suffering too badly and making sure Wang was looked after with money and a similar job elsewhere.

The business ran for two Christmases or just 19 months before I had to sell. The main cause for the eventual failure was the unreliability of most of the staff at the beginning; not only were they stealing from the business, but they were not willing or able to perform up to acceptable standards.

I had never before experienced such dishonesty nor could I realise how cunning and inventive employees could be in pilfering food, drinks and money out of the restaurant. Eventually I learnt, but by then it was too late to save the Arawak.

A lot of my customers were people from television. I was quite proud to see well-known faces in the restaurant most weekends together with patrons from the ITC and their friends. Some known faces from the world of football did turn up at weekends with their WAGS, and of course the reggae singers like Desmond Decker and Delroy Wilson, from the Caribbean who, I was told, would turn up regularly to enjoy the food and the ambiance.

A lot of our customers saw it as *their* restaurant and they were all proud to take friends and colleagues to the Arawak Inn to sample all it had to offer. It was apparently the meeting place for the upwardly mobile black professional community. Every evening myself and the rest of my dining room staff would dress up in black bow ties, white shirt and black pants or skirts in the case of the girls and perform our hosting duties to the highest standards.

Before opening, the shop front would be washed and cleaned and the sandwich board placed in front to signal we were open for business.

On duty as a manager at the Arawak Inn

There was a Jamaican painter touring the UK and some of his British friends took him to the Arawak and he too was so impressed with the whole thing he asked if he could use the restaurant to display his expensive paintings.

Of course I accepted as they did add a bit more culture and class to the place. The customers offered to purchase the paintings and as some were sold replacements were put in their place.

The restaurant was open mainly in the evenings and although there were requests for a lunchtime service, I found the extra opening would increase my costs and drive down any profit potential, although we did open for lunchtime business during the month of December for obvious reason.

We were even offered contracts for weddings and office parties but we mainly operated within our comfort zone as trying to do everything would bring down standards. And without reliable staff, you can't stretch too far so a number of requests had to be declined.

I did have a few very successful wedding receptions, as the French chef was very good at putting that together and made the event a success and a memorable experience for the guests. People enjoyed that which led to even more bookings. As word spread far and wide proprietors of other Caribbean restaurants came to check out the competition. They too were impressed and so introduced themselves and talked about the business and its future.

There was another established Caribbean restaurant I was told about in east London called the Plantation Inn which I was encouraged to visit but although the food was not bad, it was more compact and not really to the Arawak standard.

As a result of our popularity, the magazines Vogue and Harpers and Queen chose to visit the Arawak Inn to do a write up. However, they seemed to concentrate on my origins and upbringing rather than the restaurant and what it had to offer, so they wrote mostly about me having come from the ghettos of Kingston. Anyway, possibly as a result of the article we were visited by a black jazz group from either Sweden or Denmark who fell in love with the place and asked if they could perform around the piano bar area for a few weeks and, as they were prepared to work mostly for free, I agreed. Would you believe they heard about the Arawak Inn in Scandinavia, came all that way, saw it, liked it and asked if they could stay and play for free at weekends.

So they played the piano, a saxophone and guitar on Friday and Saturday nights. The music was very good so I paid them a small retainer with food and drinks thrown in, their best offer to date, and the customers loved their performance.

Anyway, I had to make arrangements for the demise of the Arawak Inn otherwise I would have gone under for sure as we were sinking despite the impression of success. My understanding was that not only would the creditors take the business away but they would take my house as well.

At one stage I was financing the business with my credit cards and after a good night I would end up counting the takings and finding out that some of the money taken were forgeries. I didn't take many cheques, 1 would take credit cards but a lot of the large notes were forged and some credit card payments too, although the companies had given authorisation and would eventually pay up. I don't know if this type of cheating had something to do with the staff but I used to lose a lot of money that way. Lots of counterfeit money was passing through the restaurant I suspect some individuals but had no proof so I couldn't act on my suspicions.

I decided to sell and I set the scene by phoning friends and family to come by for free drinks and free food during the slow periods, usually Mondays, Tuesdays and some Thursdays. The idea was to make the restaurant look popular through out the week so that whoever was buying felt comfortable about the investment, so on nights when business was slow, I would invite people round to give the right impression.

So that was what happened to me at the end of the eighties, when recession was taking hold and job numbers were falling. So I was left thinking, how the hell am I going to get out of this? Even if I managed to sell up, I was going to be left owing a lot of money.

On top of all that, something dark and mysterious was apparently going on which was having a detrimental effect on the business. It was the last thing I expected to hear mentioned in a modern place like London.

29

Like the Plague

Now, I used to have a cleaner from Guyana, South America. Very nice lady, she used to clean the restaurant each morning but would spend most of the time talking to me about anything and everything.

However, she got it in her head that people around me were envious and that they were "obeahing" me to hurt the business. Edith did talk a lot about obeah, that is witchcraft or what some people called black magic, but she couldn't convince me as I don't believe in such things. Then strange things started happening, suddenly mice and rats invaded the place and I thought "Oh, my gosh! What do I do now?" but this is not too unusual with restaurants in London.

I remember one evening when the restaurant was in full swing and as I walked towards the bar I saw a couple of things scurry by. I asked myself, "What was that?" Then I thought, it can't be. But, yes, there were mice in the restaurant.

I was anxiously looking around hoping customers hadn't noticed and praying for the session to end without incident so I could make arrangements to deal with them. As soon the restaurant closed, I got the staff to investigate where and how they were coming into the dining area and went to seek help the following morning from a firm of vermin exterminators.

They came round swiftly, investigated the problem and found a couple of holes in the floorboards covered by some loose carpets where the mice were coming in. They also looked underneath the dumb waiter and there they discovered a colony of mice, I couldn't believe my bad luck.

However, after some thought, the exterminators said that they could eradicate the mice but they reckoned that the problem originated from food falling off the dumb waiter and cautioned that all staff must make a determined effort to ensure that the four sides of the dumb waiter were properly shut when food or dirty plates were being sent from and to the kitchen. If not, their effort to eradicate the mice would be a temporary solution and they would be back.

We closed the restaurant for a few days while the holes were repaired, poison put down and the entire restaurant fumigated. I was quite upset by the careless attitude of the people working both in the kitchen as well as in the dining area, so after the restaurant was cleaned I called a staff meeting and gave instructions to all the staff that this should not be repeated and that I would be checking the dumb water for any lapse of concentration, the consequence of which would be termination. I think this speech did focus their minds.

It appears the staff from the kitchen used to put the food in the lift, close the door to one side without ensuring the other sides were also closed. The lift was then sent down to the dining room and not only did the food get cold going down from the kitchen, but food regularly fell off unto the ground below causing the pest problem, this also meant delays in customers getting their orders. I was not prepared to accept any excuses, so I made it clear that next time it happened staff would be sacked.

Anyway, eventually, I managed to get Wang to take care of all that. However, one morning I went into the kitchen and there were a couple of big rats – not mice, rats – in there. I got a shock as I thought all that problem had been resolved, so I was thinking, "How did they get in the kitchen is someone trying to sabotage the business?"

The place was supposed to be sealed and the lift properly closed. But what happened is that rats can climb and what these damned people did was to leave the lift door open after they had filled it with dirty dishes just before they went home, so the rats must have come in by climbing up the side.

Others speculated that maybe it was the boxes used to buy in foodstuff from Spitalfields market that caused the problem. The thinking was that when the boxes came into the restaurant they might have rats from the tropics in there and that they would sneak out when the boxes were opened.

Whatever their origins, those rats were brave and quite smart and I couldn't get rid of them for a long time. I tried putting down poison, they didn't take it. I tried everything suggested to me but they didn't take any of it. I tried food with poison hidden inside – they somehow avoided those too. I couldn't understand how rats could know what was inside, but somehow they got to the food without taking the poison hidden inside it.

I told the staff that at the end of each session they were to make sure everything was spotless: the plates washed and put away, surfaces cleaned, all foodstuffs securely locked away in the fridges, waste put in bin-bags and taken off the premises, and the kitchen closed off. We had a good regime going for a while but even with no other food about the rats never took the poison. And I thought how will I ever catch these bloody rats? And it happened by accident.

Well, the washing up sink was made of steel and was very deep. On one particular occasion the kitchen staff left greasy plates soaking in water and the rats must have climbed up there, slipped into the water and with all that grease in the sink, and being so slippery they just couldn't get out.

In the morning when I got in I saw these two massive rats drowned, I presumed, from exhaustion trying to get out of the sink.

I pulled them out the sink, put them in some bin bags, wrapped into more bags, still more bags and went down the road and dumped the carcases in a couple of dustbins. Afterwards, we got the place professionally cleaned and pest free.

However, some time later the restaurant was again infested this time by cockroaches and this convinced my cleaner Edith who kept saying to me, "Mr Walker you should look after yourself because dem people a obeah you."

My thoughts were that someone may have been spiteful and had come in with a few of these pests and had left them there and they had just multiplied. I didn't take her seriously at all but I appreciated her concerns. Instead, I tried to find reasons

– there had to be a logical explanation. I mean, ok, I had lots of enemies, probably the people I had sacked. People had stabbed my tyres out of spite or revenge in the past and on several occasions after closing I would go to my van only to find four flat tyres, but obeah? I didn't think so.

Once again I had to get in the exterminators and this time it took a while longer to resolve. We had to rip up all the floor covering in the kitchen, re-cover disinfect and seal everything and ensure that the entire foodstuff was safely locked away.

All this was costing me additional money that I could hardly afford together with staff pilfering compounding the problem. The staff, as I found out later, were pilfering food or taking cash received for the sale of brandy and replacing those bottles, and doing other illegal things, such as passing funny money which I'm sure they had brought in or arranged the scam with friends.

Now, with the place fumigated, things were going fine again. Wang proved to be a very good chef; very reliable, was always on time and did his job very well, so I was now feeling positive about the business.

Then, after all these problems, one Sunday morning I went in to check the state of the restaurant because, after Saturday night, you needed to have Sunday to do a big clean up.

When I got in I noticed a swarm of flies in the building. In fact, there were flies everywhere and blocking the light from the mezzanine window. I couldn't understand how they could be so many or how they could possibly have got through the glass as the place was sealed. Mice, rats, cockroaches and now flies – it sounds like the plagues of Egypt from that story of Moses in the Bible.

So I'm now very concerned and wondering how these flies got in? Then it dawned on me, the task ahead. I started thinking, bloody hell how do I get rid of these things?

You couldn't clearly see the mezzanine – there was lots of glass and, normally, you could see out through the windows into the Save the Children charity's yard next door. But not this time, the place was now black with flies! And I'm suddenly thinking obeah! Somebody must have obeahed me.

By now my mother was persuaded that's what it was and my West Indian cleaner was convinced about it all along and so she chatted with my mother about what she was certain was witchcraft being used to ruin you boy.

Edith came over to me and said, "Huh, you see those flies? A sign of obeah, you know." That was when I thought to myself, "Maybe she's right." What else could I think?

She told my mother, "dem a obeah you son. Him naa pay any mind to me so you must tell him." However, by this stage I was resigned to my cleaner's conviction. However, the immediate task was to get rid of the latest pests, so I turn on the lights and got the vacuum cleaner and started to work on those flies.

It took me about an hour to vacuum them up and get rid of the Hoover bags outside. Flies had completely covered the windows. I don't know what the attraction was, maybe it was something to do with the light at the window, but they covered every inch of glass.

Thankfully, the vacuum cleaner sucked them all in and I took the bag outside and put it into a random dustbin – not my dustbin – came back in and did more vacuuming. Eventually, I got rid of those accursed flies. I then opened up some windows to let in fresh air and to let out any other flies that I had missed.

After that experience my mum and some of her friends decided that I should go to have a "reading" with this woman who was a psychic and at this stage I thought I might as well because everything is against me; I had almost given in. The staff were not to be trusted; rats and cockroaches had invaded, and now flies and despite my strong will I was now feeling quite depressed as I saw myself on the slippery road to bankruptcy.

I decided I must go and hear what this woman has to say. The lady looked at my hands and said: "Nothing wrong with you, you know. You will be all right. Yea, you gonna be all right."

If she had said something bad that might have pushed me over the edge but she said it was going to be OK which to me was a great relief. Her words gave my confidence a boost and now I felt reassured.

She asked if I wanted to get some anointing or something like that but I wasn't into that. I was quite happy to listen to what she had to say, although she didn't say whether I had been a victim of obeah or not. Maybe she might have said it to my mum and to Edith the cleaner but she didn't say it to me. She just gave me the reassurance I needed, so that was enough for me.

30

Hurricane

After that experience I decided I was getting out of the business. I told myself I had six months, because I usually do my projecting that way. I reckoned that in six months' time if I didn't sell I would definitely be bankrupt, and hence losing the things I cherished most.

So, I went to see my accountant and asked if I could sign over the house into my wife's name but he advised that at this stage I couldn't. If I had done that some time ago, maybe, but the taxman was going to interpret that it was an intentional ploy to avoid my financial liabilities.

I thought, well, I suppose I have to bite the bullet, face the music and sort out the problem. I eventually managed to do what I said I would – sell up. A French guy bought the restaurant together with the other levels above the shop using the collateral on his house.

It was a nice restaurant and I thought a good buy providing whoever took it over was prepared to put in the effort, and anyway the property was freehold, which was a bonus. So that was how I got out of that.

I was particularly fortunate, as I'd had a heart attack while I was struggling to survive in the business. I used to drive home after the restaurant closed, usually around 2 am, but sometimes I used to have to go and do the shopping at Spitalfields in the early morning just after I closed the doors. For the drinks, I had to go to a cash and carry warehouse in Dartford, which was over 15 miles away. Sometimes they would deliver but often they wouldn't, so I had to go and collect the order myself.

I also had to make sure the restaurant was cleaned every day, either early in the morning or late afternoon. So I had to do or supervised all those jobs and still be around to ensure that the shop-front is washed and glass windows cleaned inside as well as outside before opening up to customers. I didn't have any friends or relatives working with me so I could not always depend on my staff to do a good job if I was not on the premises, and if staff were absent I would have to do the work myself until I could find replacements.

Apparently, Indian and Chinese family restaurants survive because the staff is like an extension of themselves, but it's quite different within the West Indian community; we don't operate like that. Individuals have got their jobs and that's their independence. If a family member happens to have a business, it's their look out, they will hardly get the help and support which is commonplace in those other communities. So, it's all up to me and it was not fair to ask the wife to give up her job and, anyhow, I thought that if the business didn't work out then we at least had her income to fall back on until I could sort myself out; although on occasions when we were either over-booked or the chef was sick I would get in my sister-in-law (when we were on good terms), my wife and her brother-in-law to help in the kitchen and at the bar.

When Beverly came to help out she'd bring the little one, who was a toddler by now, in tow and he would be round the back of the bar area and those waitresses would let him have as many toffee sweets as he liked. He'd be filling himself up with the after-dinner chocolates and after he ate as many as he could manage, he'd just fall asleep right there.

Apart from the occasional help, it was just me and a couple of loyal staff. So after closing I'd be going home sometimes as late as three in the morning. Although the restaurant door was shut at midnight, we would have some customers come in just before closing wanting to have cocktails so I would just close the door and they would drink and chat. I would stay with them and eventually, maybe at three in the morning, I'd get rid of them and go home.

Because of the late nights I would sometimes stay upstairs in the flat until the next day. There was a bed and other basic comforts up there, and the wife would ring me at a particular time the next morning to wake me for my trip to the market. It was hard work, and that soon began to take its toll on my health.

I gave the car to the wife and bought a post office van which I used around town to collect shopping etc. The police used to stop me a lot because of the bad state of the van and I suppose the sacked staff were always stabbing the tyres or damaging the bodywork at every opportunity; so they got their own back that way.

I remember one morning on my way up to London to get to the market, having had only a couple of hours sleep, I passed out right there in the traffic jam. I somehow managed to move the van to the side of the road. It took me about fifteen minutes to recover my senses. I'd collapsed and recovered to find people blowing their horns and staring at me. I quickly parked the van on the side of the road and went for a brisk walk, breathed deeply and swinging my arms in a desperate attempt to relax before getting back into the van to complete my journey to work. I decided it didn't matter what happened, the business must go on as long as I was able to walk and talk.

It was after that incident that I noticed I had gone down from 12 to 9 stones. It was work, work, work, with no food to sustain me as I didn't seem to have the time to sit and have a plate of food even though I worked in a restaurant, ironic as that may sound, because at times it seems I was doing everybody's job as well as paying them.

In the evenings when I opened up, we had to be looking good and eager to please. I had to do that despite my problems but it was tough at times and that incident did make me realise that I had to pack it in for my physical well-being as well as my financial good.

However, another stressful situation was caused by the alarm system which I had installed, mainly as a reassurance for the staff, with a panic button facility, and as a deterrent against anyone breaking in. The system automatically alerted the local police to any serious incidents and they would respond by checking at the restaurant or by ringing me at home.

Sometimes, when I got home thinking my job was done for that day I would be contacted by the police, so I would have to go back to the restaurant only to find that a member of staff had not closed a window properly and the wind had set off the alarm.

However, on this particular night I made sure that everything was locked before I set off home in my car. Very tired, I was looking forward to my bed: I could see the bed waiting for me. I was driving over Blackheath Hill when suddenly the car started swerving and going out of control but I just kept driving, then I felt like the vehicle was being lifted off the ground. I was so tired I thought maybe that had something to do with my erratic driving.

So, I continued home to Slade Green and staggered into the house, but as soon as I got in and was about to have a hot drink, the police rang to tell me that the alarm had gone off and they thought someone might have broken into the restaurant. Could I go and make it stop?

I said yea, OK, but after replacing the receiver I decided that I am much too tired to be bothered with that; let them break in, take what they want, the place is insured anyway. Damn it, I'm not going back now. But guess what? It was the right decision as it was that night that the hurricane that had not been forecasted struck in 1987. Apparently, I was just in front of the full onslaught of the storm all the way home. So, it was the wind moving the car and lifting it off the ground like that and I'd got home just in time. Suddenly, there was thunder, lightning and driving rain beating down outside, suddenly everything was blacked out, and the electricity had gone. The lightning was so vicious and the clapping of thunder was so frightening, and when I looked out I could see the trees being violently shaken and branches being snapped off and despite the thick velvet curtains, the glare of the lightning was getting through and illuminating the rooms.

I was drunk with sleep and with all that violence going on outside: the howling winds, the cracking of thunder and not to mention the rain, I thought I'm definitely not going back out there. Then it got worse as it was a full-blown hurricane but of course we hadn't expected one. After all, this is England, not Jamaica.

The next day, we found that roofs had been blown off and scores of trees blown down. Sevenoaks became One Oak (that was the running joke) and the roads were impassable.

I was lucky, our house was hardly damaged but the next door neighbour's roof was off. There were bits of roof and fallen trees in the street, no electricity, no heating, nothing. So everyone became very neighbourly and some who had gas were boiling water in pots and taking them over to those who didn't, and people were very united in the aftermath of this disaster.

Later in the morning I thought I might as well go up to Camberwell Green to find out what had happened to the restaurant, but I found my route blocked as all those uprooted trees were blocking the main roads. What! So I tried another route: more trees; another route: closed off. Eventually, I went back to the first route and by then the council workers were there with their chain saws cutting and removing tree trunks from the main road. I managed to get through and got to the Arawak Inn.

Here, I wasn't so lucky; the big awning across the shop-front was down the road wrapped around the top of a lamppost. The whole of the upstairs was smashed – oh it was a disaster! It was a dreadful sight, like a small bomb had exploded in there.

Anyway, I got on to the awning company and they came and took it off the lamp post and took it away to make repairs. The glass people came eventually, as there were so many people waiting for their services, to repair and replace windows. The electricity people eventually came and got the electrics working again, and with perseverance and a lot of expenditure I eventually got the restaurant fixed up, but it was off limits and out of business for over two weeks.

Most of the neighbouring businesses were in the same position. It's strange isn't it? Some were lucky, not a lot happened to them and others, like myself, had quite a bit of repairs and cleaning up to do.

It could have been worse because right at the back of the Arawak was a big tree bending towards the restaurant which, if it had toppled, would have fallen into the patio smashing through the restaurant, destroying the toilets and dining areas and probably ending up in the road at the front of the building.

The tree was just about standing in its roots – if you had pushed it, it would have fallen over, so I had the tree professionally removed and put in an emergency exit door leading into the backyard to the Save the Children property, as suggested by the local fire officer.

When I eventually completed the sale of the restaurant I went straight home to sleep and I slept for a whole day and a half. Beverly told visitors not to disturb me. "Don't wake him up. Let him sleep; he needs it."

It was great! It was so refreshing and liberating just to relieve my mind from all the trials and tribulations, if only for a day or so. It was only after I woke up that I realised how exhausted I had been.

31

Starting Over

So with the restaurant business sold, I am starting to think, what do I do now? Luckily I'd got out before it all went belly up, but that had been my livelihood. What next? Well, I had committed to a house down the road from the restaurant and with the sale of the restaurant completed I now have money to pay off most of my credit cards which had piled up during my struggles. I paid most of those off and had a few thousands left which was just enough for the deposit on the house in Camberwell Green and a little spending money left over.

So there I was with an empty house and an overgrown garden which needed serious attention. I knew nothing about landscaping and at the back the weeds were over six feet high and the neighbours now have someone to complain to about the back garden looking like a jungle. I got to work chopping my way from the back of the house to the other end of the garden and this made a big difference although not perfect.

This must have been at the bottom of the recession cycle because not many people were buying properties and although I wanted to buy the house next door as well, unfortunately my finances could not stretch that far even though I could see the rental potential and the eventual capital gain possibilities when we eventually climbed out of the downturn.

I had a car which was given to me by some Australians who could not pay their bill at the restaurant one night. They had come in to drink cocktails but drank so many that they didn't have enough money to clear the bill, so they offered me this funny French car instead which they had parked in front of the restaurant.

The Australians offered me the keys and documents *in lieu* of payment as they were going back to Australia in a few days anyway. So I accepted and took possession of the vehicle.

I had that car parked in the garage of the new house and, once I'd done some refurbishment, I decided to advertise the house for sale with car in garage thrown in, this generated a lot of interest and after a lot of hassle and false starts a guy came and gave me the full asking price, so, that was a result.

I could now relax for a bit without having to worry too much about money, but to keep my interest in work I went up the road from my home in Slade Green to an ESSO petrol station to ask for a job as an attendant. I had to do something and in any event, the money I got from the sale of the house would not last forever.

The Indian proprietor offered me the job but stressed that I would have to work weekends and nights. I realised that was the most difficult time, but I agreed to his terms and conditions and accepted the challenge.

So he showed me how to do things: how to count the money and put it through this hole in the side of the safe, which had a chute but no keys. After about four weeks the manager was both pleased and surprised at my performance on the job.

"You're doing very well", he said, "would you like to run this station?"

He even promised to increase my pay but I did not want more stress so soon after the Arawak and, besides, I would want a permanent job to be more office-based and paying a lot more money so I told him I'd think about it.

In the meantime, he sent me to another petrol station in Crayford where I worked for a while with some Tamil people from Sri Lanka.

Late nights I had to deal with all these weirdoes who took pleasure in abusing me: "Bloody black so and so" or they would fill up with petrol and drive off. I would take down the registration number and ring the manager and leave it for him to sort out.

It wasn't too long before 1 reasoned that although I didn't have an alternative job I would have to own the business to tolerate such hassle so I declined his offer to manage one of his petrol stations. On the other hand, I needed to do something that was going to earn me a regular income; so one morning as

I was driving up to London to look for work and with the radio on in the background I became aware of a particular jingle. It was an advert for an insurance company.

"Do you want to make thousands? Come and join us at Allied Dunbar." So I took the number and gave them a call and was invited to an interview at their offices in North Row opposite Selfridges in central London.

The interviewers were very positive about everything, saying things like: "You can make thousands working here. You can make serious money in this business." I did a multiple choice test and they gave me some sales material to read and said that if I passed they would send me down to Swindon to their main training centre.

I passed the test and went home to consult with the family. I asked my wife, "Do you want me to do this? It's going to be late nights, you won't see me most of the time because I will be out chasing business and I won't have weekends off either but they say I will make a good living."

Bev as always was very supportive, so I went to Swindon and there were all these people from all over the kingdom all speaking in such different regional accents it took some time to understand them, and it seemed that the only commonality was the broad English language.

In the training room the first thing we had to do was introduce ourselves to the other delegates and give a brief synopsis of our life. Some had been in the army, some had been redundant from large blue chip organisations, some were working professionals and others were dustmen or taxi drivers; a very mixed bag indeed from a cross section of our society.

Afterwards, we had to take another test to consolidate the day's training. We were then taken on for two weeks of intensive training leading to the final test and qualification to become financial advisers.

After the first week in Swindon I took the test and failed, I was supposed to get 70 per cent but instead I get 65 per cent, so I was sent back home and my report got sent to the branch manager for the process to start all over again. Anyway on the

Looking dapper at a "Kestrel" convention

second attempt I passed the various tests and went back to the branch to do the job for real.

Training on the job involved a further three weeks of mentoring by the branch manager. My Manager said, "There's a desk over there, you can share it. There is a phone, you can share that too." That desk "over there" is for a "Kestrel" and you're not allowed to use it because that privileged person is at that level because last year he made £30K worth of commission, so he's a Kestrel – a high flyer. "Remember, you're not supposed to use his space." And in that room there's also a "Falcon". Don't go in there either because Falcons are high achievers, but there are other desks over there, presumably for the plebs, if no one's using them, you can use one for that day; first come first served. At the end of each day you're expected to remove all your stuff leaving the desk clear.

I asked where were the clients I am supposed to see and was told, "Well, there's a telephone and a directory. All those people are potential customers." So you had to work it out for yourself".

Oh my gosh, it was quite a challenge, it was hard! The job itself involved cold calling people you have never met and of course you got people telling you to "F*** off!" And that was for me an eye-opener, as I have never been abused like that before on the phone.

I started scratching my head. It's all about your ability and application they said. I began to fear that it wasn't going to work and they don't pay you at the end of the month if you don't produce results; it's all based on your ability to survive.

There I was, thrown in with a pack of hungry wolves without any assistance. I rang up all my ex-colleagues from the ITC and not many of them were interested but I pointed out to them that we had known nothing about pensions during our time at the Tin Council and so I managed to persuade a few of them to take out a policy or two. That's how I started to build a client bank. I then asked those clients to refer my services to others and I also started to investigate other avenues. My wife had attended Imperial College as a student and she had an Alumni book with all these now qualified, professional individuals, hence good-quality prospects with their names, date they attended the college, and so on. This was a rich vein of prospecting and so I started calling them.

"How do I know you?" was the common response.

"Well, you don't but my wife was at Imperial College with you and she's part of your alumni. I am just calling to introduce myself, my company and to request a meeting to offer a free financial review to see if there is anything we can help you with." With that patter I got three big clients and so I continued to build this all-important client bank, earn some commission and at least get paid.

32

Heart Attack

So now with all this pressure heaped on me I had a heart attack while driving to a sales meeting one bleak winter's morning. I just slumped over the wheel of my car and could hardly move but just before the attack I had felt pins and needles everywhere up my arms. I'd had a mild heart attack before when I was running the restaurant, but I'd more or less ignored that and just got on with things. This was another heart attack, which happened while I was working for Allied Dunbar under this great pressure to achieve certain targets.

I was working on commission and had to produce monthly quotas of business in order to get money to pay my bills. To achieve that, I was rushing all over London and the south east, in all weathers, trying to speak to prospective customers; and I was working Sunday to Sunday, seven days a week and as many hours as possible.

I'd be coming home sometimes at twelve midnight exhausted, then eat a full stomach before collapsing in bed through exhaustion, and of course you're going to get a heart attack because you're not getting any relaxation or exercise, sounds familiar?

I am heading out into the country to see another client or "prospect" and driving whilst eating my lunch – it was the same thing every day: lunch on the move just to get in the business. So it was tough, coupled with all the additional pressures that the managers were putting on me; they were like the ringmaster in a circus as there income depended on our production.

Each year we had to tell the managers what our projected target was going to be – that itself was a rod for your back. They then set the annual target for you where you had to achieve one twelfth of that each month which translated into you speaking to a defined number of people each day to achieve a required number of appointments which, hopefully, would translate into actual business transactions each month. It was pressure, pressure, pressure.

Every week we had a 1:1 meeting as they wanted to know how we were doing, how many people we'd spoken to, how many appointments we'd actually made, how many appointments were successful and how much business was generated. They were constantly on our backs because a lot of managers were on this over-ride, which meant that every hundred pounds you made they would get a percentage of that, which was a major part of their income in addition to sales they were allowed to make, so they were constantly behind you, pushing you to do more and more for their bank account.

The people who become managers were those who not only relished the status of being a manager, but they had the opportunity to access "orphan" clients – customers who were not assigned to any particular advisers- and they were sales people themselves. They had first choice of all these unassigned clients, so the managers would go through the files and choose those clients more likely to generate further income for them: mostly people who had invested large amounts in the past or were currently with big insurance policies or who had substantial pension funds were targeted.

That sort of prospect provided "a good opportunity to churn" – churning being where they cancelled one policy and replaced it with another. To justify the new sale was always easy to come by, the usual one being that the replacement was "cheaper". People always heeded their advice and would take a replacement policy because it was supposed to be cheaper, but maybe in the small print they would lose some plan features important to the clients. The clients don't understand nor realise that you only get what you pay for and that there is no such thing as "a free lunch".

But in any case, the managers would get their initial commission as this change of policy was now considered new business and whoever had sold to the customer in the first place found himself out of pocket.

I was up against all that and then if you were not reaching the prescribed targets you were made to look like a failure. So I was thinking that to be successful one had to be a little dishonest and that the more crooked you were the more successful you were likely to become, particularly in this business.

In the late 1990s when the expensive London branches were sold off because of the heavy overheads, those successful advisers, the ones making thousands of pounds regularly were allowed to stay in the remaining offices in central London while plebs like myself had to go out into the sticks where some branches had relocated. So I was sent to Crawley in Surrey, and I was driving out into the country every day and during the winter life in the provinces was not very nice. The roads were icy and lonely, sometimes you were driving in fog and you couldn't see where you were going and there were many crashes particularly on the motorways.

These areas were foreign to me and none of the people out there looked like me. I tried to do business in Crawley but it wasn't possible because people out there were a bit snobbish and the body language was not encouraging. It was clear that most didn't want to deal with people of colour.

If I got an appointment it would be after people got home from their London jobs at about 8 pm, and then I would be leaving their houses at around 11.30 pm to drive all the way back to my home in south London.

So it was hard, and as it was often clear that there was no business to be had at the end of those marathon meetings, I approached the manager and told him, "Look, this is not working. I would like to be in an office close to where I live with people I feel comfortable working with". I think he got the message.

Around this time, Allied Dunbar was planning to open a branch in Bromley, so I went to talk to the manager there and was accepted on board. However, managers had the same attitude wherever you were so one had to be very cautious as they had all the cards in their hands and could and did use their privileged positions with impunity, such as "Good Practice Assessment" argument to re-broke your business.

There was nothing you could do about it; it was dog eat dog but most of us plebs were working at a disadvantage. You had the difficulty of finding your prospects in the first place, then working steadily to change them into clients, only to find that some other guy had stabbed you in the back and stolen your clients and hence your commission. If it was not your colleague, it was the so-called manager or trainee manager. In the end, you'd gone through all that process for nothing because they would be the ones getting paid.

They would ring your clients on the pretext that they were checking the suitability of the product or to ensure everything was in order with the sale and that the customer was happy with his purchase and with your service. Sometimes they would put doubts in your client's mind just to get them to cancel your policy and take out new ones with them.

Often, the clients thought that since we were representing the same organisation everything must have been ok if changes were made, but unbeknown to them, we only operated under the same brand name, within that we were all self-employed individuals struggling in the same fishpond surrounded by hungry sharks called managers or colleagues. We may have been occupying the same building, but that's where the similarity ends. We each paid for the stationery, the space we occupied, even the IT support and branch staff.

We all wanted orphans as they were "warm prospects", but only the privileged, devious or cunning ones got them and, in some cases, they were used by the managers as a bargaining chip to attract new advisers to their branch as branch production determine conventions and bonuses.

In my case, the only orphans I ever got were the ones where little information was available about the client or where it gave the impression that there was no business to be had, but I would go through these and make appointments hoping I would get lucky.

After all, we called it prospecting and the harder you dug the closer you'd get to something worthwhile. In the end I realised what they had done – what are you going to sell a 90-

year-old man? He's not going to put his money into long-term investments nor will he want life assurance, pension or a mortgage.

They'd creamed off the good prospects and given me the crap, but I did use that crap to make the appointments because although the prospect may not have been right for what you had to offer, he might have had a daughter or son who was going to inherit that house and may need advice on insurance or investments or may even have had a young family to protect.

I was using my initiative but that kind of scenario didn't happen often because the manager would go through the file and worked out that this 90-year-old man had no children to inherit anything before passing the client on to me.

On the rare occasion my colleagues and I in the sales team would strike it lucky. One adviser did ring what appeared to be a hopeless case and he got an investment of £290,000, thus earning himself £9,000 commission.

The manager had missed that one and he was gutted when he found out. The managers were livid when that case had eluded them, so after that they made sure their secretaries rang and checked people out before passing on the files to the sales team.

It was because of all that constant pressure that I had my second heart attack. On the day of this attack I was driving through Sidcup on my way to this sales meeting in Croydon and, as usual, I was rushing to get there on time.

Suddenly, I felt faint and with a feeling of pins and needles all over my arm and I could not move. I think I passed out momentarily at the wheel before I managed to get the car to the pavement and stopped in the bus lane.

I tried as best I could to attract the attention of a passer-by to get me an ambulance so this woman call the emergency services. Luckily, the hospital was only about five or ten minutes up the road and within minutes I heard the siren as an ambulance arrived with its lights flashing.

I was taken to Queen Mary's hospital where I spent two days while doctors did a full health check. The consultant advised that I was under too much pressure and needed to calm down and that there had been a heart murmur which needed to be investigated further.

After a couple of days I was sent home with instructions to attend an appointment at St Thomas hospital in central London. The consultants there did further investigations where they inserted a camera up my groin into the heart. They advised that there was an aortic valve defect and that they would have to operate.

I was told that if I decided then I might live possibly another twenty years, but if I didn't have the operation I might not live another five years. They gave me three weeks to go away and think about it. I thought about it, and about the pressure that I was under and the decisions facing me now. It was as if I was going to give myself another heart attack just trying to work out what to do. In the end, I told the wife that I was going into hospital to take my chances. I worked out that I had £50,000 left to pay on my mortgage. My wife was working part-time but she would have to go full-time.

I went to the hospital and spoke to the doctor, telling him of my family's concern and that I was scared as I'd never been in hospital before for anything major. The consultant advised me that, apart from the problem, I was fit and that was the best time to do the operation because the survival rate was very favourable if you were in good physical condition.

I asked my consultant to explain to me what was going to happen and he said, "I could tell you nice things about what is going to happen, but the truth is that we're going to saw open your chest, pull it back and make surgical corrections to your heart." When he said that I thought, "Arrrrhhhgggh!"

Now, it was a question of whether I wanted a plastic valve or a pig's one.

I asked, "What's the difference between the two?" and he said, "The pig's valve will last possibly ten years after which I would have to come back and have another operation."

I enquired, "So, what's the other alternative?"

He said, "There's an artificial valve which lasts longer, but you will be on some blood thinning medication for life."

What had happened was that one of the valves had worn out so the blood was flowing back. They had to repair it so that it would close properly. I thought about my options then said, "OK, fine. If I have to do it, I have to do it."

I went and discussed this decision with the wife, told her that I had to go into hospital but if I didn't survive, there was a little insurance, a pension, and so on. I was petrified, but I accepted my fate and from then on I was a calmer person.

I came to accept my situation, that I might not survive the operation. The way I saw it is that I was at a crossroad where my future is in the hands of the Messiah and it's out of my hands. Whatever happens, it's up to Him. If I didn't survive, then at least I had made some arrangements for my family.

Now, I've just got to put my hope in the operating team but you start hearing stories so I talked to some of my relatives with many years experience as nurses and they were saying the worse danger is not the operation, it's the anaesthetist because if you don't get enough oxygen during the procedure you could come back brain damaged even though the operation itself was successful.

I decided I was going to be extra nice to all the doctors.

My wife was worried though; more worried than I was. Anyway, I went in on the big day. I remember seeing all these flashing lights overhead as they wheeled me into this big bright room with lots of instruments on a bench. I was a bit dozy at that stage, as they had given me something to relax me. One doctor said, "Hello, Mr Walker. I'm your anaesthetist." He gave me a nice smile and then I was out.

When I woke up, I was naked in a cold room. Beside me there was a large naked white guy who was singing and carrying on. I assume different people have different reactions to the experience of surgery. These slightly built nurses came in the room and gave each of us, what they called the Australian lift, to move us from one place to another.

Some people were moaning, but I was quiet, trying to take in my surroundings. I had all these contraptions coming out of me but not really sure what had happened or where I was as I must have been between sleep and consciousness. Eventually these nurses started moving us into separate beds somewhere else from where we were propped up, but it was still cold. I was attached to various machines to monitor and regulate my heart, blood circulation, etc.

Soon after, Beverly came there to see me as the doctors had agreed it was all right for her to come in to the recovery room, but on reflection maybe it was not such a good idea. I think we were then lying down in our separate beds but when she saw me she almost fainted because I was just coming out of my stupor and she had never seen me so vulnerable. Bev didn't talk much. However, that visit assured me that I was indeed alive.

The next day, I woke up in a bed on a ward which they called the Zipper Club. I had tubes everywhere: a tube coming out of my private for me to pee and one coming from my neck and another from around my navel with monitors on my finger and elsewhere.

I can imagine how shocking it must have been for the wife to see me like that. Then I noticed this rope at the end of the bed and thought, "What's that for?" I tried to get up, but I had no strength in my stomach muscles, they were all gone. I used to have a firm, sculptured six or eight pack. That was gone. I couldn't move and the pain was unbearable and although there was one of the tubes pumping morphine into my system, I could still feel pain. As I tried to get up, I realised what the rope was for: you had to pull at the rope to get up. That was hard, really hard.

My wife was there just watching. I could see she was in shock, and then suddenly she had a huge rash on her arm. That was a nervous rash and it's been there ever since, erupting whenever she is under stress. I think Beverly went through just as much trauma as I did.

And then I was supposed to be training to walk again. The nurses initially supported me as I struggle to my feet. They insisted I should try and walk and I did eventually get up and try walking to the foot of the bed. It was difficult to walk even that short distance.

I realised that I had to get strength back onto my legs, so I started pushing myself, first to the end of the bed then to the wall and I kept doing that but resting after each attempt.

I was also told that I should be drinking lots of liquids to flush the system of all the impurities so I was trying to have all these energy drinks that people kept bringing me. I saw the stairs and that was the next challenge. I tried to walk up: two, three and then down again. Then two, three, four and down again. After about a week, I'd walk to the top of the stairs. By then, they'd taken out most of the tubes, but I had some that I could move around with and reconnected as required. I had been in that bed for about two weeks after the operation getting flabby and developing bedsores. I understood then what the doctor meant when he'd said, "You've got to be fit to undergo the operation and survive these things." Because if I was unfit by being overweight when I went in, I don't know what would have happened.

Then there were all these pills, about four types, including one I would take for the rest of my life called Warfarin to thin the blood. However, I realised that was not so bad when I saw another guy was on about ten different types of pills to take each day which would continue for most of his life. I thought, "Wow! How will he ever remember all that?"

Eventually, the doctor told me that he'd only be giving me two sets of pills to take when I leave hospital, but that I needed to take regular walks because my heart needed the exercise. So what did I do? I went back to my badminton club to play on a regular basis as soon as I was able to without telling them of my situation in case they treated me like a cripple.

I could feel the benefits of a good game of badminton; I felt good so I continued playing once or twice each week. I was also advised by the doctors to take at least six months off work but as a self-employed individual no one pays you sickness benefit.

Initially, to recuperate after they discharged me from the hospital I decided to go to my own house and get someone to come in daily to help out. A relative came in to give the nursing care I needed and to help with cooking and so on. Beverly was able go out to work as she was now working full-time, and the home care lasted for about two months.

Realising that the bills still had to be paid, I started to make arrangements to get the business in, as I knew clients were fickle and would go off elsewhere if they thought they were not being looked after.

The doctors did give me advice about possibly changing my job, but sometimes you have to be more realistic. No, I had to go back to do what I knew, despite my health issues.

Within six months, however, I was back where I'd started. The logic was, "I've got a new valve so I must be better than I was before the operation." It's like after a car has been for a service – the engine's now roaring, and I was thinking, "I've got to jump straight back in." If I hadn't, I probably would not be here today.

I now run a small property portfolio; properties which are rented out and I have launched a couple of websites. But that's it, until another great opportunity comes along. I've always been very busy. I suppose it keeps the brain working. At some stage I'm going to kick the bucket and that's it. So, there you are. That's how life is.

I started the Natural Healthcare website because I had a situation with gout and no one knew how I should deal with it. In fact, this doctor came to see me and suggested that the pain and swelling in the joints was the result of me drinking and falling over.

I suppose I should forgive him, after all he was old and might be speaking from his own experience. I had a swelling on my elbow joint and he said, "Ha ha, you've been drinking haven't you, and you fell down?" It may well have developed after years of binge drinking in the city, but I was fully sober when I got the swelling and when this doctor had come to see me.

However, the doctor couldn't be specific and the most he could do was give me strong pain relieving tablets. One year it attacked my big toe and moved up into my leg which shrunk to a third of its normal size. I couldn't walk up or down stairs and so I spent a lot of time in bed on my backside.

I decided not to accept that this is a permanent condition, so I got a diary and recorded my entire food and drink intake every day for about a year. Not only did I write what I ate and drank each day, but also how much I'd drank and eaten each day, and after a year I saw a definite pattern.

The gout erupted when I had too much alcohol, too much peanuts, too much coffee and too little water and fresh vegetables. The time when I got it really badly was when it involved a combination of the above. You see, I love peanuts. I could get through two pounds in weight in a few hours and I love brandy.

I went to another doctor for advice and he told me it's to do with the acid crystallising in the joints and all about what could have possibly caused it is good living, and over-indulgence: too much red meat and port. But it seemed that it was a sickness that people laughed at and even the doctor I'd spoken to thought it was funny. Friends also took it lightly – they were laughing about it too so I started cutting back on excesses such as coffee and peanuts and giving up brandy all together.

Abstinence made me feel much better and on those occasions I didn't have an attack of gout.

The doctors told me there was no cure but there's a tablet they called Allopurinol which, if I take about one a day will prevent an attack of gout and this helps to a degree but I found that if I drank lots of water, eat lots of fresh fruits and vegetables, keeping away from red meat and have an Allopurinol tablet every other day, I would avoid getting an attack of gout.

With all this information I decided to create a website: Natural Health Care to help sufferers out there being laughed at.

Sometime after the heart attack I decided to take my practice buy-out from Allied Dunbar put some of the money towards a house as a nest egg, using the balance to clear bills relax and have a Caribbean cruise holiday; so I rewarded myself and family to a memorable cruise around the Caribbean islands. Later on as house prices rose I was able to use the equity built up to acquire other properties.

33

The Property Game

My first venture into property started when I realised that under the right set of circumstances and at the right time property investment could bring great rewards; that is if one does not become too attached to the acquisitions. It is said timing and time in determines success or failure so after the Arawak my first instinct was to acquire a property as cheaply as possible, add some value by improvement, rent it for the income and eventually when the time was right capitalise on the equity by selling.

Well it worked with the first purchase as the time was in the depression of the early 80s and I manage to sell just before the government got rid of double MIRAS. However, as I had bills to clear and without a stable job I felt vulnerable so instead of investing the profit in other purchases I cleared my very large debts instead. Despite this decision I was constantly thinking and planning my route back into property as this seemed to be a good way of making extra cash. My opportunity realised itself one day when I walked into the offices on a development off Peckham Rye. This was a small developer who had obviously invested a lot of money on this development and with the recession in full swing sales had stagnated and it appeared the company was desperate to sell so my intervention was well timed as the agent was prepared to look at most reasonable offers. I made an offer of £83,000 for a three-bedroom terrace house with integral garage which was about 75 per cent of the true value. I was very surprised when my offer was accepted so I quickly proceeded to complete the purchase with funds from my credit cards together with some savings. This was of course a great risk to take at a difficult time of the recession and depleting all the savings I had available; but I thought with 10 years NHBC guarantee, and with reasonable mortgage repayments I could afford, close to transportation, shopping, entertainment, schools and parks; renting should not be difficult. So the Austins Court property became my first serious buy to let and later on became a cash cow as prices started to rise. I realised that I could get further advances to buy more properties and each subsequent purchase yield further advances to acquire even more properties. I decided that 12 was a good number to stop and so when I sold my financial services practice to my principle I used most of the proceeds to purchase the twelfth property, a large four bedroom semi detach house near the tube station and university in New Cross, south London. At first the rental income was just enough to cover the mortgage and insurance costs but as rates fell I was starting to feel better about my purchase. Realising the uncertainty and difficulties of letting properties I established a strict formula on how to be a successful landlord. However, as time went on I drop my guard and started trusting people to be honest and fair and it was at this stage I was conned or completely taken in by a pleasant, attractive and personable female.

My advert to rent a newly refurbished three-bedroom house with oak wood flooring throughout attracted a number of responses, three of the respondents were anxious to sign a twelve-month contract. However, this very cute Malaysian Chinese lady and her partner were very keen and offered to sign a three-year contract on our first meeting. I should have been suspicious when she offered me the full amount of deposit in cash but this Malaysian lady was very persuasive, she was friendly, calling me by my first name, smiled a lot and was personable. I must have been completely fooled by what appeared to be such a sweet and friendly person. However, I did ask them how many others in addition to them would be living at the property and whether they needed to use the dining room as an extra bedroom in order to reduce their costs; once again I should have been suspicious when the partner asked if I could remove the furniture from the small bedroom as they would be using it as an office and as Ann Choo told me that she was a self-employed beautician I just assumed she would be doing extra work from home. It was clear that Ann was in charge of the charm offensive and the partner played a supporting role. However, I caught my senses and asked them to fill in my Fact Finding sheet and to provide copies of passport, details of previous tenancy, utility bills and payslips etc. Well they provided all that except bank statements. On reflection I probably should have insisted on the bank statements and to be fair I did not confirm their documents with employer and accountants, previous landlord or immigration. I tried ringing the partner's employer and although the phone rang it was not answered and as a building firm I half expected that. Ann had advised that the previous landlord was not a nice man and probably would not give a reference. Anyway with the information I gathered it felt safe to proceed with offering the property to this nice couple. Ann wanted to pay the rent in cash but I insisted the rent be transferred into my bank account each month so we signed a contract to commence 6th April and on the 18th May (one month and a few weeks later) I went to visit the property with a surveyor. While the surveyor inspected the property the male Chinese partner made me tea and was very pleasant so I had no reason to suspect anything unusual happening on the premises.

However, about two months later on 15th July I had a call from a letting agent I had used previously. The agent gave me the phone number of one of the neighbours suggesting that I ring David urgently. I couldn't think why he wanted to speak to me so urgently so I made the call. "Hi Keith I have been trying to reach you for days, but to get straight to the point, I think your tenants are growing skunk/marijuana as there is a strong smell of the stuff in my house and in the house of the other neighbour next to you." I was lost for words "we can even smell it outside in the street" I was silent as I didn't want to believe it and wasn't sure how to respond. Then I asked "are you sure about that David", he thought for a while "well I lived in Holland for some years so I know what skunk smells like and besides we all heard a massive explosion coming from the house a couple evenings ago". That statement certainly got my attention so I immediately drove up to Peckham to investigate. As I got to the house the neighbours came out into the street and invited me into their homes to smell this thing. Well I didn't want to embarrass them because, although I could smell something a bit pungent, I was not sure it was not the smell of their houses so I said I could not smell anything unusual, but admitted I was not familiar with the smell of growing marijuana but that I have encountered the smell of burning marijuana at parties and in the streets of Brixton. The neighbours insisted that the tenants had blackened out the windows and doors and that a twist in the curtain to the front of the house had not changed for weeks and that they appeared late at night and is never seen around the property during the day.

It is clear the neighbours expected me to enter to check, so I went to the property followed by a couple of neighbours but could not enter as the lock had been changed. I tried to ring the tenants on their mobiles but got no reply and as it was late in the evening I decided to arrange with a locksmith to come the following morning at 10.00 am to change the lock, as I was not getting any responses from the tenants. I sent a text advising Ann that I would be entering the property the following morning because the neighbours advised me of an explosion inside the house. I had no response from either of the tenants, however the following morning from about 7.00 am I was getting a series of texts from Ann assuring me that everything was fine in the house and that she was in Scotland but was on her way back to the property. However, she would not speak to me on the phone.

The following morning at about 9.00 am I had a call from Peckham neighbourhood police suggesting that they turn up at the property also as the neighbours were complaining of illegal drugs being grown in the house. At 10.30 am there were about six uniform officers waiting there with me and eventually at 12.30 pm the locksmith finally arrived and was in the house in seconds. I had previously signed a police authority for them to enter the property and sergeant Cox was the first officer to enter the house, he stopped me in the hallway and from where I stood I could see very bright lights behind blackened out plastic sheets, thick electric wiring along the walls and banisters, between the railings and a collapsed ceiling in what was the lounge. I wanted to see more but was advised by the officers to stay out as the area was dangerous and in any case was now a crime scene. I could not believe what I was seeing, the derelict state of the house was shocking and I could not believe that this damage could have been caused by what appeared to be very nice people: I think I was in shock by what I had seen. It was a fine sunny day so I just stood outside a bit dazed observing the activities of the officers. Eventually a female police officer came over to me to take my statement after which I was allowed to go home to contact my insurance company. I contacted Halifax and was completely flabbergasted when they advised me that their landlords insurance did not cover malicious damage by tenants or their family members. "What was the purpose of that landlords insurance if it did not cover damage to the rented property" I asked but the lady on the phone was insistent that I was not protected under their insurance policy despite the fact this was the purpose of the policy.

The following day I was contacted by the police sergeant to advise that I was now allowed access to the property and that British Gas were called in and that they had cut the electricity and taken the meter for inspection. I could not understand why British Gas had taken the meter, as it appeared that the tenants had by-passed the official meter and installed their own instead. However, I contacted them only to be told that I would need to pay £640 to have the meter replaced. I had no choice so I reluctantly paid them this money. However, the letter their engineer left with the police stated that British Gas Revenue protection unit would not reconnect the power and meter until the cost of the illegal usage of electricity, estimated at £640, was paid in full. At this point I decided to take legal advice for a reimbursement as the contract was between the tenant and British Gas and the illegal usage did not rest with me but with the tenant.

After permission was granted to enter the property, I went to the house and was mortified by the wanton damage and deliberate destruction which confronted me. I did not actually see the forest of trees as portrayed in the local newspaper but what I saw caused me great anxiety. The Southwark paper had a photograph, which was incredible. I really could not believe that people could be so maliciously destructive. At the beginning the tenants were presented with an immaculate property with good quality furnishing, high speck kitchen and good quality wood flooring through out the property but three months later I am faced with a derelict house with water damage to the flooring in all the rooms. As a result the ceiling had collapsed in the lounge and the flooring throughout was so undulating they had to be ripped out to enable us to walk on the floor. In all the rooms they had constructed a series of wire lines suspended from large bolts in walls and ceilings and all the growing rooms had strong fluorescent lightings attached to thick wooden planks nailed to walls. There was very thick electric wiring stapled up walls, around door frames, along banisters and leading to the meter cupboard where they had by-passed the regular meter and installed their own instead. On the first floor there were large vents constructed into the ceiling venting out into the loft where they had removed bricks to create a large vent to the outside of the house. The bathrooms downstairs and upstairs were used to store their growing chemicals in large and medium size drums and there were at least five different colours of solutions together with various equipment crammed into the bathrooms and every other room had hundreds of growing pots filled with earth and fertilisers as the officers had removed the marijuana plants. All my furniture were piled up in the kitchen, patio or at the side of the house where the neighbours could not see them and some broken up and used in the loft as floor boards. Room doors and wardrobe doors were also removed and used as flooring in the loft.

Standing and looking at the destruction you can imagine the emotional journey I endured, bewilderment, disappointment, hate and of course revenge but in the end and after a few days of careful reflection I decided to put those thoughts to the back of my mind and move on.

34

Looking for Home

Where is home? How do we decide where we belong? Or is that decided for us by circumstances beyond our control? I ask the question because since my childhood I have been looking for the meaning of home and where I truly belong.

Since moving to live in England as a child I'd returned to Jamaica several times before marriage and kids. On one of those occasions I'd gone back for a holiday and discovered that my lovely grandmother, Tee, was very ill.

By then her husband, Mr De Paus, had died and his son, Leon, his heir, wasn't doing anything much with his life except producing lots of children with different baby mothers. It seemed the whole of that district was being populated by him.

On my most recent visits to Jamaica I observed that Leon had found religion and was now high up in the Rastafarian faith, and he told me that he even went to Ethiopia and lived on a commune for a while where they had teachings in their faith and pilgrimage to other regions in Africa before returning to Jamaica a wiser man.

It was strange on that occasion when I went to Hectors River only to find I had to sleep in the same bed with him, reminiscent of my youth, as there was no spare room available at that time. Anyway on the first morning I was woken early to this humming and chanting and babbling, *"Umhbbbinng-bing, umhabbingingnng-bing"*, in what sounded to me like a foreign language. He was in fact welcoming the new day.

The time before when I visited Nuts River, Leon was there with his woman and young child. However, to me it was clear that my grandma needed medical help and it didn't seem to me they cared much so despite their protestation I took Grandmother Tee to Morant Bay to try and get her a good doctor to treat her for her sickness as it seems nobody else was prepared to do anything either because they didn't care or felt it was unnecessary and expensive. I put grandma Tee in my hired car and on my own took her to Morant Bay to find her a good and caring physician.

The other family and friends were particularly concerned about the cost or that the money would be better spent elsewhere "Ah, doctors are expensive", or they would try to convince me that she will be fine in time. So I said, "I am here now anyway, I have transport and she needs treatment and medicine. Don't worry about the cost I will manage."

So, I took her to a surgery down in Morant Bay and it seems people were waiting for ages to be seen, but usually if I want something the only way I know is to push for it, so I push into the office and this absolutely beautiful half-Indian woman was just sitting there fiddling with a piece of paper. I was momentarily stunned by her beauty forgetting my reason for pushing into the office. But she was a bit annoyed at my bold action and responded in an annoying manner, "The doctor's busy, you know you have to wait." I said to her, "Calm down, calm down, my grandma needs urgent attention as you can see she is not very well. I know it's going to cost, but whatever it costs I'll pay, just get her a doctor."

She initially glared at me then looked me up and down, calmed herself, breathed in deeply and went in to the doctor's room. Moments later she came back out looked me in the eyes and said, "OK, take her in". The doctor spent a long time diagnosing grandma Tee's problem while I sat in reception trying not to look at this beautiful thing. Eventually the doctor called me in and it was a case of, "Oh, this is wrong and she needs to get this, and she needs to come back next week", and so on. "No problem", I thought as long as she got the care she needs I was happy. I must admit I did feel bad jumping the queue, but what the hell that's life isn't it? if you don't ask you don't get and door mats usually get trampled on.

I have to admit that I was really infatuated by the doctor's assistant and I could see that she was trying to avoid looking at me as much as I was trying not to look at her so just before I left I asked her the burning question; "Can I come back to see you sometime?" She said, "I don't mind." And gave me a cheeky smile as I left.

I took my grandma to some other place to collect her medicine and drove her back home and got the other people in the house to help her to wash and clean up, administer her medicine and make her comfortable. I could see grandma Tee was feeling much better after her wash and medicine so I stayed with her at the house for the rest of the day. The following day I gathered the relatives into the house advise them how they should care for her and so after a late breakfast I went down to Morant Bay to meet this girl at the doctor's surgery, and she was there waiting as promised.

We went to a local restaurant and had lunch and after we chatted a while I said to her, "Look, you need a holiday so I think you should go on tour around the island with me. Just tell your boss that you have to go and sort out some relatives in need or something." She agreed, maybe because I said I would take care of the expenses, so we went to Kingston and I asked her, "How long are you going to stay?" And she said, "As long as you want me to." Just the answer I was looking for. I asked if she'd spoken to her boss and she said she'd spoken to him and it was OK. Anyway, we went to the Pegasus hotel in Kingston and booked in for about a week, which I thought we would use as a base. I couldn't believe my luck as she seemed lovelier each day. But while I was there Sadie said she had spotted her boss, the doctor was there too. Apparently that's what professional people like him do at weekends, they'd go to hotels like the Pegasus with their girlfriends or mistresses, no doubt telling their wives they were going away on business. Sadie said she was hiding from her boss in case he spotted her and I asked if she was going out with him she said, well, he was trying to get her interested, but no, she wasn't going out with him. The relationship they have is purely platonic.

Anyway, we spent a few days there and I thought she had to be better presented as she was so beautiful and her clothe didn't do her justice, so I got my credit card out and bought her in some beautiful new clothes and she looked stunning. We decided to leave the Pegasus in case we actually bumped into the doctor, which would have been awkward for her to say the least. So, we got in the car and went to Ocho Rios and other areas on the North coast. We had a great time on the mountains leading to Ocho, enjoying the most wonderful food and drinks and later enjoying ourselves on the white sandy beaches of the northern Riviera.

However, the holiday was nearing the end and I had to go back to Kingston, I said to Sadie, "I'm flying out tomorrow and wish I could take you back with me but I can't, the authorities wouldn't allow it". So back in Kingston I gave her the fare to return home to Morant Bay but was sad I had to leave her and I don't think she was too pleased either. She was not just beautiful but wonderful in other ways too. For a change, here was a Jamaican who didn't want to fleece me who just enjoyed me for myself and I think she had a good holiday.

I was still a single man then and although Sadie was just right, and I know I could have fallen in love with her, I had to be honest with her and tell her the way it was and it would have been too complicated getting her to England. We communicated for a while but then it fizzled out. A beautiful girl like that wouldn't have been on her own for long anyway, and besides I suspected that the doctor was doing his stuff with her, although she wouldn't admit it to me. So, that was that.

My grandma did make some improvements but I don't think they kept up her treatment, although I used to send money for them to replenish the medicine and take care of her health and dietary needs.

The next time I went back to Nuts River was after my grandmother had died. I was sad because she and I had been very close. I'd spent some of my happiest times as a child at her house and I was disappointed that in her old age she had been somewhat neglected. Her passing reminded me of the death of my other grandmother: my mother's mother, with whom I stayed supervised by aunt Adlin in Rodney Hall. I was still a boy when she died and although I can't remember much about it, it struck me that one minute she was there, the next she was just lifeless: stiff and dark like a lump of wood. And you know what Jamaican funerals are like: They had this nine night set up, when people would come and tell stories, talk about her good days, drink rum, ate curry goat and made musical noises until late into the night then disappear gradually with the musicians being the last to leave. The next day people came back and did the same thing over again and this went on up until the day of the funeral, by then everyone was very intoxicated and somewhat drowsy from lack of sleep. However, on the funeral day everyone was now in their "Sunday best", though a bit unstable on their feet, there was a big outburst of emotions and crying and after the church service there was lots of sermonising and gospel singing around the grave as each man grab a shovel in turn to help with filling in the grave until the grave was completely covered. After they had committed the body to the ground "ashes to ashes, dust to dust" and all that, they wondered off back to the house to eat and drink into the late evening.

I don't remember being emotional at all. Myself and other children were sternly warned before hand to behave ourselves, no playing or running about, we understood that we had to be respectful and complied with their instructions.

The main thing I do remember about the funeral apart from stuffing my face were those funny little "maroon" men, from some mountain village, who were playing their home-made instruments and the sound was like "Dung, dung, dung," some string instrument sounding like a violin and a wind instrument sounding like a flute. It was an odd little band with a strange, morose sound during the internment but, afterwards, they came alive and it was like a party with lots of rum flowing and people getting high. As a child you took a lead from what the adults around you were doing. They were sad so you felt you should be sad too, but in reality it really didn't click. It made no great impact on me. Of course by the time grandma Tee died I was fully grown so I had a better understanding and could relate to the complex emotions and experiences at such a time, and more to the point I felt the loss deeply because I'd truly been fond of that old lady.

Funerals made me think about other people's lives and the relationship I had with them, but they also make me think about my own morality and the journey I have taken to the point I have reached right here, right now.

Life is a bit like climbing a hill. When you get to the top and take in the lovely views you tend to forget the problems you had to endure in getting to that point. The struggles fade into the past as you realise that life is really for the living and that the time we have should not be wasted on revenge and recrimination. My life journey was a bit like that but giving up or giving in, despite all the challenges, was never an option.

We tend to spend a lot of our advanced years reminiscing about the journey, and more often than not we tend to focus on the bad experiences. But sometimes we can be gracious in austerity and grateful that despite the prejudices, insecurities, injustices and sometimes brutal treatment we may have encountered along the way. I can say thank God I have managed to survive to raise a fine and balanced family – despite the hardships and against the odds.

There were times when I felt the enduring pull and desire to spend my final days back home in Jamaica where it all started. However, in the final analysis, life is where your family is so with that in mind I can see myself living out my final days in my adopted home in South London.

However, for a Jamaican rooted in the culture and tradition of a free spirit, reggae music, Jamaican labrish and a laid-back attitude to life, the camaraderie we all share – be it from the ghettos of Kingston or from the uptown smart-set in that great city – Jamaica will (despite the violence and ceaseless poverty) be my spiritual home in the sun. Harry Belafonte described it best in his songs about the sentiments of that vibrant country, in particular *Oh Island in the Sun*. And the sentiments also immortalised by one of our greatest sons, Bob Marley, in his reggae songs like, *No Woman No Cry*, goes to show that in spite of what is generally felt about Jamaican men, it cannot be denied that we love our women, our children, our mothers and our country and for those reasons I am proud to be a Jamaican.

Most people from the region are not aware of the simple fact that despite being a small island nation of under 3 million souls Jamaica is widely known and generally admired by people across the globe for what they have given to the world: Rastafarianism, reggae music, sports stars, fabulous food, respect, and an innate ability to succeed against all the odds, for example "Cool Runnings".

Yes, there have been a lot of negative attitudes towards Jamaicans, some of which, I dare say, is justifiable. And as one Jamaican policeman said to me on one of my visits to that proud land, "It is still work in progress".

On the whole, Jamaicans are a very vibrant and positive people who are all striving to succeed and, given the opportunity, they will. Cast your eyes to the UK, Canada and the USA where despite the difficulties Jamaicans have risen from humble beginnings and suppression to become successful members of those societies. And in a world of change when questions are asked about whether we can still make it in an increasingly globalised and competitive world, I can confidently repeat the well known phrase, "Yes We Can!"

As for me, the legendary Bob Marley asked a question in one of his earliest songs: "(They say) can anything good come out of Trench Town?" When I look over my life and think about the hardships, the pressures, the sheer heartache and the many barriers to overcome, which at times were like a barbed wire fence in my way, but I know I cannot dwell on those negative elements. So in balance, I must also reflect on the many opportunities, the times of grace and goodness, strength and love that have been my portion in this life.

So, yes, to answer you, Bob (or rather to answer the critics): good things *do* come out of Trench Town, and by some act of grace, I'm proof of that.

The End

Goodbye, Mango Sergeant